THE NEW GARDENER

THE NEW
GARDENER

PIPPA GREENWOOD

DK PUBLISHING, INC.
www.dk.com

A DK Publishing Book

www.dk.com

*To my mother who introduced me to gardening,
and to Alasdair and everyone else who supported
me while I wrote this book.*

Project Editor Jane Simmonds
Designers Vicky Short, Gillian Andrews
Editors Kate Bell, Jodie Jones
Editorial Assistants Melanie Tham, Claire Folkard
Design Assistant Sasha Kennedy
DTP Designer Chris Clark
US Editor Ray Rogers

Managing Editor Jane Aspden
Managing Art Editor Bob Gordon

Photography Peter Anderson

Production Hilary Stephens

Picture Research Anna Lord

First paperback edition, 1998

First American Edition, 1995
6 8 10 9 7 5

Library of Congress Cataloging-in-Publication Data

Greenwood, Pippa.
   The new gardener : the practical guide to gardening
basics / by Pippa Greenwood. -- 1st American ed.
      p.   cm.
   Includes index.
   ISBN 0–7894–3298–6
   1. Gardening. I. Title
SB453.G825 1994
635--dc20   94–6323
                                            CIP

Reproduced by Colourscan, Singapore
Printed and bound in Singapore by Star Standard Industries (Pte.) Ltd.

CONTENTS

How to Use this Book

The New Gardener provides easy access to all the information you need to plan or transform a garden, or simply to keep it flourishing and at its best from season to season. Whether you need planting suggestions for a damp, shady place, quick ideas for brightening up a dull patio, or step-by-step instructions for how to put up a fence, *The New Gardener* has the answer. The book is divided into eleven chapters, each dealing with a separate area of the garden.

Ideas for Your Garden

Each chapter begins with a whole range of design ideas and solutions. Packed with imaginative suggestions and accompanied by rich, inspirational photographs, these pages enable you to see new possibilities in your own garden and also equip you to plan the transformation in practical ways, too. Planting suggestions give you a starting point for choosing appropriate plants to fit in with your chosen design, and for selecting colors and textures you like to fill the garden with interest throughout the year.

Choosing the Right Materials

Often there is only a limited range of gardening materials at your local garden center. By looking a little further you can usually find something slightly different to suit both the style of your garden and your pocket – whether it be a container, paving slabs, or fence panels. Interspersed throughout *The New Gardener* are spreads showing a range of materials from which to choose.

Practical Projects

At the core of each chapter are the practical projects – step-by-step explanations of all the everyday gardening techniques needed to maintain and improve your garden. Photographs, artworks, and lists of exactly what you will need combine to give you complete confidence at every stage. There are also lists of plants appropriate to particular projects and advice and tips to ensure success.

Key to Symbols

The following symbols, defining the plant type and the basic conditions it will tolerate, appear in plant lists throughout the book. Additional symbols within each list have their own key at the base of that particular list. Where a name appears with more than one plant type symbol, it means that there is more than one type (e.g., both evergreen and deciduous species) within a genus, or that it responds in different ways to different climates.

- ♠ evergreen tree
- ♀ deciduous tree
- ♠ evergreen shrub
- ♤ deciduous shrub
- ⅍ evergreen climber
- ⅍ deciduous climber
- ♥ evergreen perennial
- ♥ herbaceous perennial
- ✾ annual or biennial
- ♣ perennial grown as annual
- ♦ bulb, corm, or tuber
- ✳ not hardy
- pH lime-hating

Cross-references

Throughout the book, related topics are linked by cross-references. These point you to additional information you might need – in the form of a whole chapter or project, or perhaps simply to a plant list that will provide you with extra suggestions.

Project Spread

Project spreads are at the heart of most chapters and are made up of numerous practical projects, large and small, from construction and planting to aftercare and renovation. Photographic step-by-step sequences, artworks, lists, and tips for success all combine to provide the clearest possible guide to all practical aspects of gardening.

Practical Techniques

Each chapter is packed with easy-to-follow, practical projects. Step-by-step photographic sequences show exactly how to carry out techniques in simple stages, and clear text answers common gardening questions with straightforward advice.

Tip Box

On the project pages, tip boxes (with a blue tint and sometimes an explanatory artwork) provide extra information – such as alternative methods and important aftercare reminders – to make the job easier and preempt any pitfalls.

List Box

A list box has a gray tint and contains a selection of plants relevant to the projects on that page. Symbols after each plant name tell you what sort of plant it is, whether or not it is hardy, and whether it needs acid soil (see the key to these symbols, left). Some lists have additional symbols – these have their own key at the end of the list.

Artwork

An artwork, often in cross-section, is included to clarify a technique or a particular stage in a project.

Text Box

Additional useful information – materials, different methods, and so on – is included where relevant in a text box accompanying a project.

112 Container Gardening

Planting Pots and Containers

Small containers are ideal for special plants, experimenting with new specimens, and adding an instant splash of color. They are also easily moved into a sheltered spot in frosty weather if the plants are tender. A container of tall plants, such as lilies or agapanthus, can be used to brighten up a dull border – conceal the container in a gap among other plants and remove it once the plants have finished flowering.

Large containers are perfect for growing more permanent plants, such as shrubs, perennials, and even small trees. Provided that you feed and water the plants properly, and repot them if their roots become congested, they should last for years. If you add seasonal bedding plants and perhaps a selection of spring-flowering bulbs) to the container you can create a complete miniature garden that has something to offer throughout the year.

Which Soil Mix?
Garden soil may be wonderful stuff in the border, but in a container it tends to lose its structure and harbor diseases. Specially formulated soil mixes provide a better medium. A soil-based one should normally be your first choice: it retains moisture well, and once dry is easier to wet again than peat-based products.

Soil Mixes for Large Pots
For large containers or those on balconies, peat-based and peat-substitute soil mixes are better choices since they are light and the container will be easier to move when full. Plants in these soil mixes will need more frequent feeding

Making the Most of Your Container
The larger your container, the more you can pack into it, especially if you plant at several depths. Plant large bulbs toward the base of the container and smaller bulbs or corms above; these can be left undisturbed to come up year after year. A shrub or perennial can be put in the center where it has most space to spread its roots, and then you can add annual bedding plants in the clear areas around the edge.

Central Plant
Position a large, permanent plant in the center so that its roots can penetrate deeply into the soil mix.

Watering Gap
Leave space between the surface of the soil mix and the pot rim for watering.

Bedding Plants
Plant seasonal bedding plants in the top layer of soil mix where they can be changed without disturbing the other plants.

Small Bulbs and Corms
Plant small bulbs and corms toward the top of the soil mix at about 3 times their own depth.

Lime-free Soil Mix
With containers you have a new freedom to grow plants that do not suit your soil: use lime-free soil mix to grow acid-loving plants, such as azaleas and camellias.

Large Bulbs
Toward the bottom of the pot, plant large bulbs at about 3–5 times their own depth.

Feet or Saucers?
Poor drainage can be the downfall of many plants: if the roots are always soggy they may rot. Check that your pot has enough drainage holes to let excess moisture drain away; if not, add new ones.

Feet
Terracotta or china feet are available to put under pots and raise them off the ground. This helps to keep the drainage holes clear. For a half barrel, tuck bricks under the base.

Saucers
Plastic or terracotta saucers are sometimes used under containers; these can be cleared of debris but hold water at the base of the pot, which causes waterlogging.

Container Plants for Different Seasons

Spring	Summer	Autumn	Winter
Camellias ♠ [some ✳] pH	Marguerites (*Argyranthemum frutescens* and cvs) ♣ ✳	Japanese maples (*Acer palmatum* and cvs, incl. 'Atropurpureum' and 'Dissectum') ♀	Daphnes ♠ ♤
Crocuses ♦	Begonias ♣ ✳		Winter-flowering heathers (*Erica*) ♠
Hellebores (all incl. *H. foetidus*, *H. viridis*) ♥	Fuchsias ♤ [many ✳, some ♠]	Ageratums ♣ ✳	Hollies (*Ilex*) ♠
Dwarf irises (incl. *Iris reticulata* and cvs) ♦	Helichrysum petiolare ♣ ✳	Cyclamens ♦	Junipers (*Juniperus*) ♠
Star magnolia (*Magnolia stellata*) ♤	Impatiens ♣ ✳	Chrysanthemums (*Dendranthema*) ♥ [some ✳]	Pieris ♠ pH
Dwarf daffodils (*Narcissus*, some cvs) ♦	Lobelia erinus ♣ [some ✳]	English ivies (*Hedera*) ⅍	Winter-flowering pansies (*Viola × wittrockiana* cvs) ♣
Azaleas (*Rhododendron*) ♠ ♤ pH	Nasturtiums (*Tropaeolum*) ♣ ✳	Deadnettles (*Lamium maculatum* and cvs, incl. 'White Nancy' and 'Beacon Silver') ♥ ♣	
	Geraniums (*Pelargonium*) ♣ ✳		**Key**
	Petunias ♣ ✳		⅍ Trailing
	Verbenas ♣ ✳		

WHEN TO DO A PROJECT

The season circle attached to each project provides an instant visual reference to when the project can be done, so you can plan your gardening year. Shading indicates suitable and unsuitable times.

BACKUP INFORMATION

The Appendices at the back of the book (pp.158–69) provide guidance on how to look after your garden once it's planted – by protecting plants from cold and avoiding or treating pests, diseases, and disorders. The Glossary explains a number of gardening terms.

The index that follows covers all the techniques, materials, and plants in the book, listing plants under both their common and botanical names to ensure quick and easy access to information.

MATERIALS SPREAD

Before starting to construct fences and trellises, paths and steps, and other landscape features, you need to choose the right materials. These spreads make selection easy, with photographs of a wide range of materials so you can make a more informed choice for your garden.

RANGE OF MATERIALS
Photographs clearly illustrate a representative selection of the materials available, sometimes in combination with others.

EXPLANATIONS
The accompanying text gives advice on which are the best materials to use in a particular situation, outlining their advantages and disadvantages.

"YOU WILL NEED" BOX
Accompanying each project is a box listing all the tools and materials you will need to assemble before starting.

SEASON CIRCLES

Each season circle shows at a glance when are the best and least suitable times for carrying out a project. Within a season, the shading is divided into thirds that correspond to early, mid-, and late season.

Dark shading indicates the best time to do the project.

Pale shading covers possible but not ideal times.

Times when it is not advisable to do the project are indicated by no shading.

STEP-BY-STEP PICTURE SEQUENCE
Each major project is illustrated with a step-by-step picture sequence to make every technique completely clear. Captions explain the techniques and materials shown.

PLANT NAMES

In the main text of the book and the plant lists, plants are called by their common names whenever possible. If the common name differs from the botanical name or is not widely used, the latter is given in brackets (afterward) for ease of identification and to avoid confusion. In the index, plants are listed under both common and botanical names.

·1·
TRANSFORMING YOUR GARDEN

*Any garden can be instantly improved and, in time,
completely transformed: this chapter shows you how. With the
right mixture of inspiration and practical advice as a guide,
even complete beginners will find the garden of their dreams
can soon be within reach.*

CREATING YOUR IDEAL GARDEN

Whether you have looked out on the same garden for years or for only a few weeks, transforming even an unprepossessing plot into the garden of your dreams is always possible. You may well find that the process is a lot of fun as well.

How much time and money that transformation takes up depends partly on the state of the garden now, and partly on how you would like it to be. But, however restricted your resources, with a little planning you can work wonders.

In fact, it is the thinking you do before you so much as look at a spade that will determine just how successful the finished garden is. Would you like flowers all year, are vegetables a priority, or do you just want somewhere to relax? Do you see gardening as a new hobby in itself, or a bit of a chore? Visualize how you would like your garden to look in an ideal world, then balance that picture with an assessment of how much time you're prepared to put into achieving that goal. Consider the options open to you in the following basic garden types, then mix and match elements from each to create your ideal design.

A GARDEN FOR EVERYONE
Good garden design takes into account the needs of everyone who might use it, not just the hopes and fears of those who will toil in it. If you have a family, canvass their

Family garden
Central to this design is a generous sweep of lawn, sown with tough grass varieties to withstand the rigors of children's games. An apple tree creates a visual break in the expanse of green. Deep borders planted with well-shaped shrubs and colorful annuals give an established feel, and a greenhouse and patio, both very practical features, have been attractively incorporated into the overall design.

opinions when drawing up plans – apart from anything else, you're more likely to get help with the construction if you make them feel properly involved.

If young children are to use the garden, safety will be a primary concern. Ponds may need to be "childproofed" – perhaps temporarily converted into a bubble fountain or sandbox – and plants screened for poisonous varieties. For a while it may be sensible to lay down a greater area of lawn than you might ideally like; children will play whether there is space or not, so they might as well run around on grass as on expensive specimen plants. Consider access for bikes, space for a slide or swing, and – to nurture the next generation of horticulturists – perhaps a small area for the children themselves to garden. As they gradually adopt more sedate pursuits, the lawn area can be reduced by widening and shaping borders or adding island beds.

Those who prefer to admire the garden from a horizontal position will appreciate a lounging area created with them in mind, and everyone will enjoy a patio for outdoor eating. *See also* "A Family Garden," p.14.

AN EASY-TO-MAINTAIN GARDEN
Lack of time, or inclination, can mean that a garden is left to run wild or, much worse, is blanked out completely with paving slabs or gravel. This is a great shame when, by following a few simple low-maintenance strategies, the same space could have been turned into a positive attraction with only the minimum of effort.

Forget traditional, labor-intensive garden designs, and go instead for close-packed planting (which helps keep down weeds) with low-maintenance plants that will look after themselves, plus careful use of paths and other so-called hard landscaping that creates permanent features instead of high-quality lawns. You'll find that there are hundreds of shrubs, perennials, annuals, and bulbs that need very little attention but will bring color, texture, and maybe scent into the garden.

Once a low-maintenance program has been established, the garden will be easy to look after in any spare hours plus an occasional weekend blitz. *See also* "A Low-maintenance Garden," p.15, and "Low-maintenance Borders," p.38.

Low-maintenance style
Specimen plants, selected for their different shades and shapes of foliage, combine with carefully placed paving slabs and pebbles to create a garden with an air of oriental calm.

AN ABUNDANCE OF FLOWERS

The traditional cottage garden, its borders packed with flowering and fruiting plants in glorious profusion, is an idyll that many of us aspire to. But before you get carried away with the idea, remember that the reality behind this apparently effortless style is a lot of hard work.

If you do decide you are willing and able to put in the necessary hours, it will still take a while to build up the range of plants and achieve a suitably informal style, but the wait will be well worth it. Not that you can then put your feet up – something will always need staking, deadheading, dividing, or cutting back.

If you like the idea but are short of time, you could always create a single cottage-style border and combine it with other areas that are easier to maintain. Whatever the scale of your planting, the emphasis should be on herbaceous perennials and shrubs. There are plenty of varieties to choose from according to your taste and the space available, but do try to include at least one clump each of the real cottage classics: old roses, irises, columbines, peonies, daisies, and hollyhocks.

Other quintessential cottage garden features include climber-laden arches and pergolas – preferably planted with scented roses – and a separate area devoted to fruit and vegetables. Well-worn brick paths, pretty wooden gates, and countless other rustic features can all add to the effect. *See also "A Cottage Garden," p.15.*

FINDING SPACE FOR PLANTS

Think of a garden and you'll probably picture a large expanse of lawn, surrounded with beds, borders, and trees. Yet the reality for some of us is a paved terrace or concrete backyard without so much as an inch of soil in sight.

Container garden
You don't need a garden to create inspired plant combinations, as this exuberant arrangement of containers clearly shows. The massive Nerium oleander at the rear creates a striking backdrop to a colorful mound of petunias, Helichrysum petiolare, and osteospermum gathered in smaller pots in the foreground. To support such a mass of blooms, containers must be fed weekly with a liquid fertilizer. This group would do best against a sheltered sunny wall, but there are many other plants to choose from that would thrive in more shady or exposed sites.

Fortunately, a lack of conventional growing space needn't handicap the would-be gardener in the slightest. It is perfectly possible to turn even the bleakest of spaces into a colorful haven packed with a variety of ornamental and edible plants for year-round interest.

For the best results, it is important to make full use not only of the available horizontal space, but of all the vertical areas, too. Unsightly walls, fences, and views can quickly be hidden by attractive – and sometimes even productive – climbers,

and your overall garden design will be immeasurably improved by this step into the third dimension. You may be able to lift small areas of paving around the perimeter to make more permanent beds for these climbers. However, if this is not possible, many will do perfectly well in large containers filled with good-quality soil mix.

Continue the vertical planting theme with hanging baskets, mangers, and windowboxes on house and perimeter walls. Though these containers are usually planted with summer bloomers, there are plenty of foliage plants that will thrive in them too, and if you plan the planting carefully it is possible to have color in every season.

More adventurous projects could include creating a shady arbor by training climbers over a wire frame, or wooden slats spanning the courtyard. A herb garden is easily achievable, since many herbs thrive in the free-draining conditions of a container, but have you considered creating a vegetable plot as well? A surprising range of vegetables can be grown in containers or grow bags, and in the sheltered conditions of a backyard you should be able to get excellent crops. *See also "Container Gardening," pp.104–117.*

TAKING YOUR GARDEN TO NEW HEIGHTS

If you live in an apartment, your only opportunity to garden may be on a balcony or roof garden – and both can provide a wonderful retreat from the grayness and stress of urban life. Clearly, if the area

Informal profusion
The country cottage style depends on overstuffed beds for its informal effect. Here color, form, and fragrance all play their part, jumbled into a riotous display that spills out over the gravel path.

where you intend to make your garden has not been used for this purpose before, it is vital to have the site examined by a contractor who can tell you whether it is sound and suitable for the purpose. Once you have the all clear, you are ready to begin the transformation. There are only two practical limitations to your flights of fancy: use lightweight containers and soil mix to keep the overall weight down, and, since everything will need regular attention – especially in summer – include a convenient access point in your design.

On a balcony, adorn the walls with hanging baskets, windowboxes on brackets, and mangers all planted for year-round interest, and encourage climbers to grow up the walls or spill over the front. Choose scented varieties so you can enjoy the bonus of perfume wafting in through open windows. Cluster smaller tubs and containers into attractive groups, moving them around to bring each plant to the fore during its season of glory, or simply to alter the overall effect to suit your mood of the moment.

Roof gardens can be treated in a similar fashion as balconies, with combinations Pof plants in containers. But, since roof gardens tend to be more windy, you may need to erect a windbreak or grow hardy plants around the outer edges. Using tall plants to filter the wind will also screen the garden from the envious stares of your neighbors! *See also* "Balconies," pp.106–107, and "Room at the Top," pp.108–109.

A WILDLIFE GARDEN

Gardening with the local wildlife in mind is increasingly popular in these environmentally aware times. Some may see this as a convenient way to let your garden run wild without having to feel guilty about it, but in fact a successful wildlife garden demands considerable planning and maintenance – although the diversity of wildlife it will attract more than compensates for the amount of time and effort involved.

Many of the wild plants suited to this style of garden are not as compact and upright as their cultivated cousins; this fact, coupled with their tendency to seed freely, gives a relaxed and tranquil feel to the garden and encourages wildlife to hide and feed undisturbed. However, it also means that the whole system must be kept in check by a firm hand if it is not to get completely out of control.

Wildlife garden essentials include at least one area of dense cover planted with native species and a selection of shrubs and trees to provide berries and nuts through the lean winter months. A pond is also important, since it provides breeding, drinking, and bathing sites for a huge number of creatures. And if you can create boggy areas around the margins, then so much the better, since this increases the diversity of available habitats even further.

Wildflower seed mixtures selected to suit your soil type can be used to add some color while the rest of the garden

Kitchen garden
This arch draped with scarlet-flowered runner beans shows how vegetables can be grown for ornamental effect as well as productivity.

is developing. Let the lawn grow slightly long, then allow wildflowers and clover to seed freely. The effect will be as attractive to humans as it is to insects and animals. *See also* "A Wildlife Garden," p.14.

FOOD FROM YOUR GARDEN

Nothing beats the taste of homegrown vegetables picked fresh from the garden. Though it needs a lot of attention, a productive garden proves very rewarding.

Making the site ready for planting is often hard work, but you needn't tackle the whole area at once. Establish the heart of your productive garden, and then expand gradually when you need more space and have the time to clear it.

Whatever the size of your plot, you will certainly need at least one compost pile, or preferably several, and an area set aside for a leafmold pile. Intensive cropping takes a heavy toll on the soil, so digging in lots of well-rotted organic material is essential to keep it in good shape.

Another useful addition is a greenhouse, preferably supplied with power and heat. Though this will add to your initial expenditure, it does mean you can grow some exotic crops as well as raise your own vegetables from seed and produce early and late crops. A selection of cloches and frames also helps stretch the growing season and provides winter protection.

With these basic items of equipment, you should be able to grow a good range of staple crops and a few of the more unusual varieties as the fancy strikes you. *See also* "The Edible Garden," pp.132–51.

Attracting wildlife
A well-stocked pond such as this one, with marshy marginal planting that includes cowslips, foxgloves, and marsh marigolds (Caltha palustris), *is the perfect way to lure wildlife into a garden.*

MAKING INSTANT CHANGES

A garden, old or new, that has been allowed to crumble into dilapidated disarray can be an uninspiring sight for any budding gardener. Transforming this apparent wilderness into the garden you hope for may seem an impossible task, and it can be hard to know where to start, particularly if everything seems to be in an equally poor state. But take heart – the illustrations (below and right) show a neglected garden in early summer and the

same garden a year later. None of the changes shown here is expensive to achieve or particularly time-consuming. Clearing, cultivating, thoughtful planting, and simply cutting the grass can transform even the most neglected plot within a surprisingly short space of time. Once you have tackled the basic elements, you may feel ready to undertake more radical changes – such as adding a pond or a new border, or laying a patio or path.

THE NEGLECTED GARDEN

The basic structure of this neglected garden is still visible and provides a starting point. While there are established shrubs and a mature apple tree, these have been left to become shapeless and overgrown. The patchy lawn has not been

looked after and is full of weeds, while invasive plants have been allowed to take over the borders. The boundaries have not been maintained either – the fence is broken – and the patio and shed need cleaning up and repairing.

ADDING A TRELLIS TO A FENCE
Erecting a trellis on top of the fence and planting climbers creates a little privacy. This *Clematis* 'Jackmanii' will blend with the scented rose 'Zéphirine Drouhin'.

RENOVATING A SHRUB
Pruned into shape after flowering, this lilac provides masses of color and combines well with other shrubs.

INVASIVE PLANTS
Weeds and other invasive plants, including mint, are obscuring the path.

DILAPIDATED GARDEN SHED
The old wooden shed is starting to rot in places.

PATCHY GRASS
A bare patch of ground beneath an established apple tree can detract from the tree itself.

TREATING A FENCE
Application of wood preservative and replacing damaged panels or boards (*see* p.73) restores the fence.

ROTTING FENCE
The untreated fence is decaying.

SOFT FRUIT
The neglected raspberries are full of dead canes.

WEEDS IN LAWN
Perennial weeds, including dandelions, have become established in the lawn.

NEGLECTED LAWN
The patchy grass contains both worn and overgrown areas.

SCRUFFY SHRUB
This dogwood is growing poorly and is out of shape.

ALGAL GROWTH
Algae and moss, often fostered by leaks or drips, leave unpleasant, green or blackish brown deposits that are dangerously slippery when damp.

OVERGROWN BORDER
Clogged with weeds, the border contains few plants of much interest.

UNSTABLE PAVING
Loose slabs are dangerous, and exposed ground beneath is likely to become infested with weeds.

GARBAGE
Garbage harbors slugs, rats, and other problems.

SPRING INTEREST
This compact star magnolia (*M. stellata*) has been planted for its beautiful spring flowers.

ONE YEAR LATER

The garden has been imaginatively transformed into a colorful area, with a wide range of healthy plants, including fruit and vegetables, and space to relax. In the summer, start with overall cleaning, removing any rubbish and cutting overgrown grass, which achieves an instant improvement and makes it easier for you to envisage the garden in the future. Plant up pots of annuals for a short-term splash of color. In the autumn, concentrate on renovating the lawn to improve its growth and eliminate large weeds. In the winter, prepare borders for new plants and dig over and fertilize the vegetable area. This is also the time to prune many shrubs and trim hedges. Structural features such as paths, steps, and patios may be tackled year-round, when you have the time or inspiration.

MAINTAINING SOFT FRUIT
The raspberries were pruned and tied to a support in the autumn (*see* p.147), so the current crop should be healthy.

A PRODUCTIVE PLOT
Cleared and sown with vegetable seeds, this area should crop well in its first year.

REPAIRING A SHED
The shed has been treated (*see* p.73) and rotten areas filled.

YEAR-ROUND COLOR
The dogwood moved from the patio now forms a focal point in winter and summer.

PRUNING A FRUIT TREE
The apple tree has been pruned over the winter to remove any dead and diseased branches and improve its shape. The healthy new growth should crop well.

MEADOW PLANTING
Longer grass and a selection of wildflowers make a pretty, informal area.

PLANTS FOR PROBLEM PLACES
Plants tolerant of shade and fairly dry conditions make the most of ground beneath trees. Ground-cover plants, such as this periwinkle (*Vinca*), are easy to maintain and keep down weeds.

A SHADY RETREAT
This attractive seat makes the most of the dappled shade beneath the tree.

PLANTING FOR INSTANT COLOR
Annual bedding provides a pretty stopgap if you are short of time and here allows the newly planted verbascums, lilies, and hardy geraniums to establish.

A HANGING GARDEN
This wall basket full of summer-flowering plants adds a splash of color above ground (*see* p.115).

A MOVABLE GARDEN
Containers planted with shrubs, perennials, bulbs, herbs, or annuals have brought the terrace to life.

FLORAL EDGING
Lavender creates a cheerful, cottagey effect as a path edging.

REJUVENATING A PATIO
Seeds of compact annuals sown between the paving make the newly cleaned and repaired patio less stark.

RENOVATING A LAWN
Treating weeds with a suitable weedkiller (*see* p.65) and regular cutting soon restores a lawn. Feeding and repairing bare patches may also be called for.

PLANNING A NEW GARDEN

Many new houses have what amounts to a blank space behind them – a grassed rectangle. This gives you the opportunity to create a completely new garden from scratch. Even in a garden with some established features, you can still make your mark with careful restructuring or the addition of a few new plants. Follow the guidelines below, and you can put your plan into action as you find the time. For more ideas, *see* "Creating Your Ideal Garden," pp.9–11.

PLANNING GUIDELINES

The following points will help you in drawing up your plan. Try not to leap to any decisions too quickly, and take inspiration from other gardens.

• What do you want from your garden? Do you need a children's play area, a place to relax, or perhaps fresh produce?

• How sheltered or open is your site? What is its exposure? How much of it is in shade, and for how long each day?

• Which features do want to lose or keep? List any new ones you would like – such as a lawn, pond, pergola, or shed.

• Measure the plot and make a rough scale plan that includes major existing plants and structures. Try to incorporate your preferred features and plants.

• If your maintenance time is limited, choose plants that need little attention.

• Consider whether you need a garden designer – having done all this planning, you should know exactly what you want!

THE BASIC SHAPE

The plans shown on these two pages are all based on a simple, rectangular shape. The dimensions are given below.

60ft (18m)

30ft (10m)

A FAMILY GARDEN

In a garden for the whole family, including young children, certain features take priority – perhaps a lawn for playing on, a sandbox, swing, or a slide – and these all need to be positioned where they can be used safely and easily. A family garden does not usually contain a pond, which may be dangerous, or delicate borders close to play areas. Having a family to look after may limit the time available for maintenance.

SANDBOX
A sandbox can later be converted into a pond.

PLAY AREA
The play area is screened off by bamboo planting.

PAVING
Slabs are laid out in a hopscotch pattern.

CHILD'S GARDEN
Children can grow easy, colorful annuals in their own small space.

PLANTING
Tough, thornless, and nonpoisonous plants are safest with children around.

HARD-WEARING LAWN
A lawn makes an essential play area.

SWING
A strong tree, surrounded with bark chips, is ideal for a swing.

A WILDLIFE GARDEN

Wildlife gardens are becoming more popular, although, perhaps unexpectedly, they do require considerable care and maintenance. The aim is to attract and provide both food and breeding sites for local wildlife, so native plants usually feature – from trees and shrubs to grasses and annuals. A pond to encourage newts, toads, frogs, and other water or moisture-loving creatures is vital.

POND
A well-designed pond will attract a wide range of animals and insects.

TREES AND SHRUBS
Plants with berries will provide food and nesting sites for birds.

DIVERSITY
Wildlife gardens can draw on pond, meadow, and woodland habitats for inspiration.

STEPPING-STONES
A stepping-stone path is ideal for maximum flexibility and planting space.

WILDFLOWER MEADOW
A wildflower meadow can be created using grass seed mixed with suitable wildflower seed, or by planting wild plants in an existing lawn.

INFORMAL PLANTING
Planting and plant development should appear random, with no straight lines.

A Low-maintenance Garden

This type of garden does not necessarily save you time in the first year or so, but thereafter it only needs a minimum of work to keep it looking good. All the chosen plants need little upkeep. Labor-intensive features, such as herbaceous borders that need regular watering and maintenance, are usually excluded in favor of weed-deterring groundcovers and easily cultivated shrubs and climbers. Remember that it will always be possible to add to and alter your garden if you wish to spend more time on it at a later date.

Mulching
Areas between plants are mulched to prevent the soil from drying out and impede weed growth.

Groundcover
Groundcover plants help to smother weed growth and need little attention once established.

Low-maintenance Planting
Small shrubs, with few or simple pruning requirements, are combined with low-growing perennials that need no staking.

Garden shed
Wood preservative has been mixed with coloured emulsion for a long-lasting finish.

Mowing Edge
A brick edging separates the lawn from the beds, making mowing easier.

Lawn
A straight-edged, utility-grade lawn is simple to maintain. This could be replaced by a hard surface such as paving or gravel.

Wall Shrubs
Plants such as pyracantha and elaeagnus need minimal, easy pruning and quickly clothe fences or walls.

Containers
Planted with hardy perennials, containers need minimal care to provide a good display.

A Productive Garden

Even a small area can support an attractive array of vegetables, herbs, and soft fruits, as well as a couple of fruit trees. A lawn can be small or omitted altogether to leave more space available for crops. With appropriate cultivars, the garden can provide produce for the kitchen almost year-round.

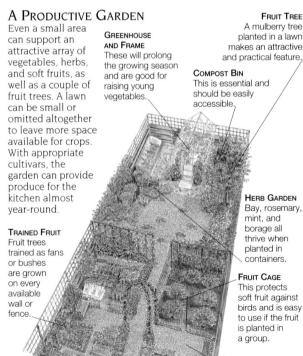

Trained Fruit
Fruit trees trained as fans or bushes are grown on every available wall or fence.

Greenhouse and Frame
These will prolong the growing season and are good for raising young vegetables.

Compost Bin
This is essential and should be easily accessible.

Fruit Tree
A mulberry tree planted in a lawn makes an attractive and practical feature.

Herb Garden
Bay, rosemary, mint, and borage all thrive when planted in containers.

Fruit Cage
This protects soft fruit against birds and is easy to use if the fruit is planted in a group.

Path
This must be wide and stable enough for wheelbarrow access.

A Cottage Garden

Here formality is banished in favor of curving, irregular lines. The emphasis is on borders packed full of shrubs, herbaceous perennials, and bulbs. Scented and traditional plants play a vital part, as do roses, especially climbers and ramblers grown over fences and arches. Cottage gardens are labor-intensive to create and maintain.

Rustic Beams
Planted with clematis, these timbers make an informal archway.

Informal Planting
Plants of all shapes, colors, textures, and scents are planted without a hint of a straight line.

Containers
Annuals and herbs in containers are an attractive mix.

Secluded Corner
A wooden bench, tucked away behind shrubs, provides the ideal place to enjoy the scents and colors of the garden.

Paving
A random mixture of stone, brick, and paving is laid informally, with plants spilling onto it from adjacent borders.

Herbaceous Borders
Plants are staked in summer to maintain the display, then cut back in winter.

DEALING WITH PROBLEM AREAS

When you take over a garden, new or old, you need to decide which of the existing features to keep. Some of these features, such as an old tree, a shed at the end of the garden, or a large lawn, may give a welcoming air of maturity to the garden; others, such as a fuel tank, overgrown pond, or unattractive view, may pose more of a problem and need to be screened or modified depending on your other plans for the garden. In this section there are several suggestions of how to cope with common problems – to improve their appearance and make them into an attractive part of your garden. Most sites contain a variety of conditions – shaded or sunny, boggy or dry – influenced by both their exposure and nearby features such as high walls and trees (see also "Microclimates," pp.22–3). Careful planting can transform these areas into assets rather than eyesores.

SHADE
There are shaded areas in most gardens, and they need not pose problems unless the shade is very dense and almost unbroken throughout the day. If the shade is caused by trees or hedges, you may be able to thin or prune to let in more light. When this is not possible, choose plants that tolerate or thrive in shade, such as woodland species or those with gold or pale leaves. For more specific examples of suitable plants, see "Plants for Different Microclimates," p.23.

Planting in shade
Many beautiful plants, here lungworts (Pulmonaria), bergenias, agapanthus, Anemone hupehensis, and ajugas, will tolerate dry shade.

HOT, DRY AREA WITH POOR SOIL
If you have an area in your garden that is subjected to high temperatures, and where the soil is dry or poor, try to improve growing conditions before starting to plant. Incorporating bulky organic matter, such as well-rotted manure, compost, or even composted bark, will help the soil to retain more moisture and can improve fertility (see "Improving Your Soil and Site," pp.26–7). You could also add some tall plants or shrubs adjacent to the area to create some shade.

Select plants that prefer arid conditions and tolerate poor soil (see "Plants for Different Microclimates," p.23) to provide you with a colorful, luxuriant, and flourishing border.

SLOPE
The simplest way to deal with a slope is to add new plants that thrive in these conditions, such as achillea, eryngium, rosemary, and thyme. If your slope already has some groundcover plants, your best plan may be to clean them up and thin, replace, or add to them where necessary. Alternatively, terrace the slope, or at least the steepest part of it. This will involve constructing a series of retaining walls – since these need to support a huge weight of soil, it is advisable to seek advice before you start.

Planting in dry conditions
Choose plants such as grasses and succulents that are adapted to drought conditions and direct sun.

UNSIGHTLY FEATURES
Fuel tanks or gas cylinders are often positioned prominently, and they are usually impossible or impractical to move. They will be less obtrusive if they are obscured with a trellis, wooden screening, or fence panels, all of which can be covered with climbing or scrambling plants (see "Ornamental Dividers," pp.82–3).

To disguise drain or utility covers, place lightweight containers filled with plants on top, but make sure these can be easily moved away for access in emergencies. If you have a tree stump that cannot be removed, drape it with cascading climbers to create a colorful focal point. Compost bins constructed out of natural materials, such as wood, need not be unsightly; plastic ones or those that are messy or covered in old carpet or plastic sheeting may, however, be rather an eyesore. Similarly, garbage cans that need to be stored in the garden are definitely worth hiding. Careful planting of individual trees, shrubs, or a hedge around the entire compost or garbage area will often do the trick. Alternatively, a trellis or wooden fence covered with a few climbing or scrambling plants can conceal unattractive views while allowing access.

BOGGY AREAS
You can waste a lot of time and money trying to ignore a boggy area in a garden – if you plant it with shrubs or perennials that do not like wet conditions, the majority simply will not last. Instead, why not work with the damp conditions to create an attractive bog garden, packed with moisture-loving plants? For details, see "Making a Bog Garden," p.127.

Alternatively, it may be possible to drain the area by constructing a system of tile drains – this is best left to professionals.

OVERGROWN HEDGE
It is worth coming to grips with an overgrown hedge as soon as possible. Cut it back to size in stages over at least two years to minimize the shock to the plants (see "Renovating a Hedge," p.85). Overgrown conifer hedges pose a particularly difficult problem: if they are cut back hard into the central area of brown foliage, most will not produce good new growth since they have few dormant buds. Either remove them and replant the hedge or mask brown areas with climbers or scrambling plants.

UGLY VIEW

A short-term solution to an ugly view is to erect a trellis or fence (see pp.72–3) in front and plant fast-growing annual climbers. If ultimately you would prefer a hedge, plant small hedging plants and erect an inexpensive fence behind them; remove the fence when the new hedge has filled out. Other effective but longer-term screens include tall-growing plants, such as bamboos and trees, or a fan-trained fruit tree (see "Ornamental Dividers," pp.82–3).

NEGLECTED POND

If you have a neglected pond in your garden, it may be possible to save it by cleaning it out and repairing any damaged or leaky areas, and then refilling and replanting it (see "Looking after Your Pond," pp.130–31). Ugly edging or a visible liner can usually be dealt with by replacing the edging with more attractive materials such as paving slabs or rocks positioned to hide the liner. If you do not want a pond, instead of removing it, why not convert it into something else? All types of pond with leaks can be filled in with soil to make water-retentive sunken beds ideal for a bog garden. Alternatively, fill an empty liner with sand to create a sandbox.

BALCONY

Balconies with chipped paint, rotting woodwork, and algal growth are not very inspiring, especially if they are full of garbage and dried-up potted plants! Have a thorough cleanup, and then wash down all the surfaces and restore the paintwork. Once you have checked that the balcony is sound, cram it full of lightweight pots planted to give year-round color and scent. Hanging baskets, wall baskets, and windowboxes also give you a chance to plant colorful flowers, and perhaps even herbs on your new, above-ground garden (see pp.106–107).

UNATTRACTIVE PATHS AND PATIOS

A simple improvement to an unattractive path or patio is to plant the adjacent area; this hides and softens the edges and draws your eye away from the paving itself. On wide or less frequently used paved areas, gaps between stones can even be filled with small, compact plants, or seeds of annuals sprinkled on to give seasonal color (see "Sowing Seeds between Paving Stones," p.100). Scented plants add interest, too – those with leaves that give off enticing aromas when bruised, such as thymes and camomiles, are suitable.

For a simple facelift, try changing the surface materials: spread a layer of gravel over concrete, or set a few cobblestones between bricks or slabs. A more radical alteration is to change the direction of a path, perhaps replacing a rigid, straight line with an easygoing, meandering route. Draw a rough sketch of the garden and experiment with various possible routes before getting to work.

Brightening up paths and patios
Plants can be positioned both within a paved area and to sprawl over and soften any hard edges.

FEATURELESS LAWN

A green square or oblong is easily transformed by a little subtle reshaping. To do this, either cut sod from the edge of one area and add it to another, or lay some new sod. Curved edges look far more attractive than straight ones in most situations and are also easy to cut out (see "Shaping a Sod Lawn," p.58).

To brighten up a dull lawn with spring and summer color, plant areas of bulbs or wildflowers. For more details, see "Planting Bulbs in a Lawn," p.63.

If your lawn is of a reasonable size, you could also create an island bed. Once you have improved the soil, plant the area to make a bed of bright drifts of color and different textures within the lawn setting. An attractive, sunken path of paving or stepping-stones will also help to break up a large expanse of green (see "Stepping-stone Paths," p.91).

HIGH WALL

Walls of buildings such as garages or sheds need not be eyesores: think of them instead as large vertical spaces for growing plants. Annual or perennial climbers or wall shrubs can be used to great effect in a situation like this, allowing you to transform an ugly expanse of brick or concrete into a beautiful wall of vibrant color.

Always check the exposure of your wall, and then select plants suited to the amount of sun or shade there, and the quantity of moisture the soil below the wall receives. Put up sturdy supports, such as a trellis or a system of galvanized wires, to bear the weight of any fully grown climber you might choose to grow. Do this before planting since it will be far more difficult later on. For more ideas on planting walls and other boundaries, see "Clothing with Climbers," pp.76–7.

LARGE TREE

Large trees are a welcome feature in a new garden – provided they are healthy and not sited too close to the house. If in doubt, seek the advice of a reputable tree surgeon who may also be able to remove low branches overhanging borders or patios. Before carrying out any work, ensure that the tree belongs to you, or ask your neighbors for permission to alter their property.

Trees often cause dense shade and dry soil beneath their branches, but this need not be a barrier to planting, since many plants will tolerate these conditions (see "Plants for Different Microclimates," p.23).

Planting beneath a tree
Provided you choose plants that are tolerant of shade, poor soil, and dry conditions, such as these Canterbury bells (Campanula medium) and foxgloves, there is no reason why you cannot enhance the area immediately beneath a tree with a display of color.

·2·
GARDEN
BASICS

Before starting any job, it is essential to learn a little about the mechanics involved – only then can you set to work with confidence. This chapter looks at how the climate and soil in your garden might affect your plans and how, with the right tools and plants, you can use them to your advantage.

SITE AND EXPOSURE

The site and exposure of a garden are two intertwined factors affecting how to plan the design and which plants will be suited to the conditions. The site relates to the topography of the garden and the area immediately around it – is it on a slope, is it sheltered by nearby trees or buildings, and what type of soil does it have? The exposure is the direction in which a particular garden faces – does it receive sun for much of the day, or is it mainly in shade? Both these factors affect the nature of the whole garden, its soil, and the plants that will thrive in it, and they combine with local weather to create a range of conditions within the garden, known as microclimates.

This page is about the site and exposure of an entire garden; on pages 20–21 the impact of different weather conditions on plants in the garden is covered; and on pages 22–3 several typical microclimates are described, with recommendations of suitable plants for each.

ASSESSING THE SITE AND EXPOSURE OF YOUR GARDEN

When you move into a new house you may have a general impression of whether the garden is quite sunny or shaded but, unless you were able to discuss the garden with the previous residents, you will need to assess fully both site and exposure before starting to plan seriously. Observe the plants that are growing well in your own and surrounding gardens to build up a picture of what you are likely to be able to grow. You can then take advantage of the conditions your own garden has to offer, choosing plants that are likely to flourish and siting them where they will do well, barring extremes and disasters.

Major factors to look out for include whether part or all of the garden is in a frost pocket or a wind tunnel. Bear in mind that city gardens are likely to be warmer than those in rural areas; coastal gardens, although perhaps affected by salt-spray, are usually less prone to extremes of temperature than inland gardens. Enquire locally about the likely weather extremes before starting to plant. Watch where the shade falls in your garden throughout the day, and at different times of year if possible – evergreen trees cast shade all year, while deciduous ones cast little shade in autumn and winter.

A north-facing garden in summer

A garden facing north will be chillier all year than a south-facing one – the soil will warm up later in the year, resulting in slower plant growth, and walls and other surfaces will retain less heat. Other areas, however, will receive a substantial amount of sun.

SUNNY AREAS
A few areas receive sun for most of the day and can be planted with sun-loving plants.

SHADE CAST BY THE HOUSE
As the sun moves around, the shade cast by the house or other buildings may affect a considerable part of the garden.

AREAS WITH SHADE AND SUN
Some areas may receive sun for only part of the day, most commonly during the early morning or late afternoon.

SHADED AREAS
Some parts remain in shade for most of the day – these areas will need to be filled with plants tolerant of quite deep shade.

A south-facing garden in summer

Much of a south-facing garden will be in sun for a large part of the day, resulting in warm air and soil temperatures ideal for a wide range of plants. The shaded areas can be used for plants that like warm conditions but will tolerate some shade.

DRY SOIL
Soil in some parts of the garden, especially next to a wall or fence, will be dry and suited mainly to plants that tolerate these conditions.

TREES
Shade cast by a deciduous tree is denser in summer than the rest of the year.

SUN PREDOMINATES
Most parts of the garden are relatively warm and sunny for much of the day.

KEY TO SHADING

The different densities of shading in the illustrations opposite indicate the areas of the garden that are in shade at various times of the day in summer.

⬜	Early morning
⬛	Noon
▨	Early evening

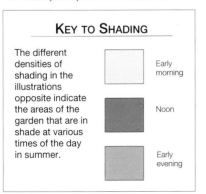

WEATHER MATTERS

Temperature, rainfall, humidity, and wind, alone or in combination, affect both plants and soil in your garden. Once you get to know the changes and extremes of local weather, you will be able to choose plants that flourish in those conditions, as many plants will withstand extreme heat or exposed situations. Weather changes with the seasons and from year to year, so there may always be times when you need to protect your plants from severe conditions (*see* "Winter Protection," pp.159–60). Plants are often described according to their ability to withstand cold – their hardiness. Use this as a guide to where to plant, positioning more tender plants in a sheltered spot or in pots that can easily be moved under cover in winter. A garden planned and planted to suit the local climate is much easier to care for and will look healthier than one planted with no regard to the weather.

FROST, COLD, AND SNOW

Frost can injure even relatively hardy plants, freezing and killing plant tissues, especially in late spring and early autumn. All half-hardy and tender plants are vulnerable, as are young growth and blossoms on otherwise hardy plants. As decreasing temperatures freeze the soil progressively deeper through winter, surface roots may be injured, and entire root balls of plants in pots may be killed. Alternate freezing and thawing of the soil is also damaging, often causing small, newly set plants to heave out of the ground. Snow helps insulate roots and low-growing plants, but its weight can cause branches to break and can permanently damage the shape of conifers.

PLANT HARDINESS

HARDY PLANT
One that normally survives the average minimum winter temperatures in a given area without the need for extra protection.

HALF-HARDY PLANT
One that undependably survives normal winter conditions. To guarantee its survival over winter it should be protected outside or brought under cover.

TENDER PLANT
One that is normally damaged or killed in winter. Bring under cover or provide winter protection.

WIND

Some air movement is needed to reduce humidity and lower air temperatures; it also keeps many diseases at bay, and helps to disperse pollen. However, excessive wind can scorch foliage and flowers, distort growth, and may even break or uproot plants, as well as dry out soil. Salt-laden coastal winds can cause severe scorching, and salt from sea spray can kill plants if it reaches their root systems. In windy conditions, spraying against pests and diseases is difficult. Fewer fruits may set since pollinating insects are less active.

A windy site can usually be planted successfully behind a living or artificial windbreak; this must allow about 50 percent of the wind to blow through to be most effective (*see* "Wind Tunnels," p.22).

Damaged stem

Blackened leaves

Wind scorch
Wind scorch causes leaves or parts of leaves to wither and dry out. Plants particularly prone to wind damage, such as this maple, should be planted in a sheltered place or behind the protection of a windbreak, especially if your garden is situated on an exposed hilltop or near the coast.

Coastal sites
For exposed gardens, choose plants that are tough enough to withstand salt-laden coastal winds. Low-growing plants suffer less from wind damage than tall, willowy ones; group them together to give the best protection. Strong winds have an extremely drying effect, so choose succulents and plants with tough leaves; these will retain moisture more effectively than those with tender, green shoots and leaves.

Frost-damaged leaves

Vulnerable young stems

A frost-damaged pieris
The young, tender shoots of the pieris are easily damaged if exposed to frosts in early spring.

HEAT AND HUMIDITY

High temperatures and bright sunlight can be very damaging, and are often combined with low moisture levels in the soil. Heat damage causes wilting, scorching, and, ultimately, withering of the plant due to moisture loss from both plant and soil. Add organic matter to the soil to encourage moisture retention, and choose plants that tolerate sunny, hot, or dry conditions – these plants have leaves that retain moisture well (*see* right and below).

Certain plants need high humidity to grow well – tropical plants and ferns are examples – but this often causes a multitude of problems. When the air has a high moisture content, more moisture is retained by plant leaves, encouraging diseases such as mildew and fungal scab infections. The soft growth of the plant is also more prone to damage and attack by pests.

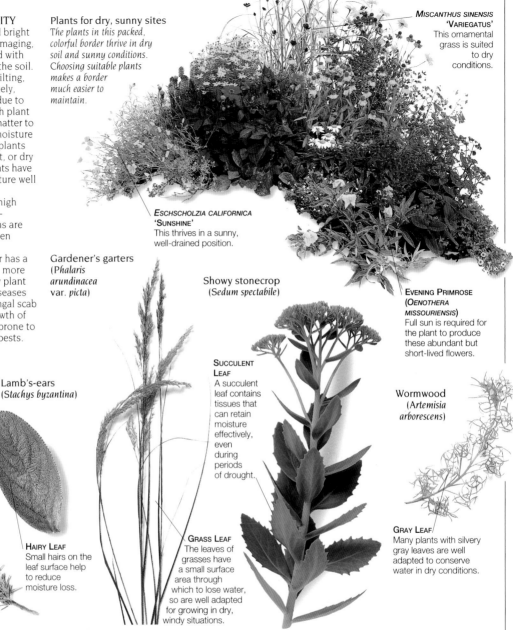

Plants for dry, sunny sites
The plants in this packed, colorful border thrive in dry soil and sunny conditions. Choosing suitable plants makes a border much easier to maintain.

MISCANTHUS SINENSIS 'VARIEGATUS'
This ornamental grass is suited to dry conditions.

ESCHSCHOLZIA CALIFORNICA 'SUNSHINE'
This thrives in a sunny, well-drained position.

Gardener's garters (*Phalaris arundinacea* var. *picta*)

Showy stonecrop (*Sedum spectabile*)

EVENING PRIMROSE (*OENOTHERA MISSOURIENSIS*)
Full sun is required for the plant to produce these abundant but short-lived flowers.

Rosemary (*Rosmarinus officinalis*)

Lamb's-ears (*Stachys byzantina*)

SUCCULENT LEAF
A succulent leaf contains tissues that can retain moisture effectively, even during periods of drought.

Wormwood (*Artemisia arborescens*)

HAIRY LEAF
Small hairs on the leaf surface help to reduce moisture loss.

OILY COATING
The tough, oily surface slows water loss through the leaves.

GRASS LEAF
The leaves of grasses have a small surface area through which to lose water, so are well adapted for growing in dry, windy situations.

GRAY LEAF
Many plants with silvery gray leaves are well adapted to conserve water in dry conditions.

RAIN

Rain is essential for the survival of all plants; it also helps to keep foliage and flowers free of dust and other deposits. Too much rain can pose problems since it leads to waterlogged soil (where the amount of water entering the soil exceeds the amount draining out) and leaching of nutrients, thus preventing plants from growing properly. If plants are exposed to waterlogged conditions for long periods, the roots may become "asphyxiated" and die. Few plants, except specially adapted marginal water plants, will establish well on permanently waterlogged sites. To improve the soil in waterlogged areas, try adding organic matter and grit or, in extreme cases, putting in a drainage system. You can also choose plants that are specifically suited to moist conditions (*see* "Plants for a Bog Garden," p.127). Avoid walking on waterlogged soil since it is easily compacted.

STORM DAMAGE

On slopes, soil may be washed away by torrential or heavy rainfall, and the soil structure may also be quite severely damaged elsewhere in the garden. The force of heavy rain can sometimes bruise or even tear soft, tender foliage and flowers. More extreme problems may be caused by hail, which can literally puncture foliage. Lightning damages or kills any trees that it strikes.

MICROCLIMATES

It is rare to find a garden that has uniform conditions throughout. Within even the smallest plot there are different areas that are like miniature gardens in themselves, each with a slightly different set of growing conditions. These microclimates can cover a range of extremes – there may be densely or partially shaded areas which in turn may be kept moist or constantly robbed of water; or south-facing raised beds that provide a warm area where plants move into growth early in the year; or there may be dry areas, perhaps next to a wall. Each microclimate provides an opportunity to garden in a different way, to use the site to its best advantage, or to play down its difficult points by careful choice and maintenance of plants. Once you get to know the whole range of different growing conditions offered in your garden, you will be able to choose the most suitable plants for each spot.

FROST POCKETS

Because cold air is heavy and dense, it flows down slopes and settles in low-lying areas such as valleys and hollows. Frost is more likely to occur in these areas (which are known as frost pockets) than in neighboring areas. A frost pocket may also occur behind a wall or hedge – thinning the obstruction will help to prevent the cold air from being trapped behind it. Plant only the hardiest, deepest-rooted plants in a frost pocket, or be prepared to provide protection (*see* pp.159–60).

Two examples of a frost pocket

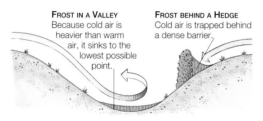

FROST IN A VALLEY
Because cold air is heavier than warm air, it sinks to the lowest possible point.

FROST BEHIND A HEDGE
Cold air is trapped behind a dense barrier.

WIND TUNNELS

Gaps between buildings or trees in or near the garden may force wind through the narrow space at great speed, resulting in a wind tunnel. Any wind damage to plants, such as scorching and breaking, will be much more severe in these circumstances. Always bear this in mind when planting new trees or siting a shed or greenhouse. If you have a wind tunnel in your garden, construct a windbreak to provide shelter and plant wind-tolerant plants (*see* opposite). Windbreaks should allow about 50 percent of the wind to blow through; solid barriers deflect the wind upward, then back down on the other side of the barrier.

A wind tunnel

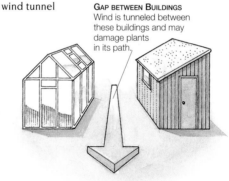

GAP BETWEEN BUILDINGS
Wind is tunneled between these buildings and may damage plants in its path.

HOT SPOTS

Areas within a garden that receive a lot of sunshine and are not cooled down by winds because they are sheltered may become very hot and dry, especially during the summer. A south-facing wall and the nearby soil are particularly likely to develop these conditions as the sun is absorbed by the wall, which then releases heat gradually. A corner where two walls meet, both of which absorb a lot of heat from the sun, will create intensely hot conditions. Improve the soil's ability to retain moisture as much as possible (*see* "Improving Your Soil and Site," p.27) and select drought-resistant plants.

A hot corner between walls

HIGH TEMPERATURE
Heat is released from the walls back into the corner; breezes have little cooling effect.

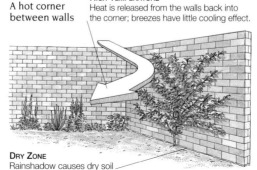

DRY ZONE
Rainshadow causes dry soil near the wall base.

OTHER MICROCLIMATES

SLOPES
Rain may wash damp or sandy soil down a slope, gradually removing the topsoil and with it many plant nutrients. Ground-cover plants help to hold the soil in place since their roots form a network, enabling other plants to become established. They also protect the soil from the damaging effects of wind and rain and usually need little maintenance. Plants on warm, sunny slopes develop and flower quite early. For a wet slope, terracing can be used, with horizontal planting areas held by retaining walls.

POLLUTED AREAS
Water, soil, and air all suffer the effects of increasingly widespread pollution. In certain areas, gardens may be affected by pollution from factories or power plants. Parts of a garden that border a busy road will also receive high levels of pollution. Little can be done about water or ground pollution in the garden, but some air pollutants, such as lead, can be partially kept out by dense planting around the edge of the garden.

SALTY AIR AND SOIL
In coastal gardens, winds are laden with salt spray. This can damage the foliage, and any buildup of salt in the soil will harm roots. Select salt-tolerant plants for these conditions.

SHADE

Large, overhanging trees or nearby buildings produce areas of shade. If the tree's roots or the building's walls are close by, the shaded soil in the area will be dry; if there is any water source nearby, the soil will be moist. Heavy or clay soils retain more moisture than sandy soils.

MOIST SHADE

The bottom of a slope is a typical moist shade area – water is washed down the slope, and moisture from farther up seeps down through the soil to the base, which is often shaded by plants growing above.

DRY SHADE

Dry shade is common beneath trees since moisture is removed from the soil by the roots. Trees that are well established or closely planted may also cause very dry areas. Dry shade sometimes occurs near a wall or fence where the structure creates an obstruction to rain on one side, creating a rainshadow. In addition, brick walls absorb soil moisture. Although these conditions are hard to combat, a number of plants tolerate dry shade.

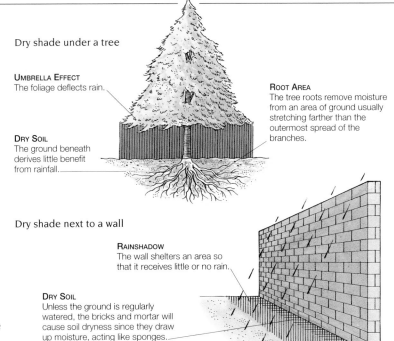

Dry shade under a tree

UMBRELLA EFFECT
The foliage deflects rain.

ROOT AREA
The tree roots remove moisture from an area of ground usually stretching farther than the outermost spread of the branches.

DRY SOIL
The ground beneath derives little benefit from rainfall.

Dry shade next to a wall

RAINSHADOW
The wall shelters an area so that it receives little or no rain.

DRY SOIL
Unless the ground is regularly watered, the bricks and mortar will cause soil dryness since they draw up moisture, acting like sponges.

PLANTS FOR DIFFERENT MICROCLIMATES

WIND-TOLERANT PLANTS
Achilleas 🌿 [some ◇] 🔽
Pearly everlasting (*Anaphalis*) 🌿 [some ◇]
Anchusas 🌿
Wormwoods (*Artemisia*) ● 🌿
Darwin's barberry (*B. darwinii*) ⊛ ❂
Canna x generalis and cvs ◊ ❋
Hornbeam (*Carpinus betulus*) ♀
Knapweeds (*Centaurea*) [some] 🌿 ❂
Mexican orange blossom (*Choisya ternata*) ●
Crocuses ◊
Brooms (*Cytisus*) ●△◇🔽
Carnations and pinks (*Dianthus*) 🌿
Elaeagnus pungens and cvs, incl. 'Maculata' ● ◇
Fleabanes (*Erigeron*) 🌿 ❂
Escallonias ●◇
Euonymus fortunei and cvs ●◇🔽
Beech (*Fagus sylvatica*) ♀
Summer hyacinth (*Galtonia candicans*) ◊ [some ◇]
Spanish gorse (*Genista hispanica*) △
Hardy geraniums (most, incl. *G. sanguineum*) 🌿🔽
Griselinia littoralis ●◇🔽
Canary Island ivies (*Hedera canariensis* and cvs) 🍃❂
Hollies (*Ilex*) ♦●△

Junipers (*Juniperus*) ♦●◇
European larch (*Larix decidua*) ♀
New Zealand tea tree (*Leptospermum scoparium*) ●❋
Daffodils (*Narcissus*) ◊
Phormium tenax 🌿❋
Prunus lusitanica ♦●
Pyracanthas ●🍃
Rugosa rose (*Rosa rugosa*) △◇
Yews (*Taxus*) ♦●
Arborvitae (*Thuja*) ♦●
Laurustinus (*Viburnum tinus*) ●

DROUGHT-RESISTANT PLANTS
Achilleas [most] 🌿 [some ◇] 🔽
Arabis 🌿🔽
Aubrietas 🌿🔽
Trumpet creeper (*Campsis radicans*) 🍃❂
Rock roses (*Cistus*) △❋🔽
Sea hollies (*Eryngium*) 🌿 [some ❋] 🔽
Flannel flowers (*Fremontodendron*) ●
Brooms (*Genista*) △
Hypericums △🔽
Junipers (*Juniperus*) ♦●🔽◇
Sweet alyssum (*Lobularia maritima*) ❂◇
Catmint (*Nepeta*) 🌿🔽
Moss rose (*Portulaca grandiflora*) ❂❋
Rue (*Ruta graveolens*) △
Rosemary (*Rosmarinus*) ●🔽
Santolinas ●

Sedums 🌿
Tamarisk (*Tamarix*) ●△◇
Crimson glory vine (*Vitis coignetiae*) 🍃
Weigelas △

PLANTS FOR DRY SHADE
Alchemilla mollis [most] 🌿
Coral plant (*Berberidopsis corallina*) 🍃
Boxwood (*Buxus sempervirens*) ●
Spurge laurel (*Daphne laureola*) ●
Elaeagnus (most, incl. *E.* x *ebbingei*) ●◇
Epimedium pinnatum 🌿🔽
Canary Island ivies (*Hedera canariensis* and cvs) 🍃❂
Hypericums (most, incl. *H.* x *inodorum* 'Elstead') △🔽
Hollies (*Ilex*) ♦●△
Stinking iris (*Iris foetidissima*) 🌿❂
Deadnettles (*Lamium*) 🔽
Japanese honeysuckle (*Lonicera japonica* 'Halliana') 🍃
Mahonias ●
Butcher's broom (*Ruscus aculeatus*) ●❂
Symphytum grandiflorum 🌿🔽
Fringecups (*Tellima grandiflora*) 🌿
Periwinkles (*Vinca*) 🍃🌿🔽

PLANTS FOR MOIST SHADE
Akebia quinata 🍃
Anemone x hybrida 🌿
Arum italicum 'Pictum' ◊
Goat's beard (*Aruncus dioicus*) 🌿
Bergenias 🌿❂🔽
Camassia leichtlinii ◊
Lily-of-the-valley (*Convallaria majalis*) 🌿
Foxgloves (*Digitalis*) 🌿❂
Snowdrops (*Galanthus nivalis* and cvs) ◊
Hellebores 🌿❂
Hostas 🌿❂🔽
Golden hop (*Humulus lupulus* 'Aureus') 🍃
Mountain laurel (*Kalmia latifolia*) ●ᵖᴴ
Snowflakes (*Leucojum*) ◊
Honeysuckles (*Lonicera*) ●🍃🍃
Paeonia suffruticosa and cvs △
Pieris ●ᵖᴴ
Pittosporums ● [some ❋]
Primroses (*Primula*) [most] 🌿
Rhododendrons and azaleas ●△ᵖᴴ
Sweet box (*Sarcococca ruscifolia*) ●🔽
Skimmia japonica ●

KEY
◇ salt-tolerant
❂ pollution-tolerant
🔽 groundcover plant

MAKING THE MOST OF YOUR SOIL

Soil is composed mostly of mineral particles, air, water, and organic matter in varying quantities – plants need all of these to live. The proportions of each determine the type of soil you have. If your soil is light and drains rapidly, it is probably sandy. If it is heavy, sticky, and becomes waterlogged, it is probably clay. And if it is moisture-retentive yet well drained, it is a medium loam. Finding out your soil's texture is a starting point for determining which plants will thrive there and which just survive, although most soils support a range of plants. The pH of the soil (whether it is acid or alkaline) also determines which plants grow well. Although you can alter the pH, it is hard to change it substantially in the long term; a better solution is to select and grow plants that are suited to the pH.

IDENTIFYING YOUR SOIL

Garden soil consists of three layers – the topsoil, the subsoil, and, at the bottom, the bedrock. The topsoil, in which you dig and plant, is uppermost and is regularly enriched and altered by organic matter, which gets mixed in by soil organisms. Usually dark in color, it is full of nutrients, soil creatures, and microscopic organisms. Subsoil is lighter in color and has a much lower level of nutrients and organic matter. In new gardens, the topsoil may have been buried or cleared; if so, you need to add organic matter or even topsoil before planting.

Soil texture is determined by the size of the soil particles. The two extremes are sand (larger) and clay (smaller). Sandy soil does not retain water well; although easy to dig, it is low in fertility. Clay soil is moisture-retentive, drains slowly, and is harder to work but usually very fertile. A good mix of the two – a medium loam – is ideal.

The ideal soil
Medium loam has a fine, crumbly texture. It retains water well without becoming waterlogged and contains a balance of nutrients, making it a fertile growing medium.

Soil structure
If you dig straight down into your soil, the subsoil may be visible as a lighter layer below the topsoil. It also tends to be stonier since it is derived directly from the bedrock (parent rock).

Soil texture
Sandy soil is usually light in color and rough to the touch, with few changes in texture since it is mostly made up of sandy particles. Clay soil has a smoother, more solid feel and may be molded into shapes if pressed.

SANDY SOIL
This has a light, loose texture and a rough, gritty feel when rubbed.

CLAY SOIL
This is sticky, smooth, and easily molded when wet.

TOPSOIL
This is the uppermost layer of the soil, often a dark, rich brown in color. It should have a high level of organic matter and be full of both large and small soil organisms.

SUBSOIL
The subsoil usually contains a much lower level of organic matter and nutrients than the topsoil, very few soil organisms, and is often lighter in color.

WHAT IS SOIL pH?

The soil pH is the level of acidity or alkalinity measured on a numerical scale of 1–14; soils of neutral pH have a value of 7. The pH determines the solubility of nutrients, indicating which are readily available and which in short supply. Many testing kits use a color rather than a numerical scale (*see* right).

Yellow-orange color

Bright green color

Dark or bluish green color

Acid soil
This yellow-orange color indicates a pH value below 7 and therefore an acid soil.

Neutral soil
A bright green soil test indicates a pH value of 7 and the soil is therefore neutral.

Alkaline soil
A pH above 7 produces a dark green color, indicating an alkaline soil.

CHOOSING PLANTS FOR YOUR SOIL TYPE

When you take on a garden you take on the soil – and chances are you will be unlikely to find yourself in possession of the perfect medium loam. A basic knowledge of your soil type will mean you are less likely to make too many expensive mistakes by growing plants that are unsuited to your conditions. Flourishing gardens, and those easiest to maintain, are usually filled with plants that suit the soil type. Whether it is clay, loam, or sand, you need to look after it by regularly mulching and adding organic matter. If you regularly feed and water the plants, your garden should thrive, even if your soil is not ideal.

Listed below are plants for different soil types. Those for clay soils need plenty of nutrients and tolerate constantly moist, sometimes waterlogged roots. Slightly alkaline soils support a wide range of plants; those given below tolerate highly alkaline conditions. Plants listed as requiring acidic soil are those that will not flourish in any other soil – many other plants also grow well in acidic soils. Plants for poor, sandy, and shallow soils tolerate dry roots or do not need large quantities of nutrients to survive.

Marigold growing in stony, shallow topsoil.

Buttercup growing in heavy, deep topsoil.

Free-draining chalky layer

Slow-draining clay layer

Alkaline soil
This is usually free-draining, pale, and stony, with a shallow layer of topsoil. It is usually fairly fertile.

Clay soil
This is dense and slow-draining, with a tendency to become waterlogged. It is usually high in nutrients.

PLANTS FOR DIFFERENT SOILS

CLAY SOIL
Maples (*Acer*) [many] ♀△ [some ᵖᴴ]
Juneberries (*Amelanchier*) ♀△
Aucubas ●
Bergenias ☙
Bellflowers (*Campanula*) ☙
Cornus [many] ♀△
Cotoneasters ●△
Forsythias △
Hardy geraniums ☙
Hellebores ☙
Hostas ☙
Kerrias △
Laburnums ♀
Honeysuckles (*Lonicera*) [many] ●ᕗ
Crabapples (*Malus*) [many] ♀
Philadelphus △
Roses (*Rosa*) △ᕗ
Coneflowers (*Rudbeckia*) ☙❀
Sedums [many] ☙
Spiraeas △
Sages (*Salvia*) [many] ☙
Lilacs (*Syringa*) △
Viburnums [most] ●△

ALKALINE SOIL
Bear's breeches (*Acanthus*) ☙
Maples (*Acer*) [some]♀△
Achilleas ☙
Horse-chestnuts (*Aesculus*) ♀

Aethionemas ☙
Hollyhocks (*Alcea*) ☙❀
Alchemillas ☙
Alliums ♂
Alyssums (*Alyssum*) ❀
Windflowers (*Anemone*) ☙
Columbines (*Aquilegia*) ☙
Arabis ☙
Wormwoods (*Artemisia*) ●☙
Michaelmas daisies (*Aster*) ☙
Aubrietas ☙
Aucubas ●
Aurinias △❀
English daisy (*Bellis*) ☙
Bergenias ☙
Buddleias ●△
Boxwoods (*Buxus*) ●
Bellflowers (*Campanula*) ☙
Caryopteris △
Ceanothus ●△ [some ᵖᴴ]
Knapweeds (*Centaurea*) ☙❀
Ceratostigmas △☙
Flowering quinces (*Chaenomeles*) △
Chimonanthus △❀
Clarkias ❀
Clematis ᕗᕗ
Colchicums ♂
Cosmos ☙❀ [some ❉]
Hawthorns (*Crataegus*) ♀△
Montbretias (*Crocosmia*) ♂
Fuchsias △ [many ❉]
Gypsophilas ☙
Heuchera sanguinea and cvs ☙

Kerrias △
Laburnums ♀
Lavenders (*Lavandula*) ☙
Tree mallows (*Lavatera arborea* and cvs) △
Honeysuckles (*Lonicera*) ●ᕗ
Stocks (*Matthiola*) ❀
Penstemons ☙ [some ❉]
Polemoniums ☙
Lungworts (*Pulmonaria*) ☙
Pyracanthas ●ᕗ
Flowering currants (*Ribes*) △
Coneflowers (*Rudbeckia*) ☙❀
Elders (*Sambucus*) △
Campions (*Silene*) ☙❀
Lilacs (*Syringa*) △
Thymes (*Thymus*) ☙☙
Tulips (*Tulipa*) ♂
Verbascums ☙
Viburnums ●△
Weigelas △
Wisterias ᕗ

ACIDIC SOIL
Bearberries (*Arctostaphylos*) ●△ᵖᴴ
Heathers (*Calluna*, *Erica*) ☙ [most ᵖᴴ]
Camellias ● [some ❉] ᵖᴴ
Daboecias ☙ᵖᴴ
Enkianthus △ᵖᴴ
Eucryphias ●△ᵖᴴ
Fothergillas △ᵖᴴ
Gaultherias ● [some ᵖᴴ]

Kalmias ●ᵖᴴ
Chilean bellflower (*Lapageria rosea*) ●❉ᵖᴴ
Lithodoras [some] ●☙ᵖᴴ
Magnolias [most] ♦♀△ᵖᴴ
Nomocharis ♂ᵖᴴ
Black gums (*Nyssa*) ♀ᵖᴴ
Pernettyas ●ᵖᴴ
Philesia magellanica ●ᵖᴴ
Phyllodoces ●☙ᵖᴴ
Rhododendrons and azaleas (*Rhododendron*) ●△ᵖᴴ
Vacciniums ●△ [some ❉] ᵖᴴ

POOR, SHALLOW, OR SANDY SOIL
Abutilons [some] △☙❉
Achilleas ☙
Ceanothus ●△
Judas tree (*Cercis siliquastrum*) △
Cotinus ♀△
Elaeagnus ●△
Hardy geraniums ☙
Jasmines (*Jasminum*) ᕗᕗ [some ❉]
Kerrias △
Laburnums ♀
Lavenders (*Lavandula*) ● [some ❉]
Mahonias ●
Perovskias △
Mountain ash (*Sorbus*) [many] ♀
Verbascums ☙❀
Wisterias ᕗ

IMPROVING YOUR SOIL AND SITE

Preparing your soil well, and in some cases improving its structure and fertility, gives it the potential to support plenty of beautiful and productive plants, and is well worthwhile in the long run. In a new garden, or if you are planting in a previously uncultivated area, your first task will be to clear away any debris and weeds. You can then start on soil improvement. Soil texture, its moisture-retaining and nutrient-holding characteristics, and its fertility can all be altered considerably by digging and forking and by incorporating plenty of suitable organic matter. Organic matter is the nonmineral element in the soil – it helps to maintain soil structure and enables organisms such as worms to survive. Which other materials you add will depend on what type of soil you have to start with, and how much time and money you are prepared to spend on improving its condition.

CLEARING A NEGLECTED SITE

On an uncultivated area, weed control is best tackled by a combination of cutivation and chemical techniques. If an area is heavily infested with perennial weeds, a weedkiller will save you a lot of work; otherwise, you will need to dig over and take out every piece of root. Remove further weeds as they appear. Control annual weeds by regularly hoeing and digging while they are still small, so that they do not compete with other plants or set seed. Hand-weeding also works well and is easiest for removing weeds without damaging adjacent roots.

CHOOSING A WEEDKILLER

Always select the right weedkiller for the job. Nonselective weedkillers kill all green plant material they come into contact with. Other weedkillers are selective in their action, killing only certain types of plant without harming others. Contact weedkillers are effective purely on the parts of plants that they come into contact with. In contrast, systemic weedkillers are translocated – carried right through the plants to the roots – making them especially useful for controlling perennial weeds. Most weedkillers act through the foliage, but some are soil-acting. Whichever type of weedkiller you choose, use it with great care to avoid damaging plants you want to keep. *See also* "Weeds," p.168.

APPLYING WEEDKILLER

Apply weedkillers when the weeds are growing strongly – in late spring and early summer – in the quantities and rates recommended by the manufacturer, and never on a very warm or windy day. Wear protective clothing if this is recommended.

Clearing woody weeds
Before spraying or digging out perennial and annual weeds, clear any woody ones. Cut down the top-growth, then dig out the roots or stumps, carefully removing every piece of the root.

SUPPRESSING WEEDS

Black plastic, landscape fabric, and old carpet will all suppress the growth of new weeds on an area cleared of weed growth. These materials are best for an out-of-the-way corner, since the covering looks ugly. Secure the covering close to the soil surface; without light, the weeds will die off, although perennial weeds may take a few seasons to be killed.

Laying black plastic
Cut the weed growth close to the ground, then lay heavy-duty black plastic over the area. Make slits in the soil with a spade, and anchor the plastic by sinking the edges into the slits.

DIGGING AND FORKING

Simply digging or forking over the soil helps to break down compacted areas, increasing aeration and encouraging good plant growth. Turning over the soil also brings large stones to the surface. The deeper you dig the better, but never mix the subsoil with the topsoil.

Avoid digging when the soil is wet, since this will damage the soil structure. If a heavy soil can be dug and left clear over the winter, the weathering effects of frost and cold will help to break down lumps of soil. If the soil already has a reasonable texture, forking well is usually sufficient, and it saves work if you incorporate organic and inorganic matter as you go. When the soil has been dug or forked over, it may look rough and lumpy. Before starting to plant or sow, dig or fork it over again and then break up any clods or lumps on the surface with a rake. This produces a fine tilth – a topsoil layer with evenly sized particles over the surface – that is ideal for the plants' roots.

Digging
Drive the blade of the spade into the ground, then pull back the handle to lift the soil. Do not bend your back – use your knees and elbows.

Forking
Drive the fork into the ground, then lift and turn the fork over to break up and aerate the soil. Remove any stones you bring to the surface.

IMPROVING SOIL TEXTURE AND STRUCTURE

Although digging or forking alone is beneficial, for the greatest improvement you should incorporate plenty of organic and inorganic matter at the same time. This will help to improve aeration, moisture retention, and, in some cases, soil fertility. Organic materials can also be spread on the surface in autumn – they will have worked down into the soil by the following spring when they are needed.

Organic additives include well-rotted manure, leafmold, the contents of old grow bags, composted shredded bark, mixtures based on various plant fibers, and compost, all of which improve soil structure and hold moisture in the soil. Spent mushroom compost is also good, but it makes the soil more alkaline. Inorganic additives include coarse sand and grit, which lighten and improve drainage on heavy soils, and lime, which improves the structure of clay soil by breaking it up. Since lime is alkaline, avoid using it near acid-loving plants.

MAKING COMPOST AND LEAFMOLD

The best compost is made in specially constructed bins (see below); these are available ready-made, in kit form, or can be built from scratch. Ensure that the compost is well rotted before adding it to the soil. Make leafmold by putting fallen leaves in a bin or large black plastic bag with several air holes. The leaves should be decomposed and ready to use after six to twelve months.

Making your own compost

A good compost needs the nitrogen from grass clippings, manure, or annual weeds, mixed with bulkier material, such as kitchen waste and woody chips from pruning. The materials decompose as the temperature rises. With regular turning, the compost should be ready in 3–4 months.

Well-rotted manure
Manure is best dug in, but if used as a mulch and spread on the surface it will gradually be taken down into the soil by earthworms.

Mushroom compost
This can be dug into the soil. It is alkaline and so cannot be used where lime-hating or acid-loving plants are to be grown.

Lime
This can be added to heavy or compacted soil to help to break up lumps to form crumbs. It raises the soil pH.

Coarse sand
This can be dug into a heavy soil to open it up and improve drainage to an extent.

IMPROVING SOIL FERTILITY

Most soils are naturally quite fertile, but to maintain this, fertilizers are sometimes needed. Organic and inorganic fertilizers contain a range of nutrients in different proportions. On most soils the nutrients that need to be added regularly are nitrogen for vigorous growth, phosphorus (phosphate) to encourage flowering and fruiting, and potassium (potash) for strong roots. The packets usually indicate the respective proportions under the chemical symbols N, P, K (see also the nutrient content chart, below). A balanced fertilizer contains roughly equal proportions of the three main nutrients; a complete fertilizer also contains equal amounts of N, P, and K, but includes a range of other minerals, too. At certain stages in a plant's life, a fertilizer rich in a particular nutrient may be more appropriate. For details about how to apply fertilizers, see "Feeding," p.47.

INORGANIC FERTILIZERS

Inorganic fertilizers may be your only option in a small garden where there is no space to store bulky organic fertilizers. They can be combined with homemade compost and leafmold.

ORGANIC FERTILIZERS

Bulky organic fertilizers, such as well-rotted manure, contain fewer nutrients by weight than inorganic fertilizers, but improve the soil in other ways: they add important trace elements and help improve soil structure.

KITCHEN WASTE
A layer approximately 6in (15cm) deep of kitchen waste, such as peelings, can be mixed together with garden debris.

GRASS CLIPPINGS
Mix a thin layer of grass clippings, preferably with manure or a commercial compost activator, to speed up the process of decomposition.

TWIGGY MATERIAL
A thick layer of light, twiggy material at the base allows air to circulate through the compost pile.

TYPE OF FERTILIZER	% NITROGEN (N)	% PHOSPHORUS (P)	% POTASSIUM (K)
INORGANIC			
Ammonium nitrate	35	–	–
Superphosphate	–	20	–
Potassium sulfate	–	–	49
ORGANIC			
Manure	0.6	0.1	0.5
Compost	0.5	0.3	0.8
Seaweed meal	2.8	0.2	2.5
Mushroom compost	0.7	0.3	0.3
Bone meal	2.	14	–

NUTRIENT CONTENT OF FERTILIZERS

CHOOSING PLANTS

Whatever type of plant you buy, selecting a healthy specimen is vital. Plants can be bought in various forms. Container-grown plants have been raised in containers. Bare-root ones are grown in open ground, then lifted and sold when dormant with no soil or soil mix around their roots. Containerized plants are grown in open ground, then lifted and planted in a container. Balled-and-burlapped plants are sold with their roots and surrounding soil wrapped in burlap or netting.

Container-grown plants are the most expensive but often establish more easily than other types since their root systems are well developed. Advice on buying woody plants – those with hardened, woody stems that form a long-term branch structure – is given on these two pages. Herbaceous plants – those that die down to the ground at the end of each year – are covered on pages 30–31.

WHAT TO LOOK FOR

Before you buy, check that the plant is suitable for the spot you have in mind. Will it look good with its neighbors? Does it need sun or shade? Is it hardy or will it need protection? Will it thrive in your particular soil conditions?

How tall and wide will the plant grow? Is it an irritant or even poisonous? The plant label should provide you with all the information you require (see below) but if not ask at the garden center or nursery before buying.

CHOOSING A TREE

Trees are sold container-grown, containerized, bare-root, and balled-and-burlapped. Young trees are cheaper and quicker to establish than larger ones. The crown of the tree should be well balanced and free of spindly, damaged, or crossing branches. Most trees do not need extensive pruning; if a lot of growth has been pruned out, the plant may be unhealthy or prone to dieback disease – if in any doubt, do not buy it. If the tree is bare-root, the roots should be firm and evenly spaced with some fibrous growth. For details about how to plant a tree, see p.43.

Peony
'Sarah Bernhardt'

Peony
Paeonia 'Sarah Bernhardt'

SEASON OF INTEREST: In late spring to midsummer, produces masses of large, scented, double flowers that have papery, rose pink petals with paler edges. This showy plant makes an ideal summer focal point.

HEIGHT: 3ft (1m)

SPREAD: 3ft (1m)

HARDINESS: Very hardy, but young growth can be damaged by late spring frosts.

SOIL TYPE: Rich and well-drained.

EXPOSURE: Prefers full sun, but will tolerate light shade.

Evenly spaced branch framework

Container-grown tree (oak)

Healthy-looking foliage

Soil mix free of weeds, liverworts, and algae

Firm, healthy roots, reaching to the edge of the soil mix but not filling the pot

SPR · SUM · AUT · WIN

WOODY PLANTS

• Trees are deciduous or evergreen woody perennials, often with a single trunk, and are the tallest and longest-lived plants.

• Shrubs (including roses) are perennial, deciduous or evergreen woody plants, usually bushy and multistemmed.

• Climbers are evergreen or deciduous plants, generally perennial and woody, but a few are herbaceous or annual.

TREE ROOTS IN MESH

Mature trees may be sold with their roots in mesh within a pot; if left on too long, the mesh may retard the trees' development. The root balls are often small in relation to the top-growth. Before planting, cut the mesh away and soak the root ball to make it easier to spread out the roots.

CHOOSING A SHRUB

Shrubs are usually sold container-grown but may also be available bare-root, balled-and-burlapped, or containerized. Choose a plant with a well-developed root system. To inspect the roots of a container-grown shrub, place one hand on top of the root ball, invert the plant, and slide off the pot. The roots should be firm and healthy with white tips. If the root system is poorly developed, the soil mix will fall away as you remove the pot. A mass of congested roots, on the other hand, indicates that the plant is potbound. Make sure that the soil mix surface is free of algae (a green or brownish green layer), liverworts (flattish, green growth that develops when a plant has been in the pot for too long), and weeds. The stems should look healthy, vigorous, and evenly distributed, with plenty of foliage. For how to plant a container-grown shrub, see p.42.

Container-grown shrub (skimmia)

Healthy, well-spaced top-growth

Foliage not yellowing or withered

Plenty of fibrous roots

Potbound shrub

Root system is potbound

see p.42

BALLED-AND-BURLAPPED TREES AND SHRUBS

Trees and shrubs are often available as balled-and-burlapped plants. These tend to grow better than bare-root specimens. Choose a plant with the largest possible root ball, and squeeze the soil to check that it is moist and firmly packed; the burlap or netting should be intact. Loose soil, damaged burlap, and large-mesh netting all expose the root ball to the drying effects of air. Fibrous root growth should be visible when the ball is unwrapped. For how to plant a balled-and-burlapped tree, see p.43.

Moist soil around root ball

Burlap intact to keep root ball as firm as possible

see p.43

CHOOSING A ROSE

Roses are usually sold bare-root while dormant, and container-grown or containerized in the growing season. Buy a bare-root rose only if you can plant or heel it in immediately. Stems should be sturdy and free from signs of damage or disease, with no crossing branches or distorted growth. Buds should be plump, not withered. The graft union, a woody lump at the stem base where the rose's top-growth has been grafted onto the roots, should be complete and firm. Roots should be healthy, even, and unbroken. Avoid plants with lopsided or severely cut-back roots, since these will neither anchor the rose nor reach moisture and nutrients.

Select containerized roses in the same way as shrubs (above), checking that the foliage looks healthy, and inspect the roots. For details of how to plant a rose, see p.43.

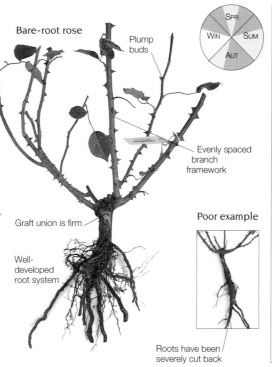

Bare-root rose

Plump buds

Evenly spaced branch framework

Graft union is firm

Well-developed root system

Poor example

Roots have been severely cut back

see p.43

CONTAINERIZED PLANTS

Containerized plants should not be confused with container-grown plants; their root systems are far less well developed and do not establish as quickly. They are usually potted the season before they go on sale, so the soil mix often looks fresh with no algae or weeds on the surface, and tends to fall away if you remove the pot. Roses are often sold in this way. Plant as for bare-root plants; see p.43.

Check for new, healthy roots.

Large roots have been cut before potting.

Soil falls away when pot is removed

see p.43

CHOOSING PERENNIALS

Perennials are usually available all year, but the widest selection is found in spring. This is the best time of year to buy, since both foliage and roots can be easily examined and the plants establish quickly.

Most herbaceous plants are sold in containers. These should be intact, or else the roots may have been damaged or have dried out. The foliage should be healthy, vigorous, and disease-free, and there should be signs of new growth at the crown. If the plants are dormant or naturally dying back, check the crown to ensure it is firm and undamaged. If buying in early spring, ensure that the perennial has plenty of good, strong buds or shoots. Examine the roots to check that they are firm and healthy. They should be white, indicating new growth, and sufficiently well developed to hold the soil mix in place when the pot is removed, but not be potbound or too tightly packed. Dead roots look blackened and may indicate that the plant has suffered moisture or nutrient stress. The soil mix should be moist, but not soggy, and the surface free from weeds, algae, and liverworts.

NONWOODY PLANTS

• Perennials are nonwoody, mostly herbaceous plants that die down at the end of the year, lie dormant in winter, and produce new growth the following spring. A few nonwoody plants are evergreen. Some tender perennials are grown as annuals.

• Annuals are nonwoody plants that germinate, flower, set seed, and die within the space of one year. Many (the half-hardy annuals) survive only during mild weather, and are raised to flower in the same year. Hardy annuals tolerate frost but will not survive hard winters.

• Biennials are nonwoody plants that produce leafy growth the first year and then flower, set seed, and die in their second. They often establish themselves in the garden through reseeding.

Container-grown perennial (lupine)

Healthy, green top-growth

Soil mix just moist

No weed growth visible on soil mix surface

Roots visible around the root ball, but not congested

Sturdy, new shoots

Roots growing strongly and free from any signs of dieback

Weak perennial

Top-growth is thin, sparse, and weakened

Soil mix falling away because the roots are poorly developed

Potbound perennial

Discolored foliage

Tightly packed, congested roots

PLANTS WITH THEIR ROOTS IN MESH

Some perennials and annuals are sold with a mesh, usually made of perforated plastic, around the roots. The roots should be able to break out of the mesh and become established in the soil mix. However, less vigorous plants may be unable to push through so their roots become potbound, even if there is good soil mix beyond. Before planting, carefully cut through the mesh in several places to allow the roots to grow out more easily.

Root ball within mesh
The mesh around the roots may be visible at the surface of the soil near the base of the stem.

BULBS, CORMS, RHIZOMES, AND TUBERS

• Bulbs are underground storage organs, formed from modified leaves or leaf bases. They often have a dry outer layer (the tunic). Each year bulbs produce new leaves which die down after flowering.

• Corms are the swollen, underground bases of stems, often with an outer layer or tunic. New leaves are produced and die down each year.

• Rhizomes are swollen, underground stems that grow horizontally. They produce new leaves each year which die down when the plants are dormant.

• Tubers are swollen, irregularly shaped stems or roots. They produce new leaves each year which die down after flowering.

CHOOSING BULBS

Bulbs, corms, rhizomes, and tubers are, botanically, quite distinct, but they are grouped together here as bulbs since you need to look for similar qualities in each when buying. Bulbs are sold loose or in packages. They should be stored in a cool and well-ventilated place. A bulb should feel firm to the touch, and its exterior should be free from blemishes or insect attack. Growth points, if present, should look healthy without having started into active growth, and there should be no fresh root development. Although large, heavy twin-nosed daffodil bulbs are desirable, an undersized twin-nosed bulb may produce fewer, smaller flowers than average, or perhaps none at all, in its first year.

Single-nosed daffodil – good example

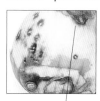

Undamaged nose, not yet starting into growth

Tunic intact

Firm base without new root growth

Daffodil – poor examples

Tunic removed to reveal patches of deterioration beneath

Offset too small to flower in the first year

CHOOSING ANNUALS

Annuals are usually sold in packs or trays but occasionally in small pots or as individual plugs. Some are available in batches of single colors, allowing you to restrict the color combinations you use. Annuals are relatively short-lived, so choose healthy plants without rotting leaves or mildew. The roots should be well developed, but not potbound or discolored, and with no signs of dieback or rot.

The soil mix should be just moist but not covered in algae. Young seedlings in plugs are cheapest, but they need to be grown on in pots until they are well established. More mature plants should be full of buds with sturdy stems and unyellowed leaves; they should start flowering soon after planting. Most summer-flowering annuals should not be planted or left outside until all danger of frost is past.

BUYING SEEDS

When buying seeds, check that the packets are displayed in a fairly cool but dry environment since the seeds may deteriorate if exposed to baking sun. The packet should give an outline of conditions needed for germination and a brief description of cultural requirements. Always check the "sell by" date to make sure you are not buying old stock at the full price. Many seeds available are F1 hybrids, which, although more expensive, produce larger and more uniform crops.

Some small seed is available with a coating that makes handling and spacing easier. This pelleted seed is, however, considerably more expensive than other seed and is not yet available for a wide range of plants.

Tray of healthy annuals (pansies)

Compact, vigorous growth

Buds developing

Weak plant

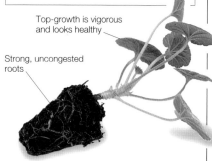

Top-growth is vigorous and looks healthy

Strong, uncongested roots

Moist soil mix

Container intact

Straggly stems with sparse foliage

Fungal growth on dead leaves

Seedling plugs

Seedlings can be obtained in individual plugs of soil mix, ready for planting in small pots or trays. The root balls are well developed, so damage to the plants while transplanting is reduced.

TOOLS AND HOW TO USE THEM

A few carefully chosen tools and pieces of basic equipment are all that you need for starting, maintaining, and improving your garden. The range you select depends on the type of garden you have and how frequently you are going to do any one job. Start with the basics, shown on the next three pages, and build your collection as you need to. A selection of the most useful lawncare tools is shown on p.35. Try to buy as good a quality of tool as possible – regular replacements of poorly made or badly designed tools will become expensive in the long run, whereas good-quality tools will last for years if they are well looked after. To make sure you choose the right tool for the job, insist on handling each one before you buy it and check that it is the correct size for you, that it is neither too heavy nor too light, and that it is comfortable to hold.

HAND FORK AND TROWEL

Use a hand fork or trowel for small-scale tasks, such as light weeding and gardening in confined spaces. These hand tools can also be used for planting, moving, or dividing young or small plants and bulbs, and they are ideal for mixing up small amounts of soil mix or top-dressing.

HANDLE
Choose a wooden or plastic handle that fits your hand well.

PRONGS
Hand forks have three or four prongs. Both designs are satisfactory.

BLADE
The small blade is ideal for use in containers, rock gardens, and raised beds.

STAINLESS OR COATED STEEL?
Stainless steel tools do not rust but are costly; coated steel ones are cheaper and last well if kept clean.

SPADE AND FORK

A good quality spade and fork are essential since these will usually be the tools you need most. They should be sturdily constructed if they are to perform and last well. A spade is used for digging over the soil and preparing large holes. A fork is good for turning over soil or lifting root vegetables – a flat-pronged potato fork is specially designed to minimize root-crop damage. A fork is also handy for transplanting or dividing plants, forking in manure, and spreading mulches.

Straight back

Correct digging
When digging, keep your back straight to avoid straining it. A tool of the correct length, size, and weight will be easier to use than one that is too heavy or small. These guidelines apply to forking, hoeing, and raking, too.

HANDLE
A D-shaped plastic handle is the most common type.

SHAFT
This is usually wooden, but it may be metal. It fits into a long socket in the neck.

HEAD
The neck and head should be molded from one piece of metal for added strength.

TREAD
A tread relieves pressure on your instep and improves grip.

BLADE
The coated blade is easy to clean and should not rust.

PRONGS
The prongs of a digging fork are usually square, but on a potato fork they are flat.

GARDEN RAKE

Use a garden rake to collect up fallen leaves and other debris, to break up lumps of soil, and to create a fine, level area for planting and sowing.

Using a rake to clear
To collect up stones and break up lumps of soil, position the rake with the teeth downward and draw it toward you.

Using a rake to level
With the flat edge of the head downward, draw the rake back and forth, then work at right angles to this.

RAKE HEAD
The head has molded or riveted teeth and is usually available in various widths.

DUTCH HOE

There are various types of hoe, but the best to choose is a Dutch hoe since it can be used for a wide range of jobs. It is ideal for weeding between young and established plants and for marking out and making drills for sowing and planting.

Using a hoe for weeding
Keeping your back straight, hold the hoe handle in a comfortable position with the blade parallel to, and just below, the soil surface. Push and pull the hoe, skimming the soil to remove surface weeds without damaging the roots of nearby plants.

Using a hoe to aerate the soil
Hold the hoe so that the blade is at right angles to the ground. Push the blade gently into the soil to break up the top layer.

SHAFT
A 5ft (1.5m) shaft suits most gardeners. Longer ones may be available. Wooden shafts can easily be replaced if they are broken.

BLADE
The hoe blade is flat and sharpened. It is slightly angled to slide easily through the soil.

PRUNERS

A good pair of pruners can cut all soft stems and tackle woody ones up to about ½in (1cm) in diameter. Pruners are also good for taking cuttings for propagation. There are various types of cutting action; whichever type you choose, the pruners should be of high quality, sharp, and produce a clean cut without damaging or crushing the stem.

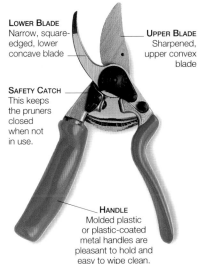

LOWER BLADE
Narrow, square-edged, lower concave blade

UPPER BLADE
Sharpened, upper convex blade

SAFETY CATCH
This keeps the pruners closed when not in use.

HANDLE
Molded plastic or plastic-coated metal handles are pleasant to hold and easy to wipe clean.

WATERING CAN AND HOSE

Use a watering can for plants in greenhouses and containers, and for individual plants as well as seedlings. Do not buy one that will be too heavy to lift easily when full. For large areas, a hose is easier to use.

ROSE
Position a detachable rose facing downward for a coarse spray and upward for a fine spray.

HOSE ATTACHMENTS
Many different snap-on hose-end attachments are available to spray, sprinkle, provide a strong jet or fountain, or feed.

Using pruners
Grip the handles of the pruners firmly and make a clean cut without twisting.

An angled cut
For stems with alternate buds, use an angled cut just above and sloping away from the bud.

A straight cut
Use a straight cut to prune stems with opposite buds.

KEEPING YOUR TOOLS CLEAN

Your tools will do a better job and last much longer if you maintain them well.

Store them in a dry place and never leave them out in the rain. Clean off dirt and debris after use and oil metal tools so that they don't rust. Sharpen blades from time to time.

Service power tools regularly so that they are always safe and ready for use when you need them.

GARDENING GLOVES

For general use, fabric gloves with suede reinforcements are best. Try several types to see which fits and suits you.

CUFFS
Cuffs protect against thorns.

HOSE LENGTH
Hoses come in different lengths. Buy enough to reach all areas of your garden.

HOSE CARE
Keep the hose free from kinking and protect it from freezing since this might weaken it.

SHEARS

Shears are useful for trimming hedges – a sturdy pair of shears will cut through even woody stems with ease. They can be used for cutting back herbaceous plants and for general trimming. Shears are handy for more delicate jobs, too, including cutting small areas of grass and neatening up edges that are difficult to reach. Choose ones that are not too heavy to use comfortably. After use, wipe the blades clean, dry them, and rub over with an oily rag. Have them sharpened as necessary.

Cutting straight
To achieve an even, level cut, keep the blades of the shears parallel to the line of the hedge. If the hedge is straggly, use string stretched between two stakes as a guide for cutting straight.

NOTCHED BLADE
Choose shears with a notched blade to hold larger stems during cutting.

HAND-SPRAYER

This is useful for misting plants, both indoors and outdoors, that need a moist atmosphere. The most usual type of hand-sprayer works on a compression system, where the water is pumped up before use. The nozzle can often be adjusted to produce a strong jet or a fine spray. Hand-sprayers can also be used for applying small quantities of pesticide, weedkiller, or foliar feed – and reserve one sprayer for using with herbicides exclusively. Wash out after use.

NOZZLE
This is adjustable, enabling you to control the strength of spray.

WHEELBARROW

If you need to move heavy or bulky materials, a wheelbarrow will save you a lot of time and energy. A galvanized metal wheelbarrow will probably last longer than a painted metal or a plastic one, but, it may cost more initially. Most traditional wheelbarrows have one solid wheel. For transporting very heavy or large loads, a garden cart (with two side wheels) is preferable to a wheelbarrow.

LOADING A WHEELBARROW
For ease of use and to minimize the risk of back strain, never try to take too much in the wheelbarrow each journey. Always distribute the load so that the greatest weight is positioned at the front. Provided that you do not overload the barrow, it should move well over most surfaces.

TRAY
The tray is deeper at the front to allow more weight to be carried.

PRUNING SAW

A general-purpose pruning saw, preferably one with heat-treated, hardpoint teeth, is useful for pruning branches over 1in (2.5cm) in diameter. The blade is shaped so that it can be used in confined spaces. Models with wooden and plastic handles are available; check which is easiest to grip and feels most comfortable.

BLADE
Usually no more than 18in (45cm) long, the blade may be fixed or can be folded down into the handle when not in use.

HANDLE
A curved handle gives a good grip when sawing.

KNIFE

A good-quality, general-purpose knife with a folding carbon-steel blade should last for years. Use it for taking cuttings, picking flowers and vegetables, and pruning small plants. Always wipe the blade dry and rub with an oily rag after use.

HANDLE
In winter, a wooden or plastic handle is not as cold as a metal one.

MESH
A fine mesh will sieve soil mix over delicate seeds.

SIEVE

A sieve is used for removing lumps and stones from soil and for sifting soil mix over seeds. Choose one with a sturdy wire mesh for greater durability. A sieve with a fine mesh of about ⅛in (3–4mm) can be used to sieve soil mix over tiny seeds after sowing, one with a large mesh of about ½in (1cm) will remove stones and debris from soil, and a medium mesh between these two will separate out lumps in soil.

OTHER EQUIPMENT

Plant pots, biodegradable fiber pots, cell packs, and **seed trays,** all in a range of sizes, are useful for sowing, planting cuttings, and raising plants. Use **labels** to help you identify newly sown seedlings. A **dibble** is ideal for making holes for transplanting, or for planting cuttings. The spatula-like end of a **widger** is useful for lifting delicate cuttings and seedlings. Use **twine, twist ties,** or **ring ties** for restraining plants and tying in climbers. **Bamboo stakes** singly or tied together will support large plants or groups of plants. Other **wooden stakes** are handy for smaller plants in pots.

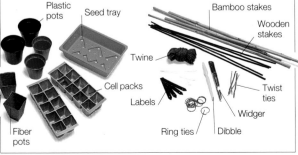

Plastic pots

Seed tray

Twine

Bamboo stakes

Wooden stakes

Cell packs

Labels

Twist ties

Widger

Fiber pots

Ring ties

Dibble

LAWNMOWERS AND TRIMMERS

Lawnmowers can be manually driven or powered by electricity or gas. They are available with one of two cutting actions: a cylinder mower may be manual or powered and has a spiral of blades that moves around, cutting against a fixed blade at the bottom; a rotary mower is always powered and cuts with a single rotating blade. Manual mowers are usually the cheaper option; they are simple to maintain and ideal for small areas. Power mowers cope well with large areas. Cylinder mowers are heavy and tiring to operate, but they give a neat cut on a good-quality lawn. Rotary mowers, on the other hand, perform well on long, uneven grass but do not produce such a neat finish.

Trimmers use a nylon line that spins around at great speed to cut the blades of grass. A trimmer can also cut through weed growth and is especially useful in small or tight areas. Trimmers are powered by gas or electricity. Electric ones are lighter, cheaper, and easier to maintain, but can only be used close to a power source and not on wet grass.

Nylon-line trimmer

POWER SWITCH
The switch operates the trimmer when pressed and cuts out when the grip is relaxed.

SHIELD
This controls the line to keep the trim even.

EDGING TOOLS

To neaten lawn edges you may need some long-handled shears and a half-moon edger. Long-handled shears are useful for trimming long grass that overhangs the lawn – alternatively, a nylon-line trimmer with an adjustable head can be used. A half-moon edger is used for neatening or reshaping a lawn edge that has become scruffy; it can also be used to cut out pieces of sod. Both the shears and edger need to be held vertically to cut well.

Rotary action
The flat blade rotates to cut horizontally, and directs the grass clippings into the bag attachment.

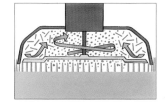

Mulching mechanism
A variation on the usual rotary action, this shaped blade chops up the grass clippings, producing a fine mulch that does not need to be gathered up or discarded in landfills.

Power rotary mower

BAG ATTACHMENT
The clippings are collected in this bag and can be easily added to the compost pile.

HANDLES
The handles need to be long enough for you to use the shears without bending.

SHAFT
This is available in wood, steel, or plastic-coated steel – all are strong.

BLADE
This needs to be kept sharp so that it cuts effectively.

Power cylinder mower

BLADES
These provide a close-cut finish for a very high-quality lawn.

Cylinder blades
A spiral of blades arranged as a cylinder cuts against a fixed blade at the bottom.

SPRING-TINED RAKE

A spring-tined rake has thin, flexible wire tines. It is useful for raking fallen leaves or other lightweight debris, allowing the lawn grasses beneath to grow unhindered. It is also the best basic tool for scarifying a lawn and removing moss that has been killed by a mosskiller. Hard raking lightly aerates the lawn, too.

TINES
Flexible wire tines can reach the base of the grass to remove accumulated debris.

·3·
BEDS AND BORDERS

*Formal or relaxed, high-maintenance or easy-to-keep, a single
color or rainbow-tinted – every border is unique, reflecting the
nature of the gardener who created it. Designing a bed
provides a glorious opportunity to splash out with color,
form, and texture, so let your imagination run riot.*

PLANNING BEDS AND BORDERS

A well-designed border is a joy to behold, bringing together a range of plants that complement each other and their situation to create a particular mood or effect. In contrast, the average border is rarely much more than a strip of soil supporting a haphazard collection of plants.

For the new gardener, taking on an established border is something of a mixed blessing. On the plus side, you are likely to inherit a selection of mature shrubs that can provide an instant framework for your plantings. On the minus side, some of them may well be growing in the wrong place but, fortunately, many will quickly reestablish if moved in autumn or spring.

In the short term, personalize your newly acquired borders by the judicious addition of one or two favorite plants. For long-term success, however, it is sensible to leave the existing design for one full growing cycle, noting its strengths and weaknesses, ready for a redesign in the following year.

In a brand-new garden, you have a wonderful opportunity to create borders from scratch, with the choice of size, shape, and contents completely unhindered by existing features. Yet once again, the key to success is to take your time. Draw up detailed plans, implement them gradually, and be prepared to make modifications as flaws become apparent.

Whether starting to plant from square one, or modifying a border, it is important to take site and exposure into account (*see* p.19). Assess existing plants for site suitability, and be prepared to move – or even discard – them if necessary. Armed with a list of suitable plants, you are ready to plan with confidence.

BORDERS IN FULL SUN

If your garden has only sunny borders, you are indeed fortunate. Many plants grow sturdy and strong in full sun, flowering varieties will give a fine display of blooms,

A border with a fully sunny exposure
Make the most of any really sunny sites, packing them with a mass of colorful annuals and perennials that will thrive in the conducive

and color in virtually any shade or hue is yours for the taking. The majority of us, however, have at most a couple of truly sunny beds, with others that brighten and darken through the day – and the seasons.

Make the most of sunny spots with a range of shrubs, perennials, bulbs, and annuals that will really relish conditions there. Annuals in particular often need a lot of sunshine to produce a good display. Use the rapid color they can provide to fill gaps while other plants are establishing or

atmosphere. Remember that such a densely planted border will need to be fed and watered regularly if it is to give its best over a prolonged season.

as an ornamental edging that you can change from year to year. Most natural colors combine surprisingly well, and a mixture looks cheerful in a sunny spot.

SHADY BEDS AND BORDERS

A bed or border that spends a large part of each day in shade may present a bit of a design challenge, but it can look stunning. Shade-loving plants are generally notable for their foliage and can be combined to create exquisite contrasts of form, texture, and subtle color.

Spring plants make a pretty start to the year, especially those woodland natives accustomed to low light levels. Choose from crocuses, fritillaries, wood anemones, snowdrops, and countless others.

Even without the familiar collection of summer-flowering plants, a shady border needn't be dull. From the glossy, dark greens of camellias and rhododendrons, to the soft, silvery deadnettles (*Lamium*) and bold, brownish purple bergenias, the diversity of foliage available is truly breathtaking. As a bonus, many of these varieties flower as well, although with a few notable exceptions (such as camellias and rhododendrons) the blooms do tend to play second fiddle. For more plant ideas, *see* "Plants for Different Microclimates," p.23.

Grouping for a shady corner

Fill darker areas in the garden with a lush collection of foliage plants. Hostas thrive in damp, shady conditions and their wonderful, sculptural leaves will make a real impact, especially when several different types are planted together. Here, they form a striking contrast with the feathery, blue-green leaves of rue, and the variegated ivies.

Successful island bed planting
An island bed can be planted with almost any variety suited to the soil and exposure, provided it is not too invasive or sprawling in habit. This bed is full of compact and easy-to-maintain plants.

Make use of height
The most effective border designs work in three dimensions. Here the eye is led in a single sweep from the clumps of herbaceous geraniums and purple sedum in the foreground, right up to the glorious clematis on the wall behind. A limited color scheme has been used to help unify the planting.

BASIC DESIGN CONSIDERATIONS

It is not sufficient to know that a plant will grow on your chosen site; you must also be aware of how fast and large it will grow.

Unless you know the eventual height and spread of a plant, it is impossible, for example, to plan whether you need to grow several plants of the chosen variety in a clump, or if a single specimen will do the job, given time. Without this information you are likely to fall into the trap of overplanting – one of the cardinal sins of gardening. Not only is overplanting unnecessarily expensive, but borders that look good initially will quickly become crowded, requiring thinning almost as soon as they have settled down. Resist the temptation, and fill temporary gaps with seasonal bedding plants instead.

Knowing its ultimate size also helps you to position each plant for greatest effect. A tall plant could form an unobtrusive backdrop, or bring it forward in the bed to make a striking feature in its own right.

The traditional border follows a tiered plan, with ground-huggers at the front rising to medium and tall varieties; this also prevents the tall plants from overshadowing low ones. In practice this might produce a border where tall hollyhocks give way to lupines and polemoniums, with herbaceous geraniums and dicentras at the front. However, it can also be fun to experiment with the conventions – perhaps combining plants of varying heights within the run of a border to create an undulating effect.

LOW-MAINTENANCE BORDERS

The traditional herbaceous border takes a lot of preparation and continues to demand a great deal of attention throughout its life. Clearly not everyone has the time, or the inclination, to spend every spare minute pruning, staking, tying, and dividing. If you fall into this category, choose plants that need the minimum of care – but remember that every plant benefits from feeding, watering, and deadheading as required.

Shrubs, groundcover plants (including groundcover roses), and bulbs can all be grown with amazingly little effort – some may require an occasional trim, but that takes next to no time. As with any other bed or border, of course, you will need to take exposure and soil type into account when choosing your plants, but if you do concentrate on slow-growing shrubs, perhaps underplanted with spring- and summer-flowering bulbs or groundcover plants (which, as a bonus, will help to exclude weeds), then you will have set yourself an easy job for the future.

To finish off a low-maintenance border, lay down a deep mulch of compost or, more attractively, bark chips. Not only will this mulch help to retain valuable soil moisture, it will also keep most weeds firmly in check.

PLANNING ISLAND BEDS

A large expanse of grass, unless used as a play area, will almost always look a lot more interesting if broken up by a well-placed, well-stocked island bed.

There is nothing to stop you from creating an island bed anywhere in the lawn, provided you remember to leave enough space so that it can be walked around with ease. This is important both for maintenance of the arrangement, and so that it can be admired from all sides – unlike a conventional border, an island bed is planted to look good from any angle.

Any plants suitable for the soil type and exposure can be used, although invasive or floppy varieties may trespass onto the grass. Like any other bed, a combination of heights can be used to create an interesting effect. However, unlike conventional beds, the tallest varieties should be planted toward the center of the bed, with plants gradually decreasing in size out toward the edges.

Island beds can also be planted with symmetrical arrangements of perennials planted around a central shrub, or with a composition of brightly colored annuals.

NARROW BEDS

Although we are perhaps used to thinking of borders as grand herbaceous extravaganzas, clearly they can be made to any size to suit your garden.

A narrow border – say one of 2ft (60cm) or less – will require special care if the planting is to be a success. One approach is to confine yourself to a single variety along the border. If the bed is beside a path, perhaps plant compact, fragrant lavender to release a cloud of perfume as you brush past. A narrow bed against a wall can be a challenge, since this sheltered ground is likely to be very dry, but the chocolate vine (*Akebia quinata*) and some other climbers would thrive there.

In general, avoid plants with a spreading habit, and concentrate on fairly upright varieties. Follow this basic rule, and your narrow border can be stocked with almost any plant you like to bring color, shape, and scent to the garden, provided it stays in proportion with other features.

CORNER BEDS

Making a border or bed in a corner turns an empty space into a focal point of interest and color. When planning your design, bear in mind that the woody roots of certain large plants may interfere with house foundations or brickwork, so a border next to a house is best stocked with a selection of perennials and annuals rather than vigorous large shrubs and trees. Include some scented plants to enjoy their perfume wafting through the windows, and use climbers or wall shrubs to increase the impact of the planting without taking up too much valuable ground space.

Alkaline corner bed
Meeting the twin challenges of a corner site and an alkaline soil demands careful planning, although the potential planting list is long. Here, deadnettles, dahlias, achilleas, and heucheras, among others, fill the front of the bed, while asters, penstemons, and gauras bring height to the arrangement.

ALKALINE OR ACID BORDERS

A soil that has a high pH value provides an alkaline environment in which many plants will fail to flourish and some will suffer severe, even fatal, nutrient deficiencies. Likewise, a dark, peaty soil with a low pH value provides acid conditions that, although ideal for a wide range of plants (including some that like only acid soil), are not suited to others. However, forewarned is forearmed, and if you know which category your soil falls into (*see* "Identifying Your Soil," p.24), you can choose from the many plants that prefer alkaline or acid conditions to create a flourishing border.

MOIST BEDS AND BORDERS

If you have a moist area in the garden, rather than leaving it to the moss and weeds, you have the perfect opportunity to create a habitat for the many plants that will thrive in these moist conditions and reward you by responding with masses of luxuriant growth.

Hostas are a prime example. They love to have moist roots and will form dense mounds of bold variegated or ridged leaves at a tremendous rate in suitably moist conditions. Plant astilbes alongside, where their finely divided leaves, topped with plumelike flowerheads in shades of pink, red, or white, will form an attractive contrast. Both hostas and astilbes are small to medium in height and hence look good toward the front of a graduated border, or grown in massed plantings as groundcover.

Hellebores, especially *Helleborus orientalis*, should do well in a moist bed, and many of the brightly colored mimulus varieties also thrive in a moist spot – annual species will flower just a few months after they have been sown. For a quirky, modernist planting try *Houttuynia cordata* 'Chamaeleon', which produces masses of crazily colored, aromatic foliage and flourishes when its roots are in damp soil. Traditionalists may prefer to grow foxgloves, which look particularly attractive if grown in groups and then allowed to self-seed.

If the soil is acid as well as moist, then you have a wonderful opportunity to grow azaleas and rhododendrons, *Kalmia latifolia*, and pieris – all plants that are unlikely to perform well in dry areas. If the moist spot is fairly shaded as well, most of the plants suggested for shady borders will thrive there. For more plant ideas, *see* "Plants for Different Microclimates," p.23.

A moist and shady area
Often regarded as an insurmountable headache and abandoned to the weeds, a moist, shady area can in fact be used to great advantage. Here an informal planting, including astilbes and candelabra primroses, creates a naturally pretty effect which, as a bonus, will attract wildlife.

CHOOSING PLANTS FOR THE BORDER

Finding the right plant for the right place can be a daunting task. Faced with apparently unlimited choice, it is sometimes tempting just to close your eyes and grab at the nearest container in the nursery or garden center. Needless to say, this course of action is unlikely to produce well-balanced designs.

When choosing plants, the first step is to look long and hard at the bed to be planted – both on its own and in combination with its neighbors. The relationship between beds in a garden is as important as the relationship between plants in a bed. In either case, the proximity of one to another can produce an effect which is restrained and harmonious, or bold and clashing. But those effects should be intentional, not the unexpected outcome of a poor combination.

Visit local gardens and nurseries with an eye open for plants or plant associations that you particularly like. Magazines, books, and even paintings are all good sources of inspiration, and the categories discussed below should prove helpful as you explore the range of available options.

But remember there is no need to rush. You can always temporarily fill a border with colorful annuals and plan the long-term planting over a season or two.

FRAGRANCE
Part of the joy of a good border is not only its appearance, but also its scent. Try to include a few plants chosen specifically for their scented blooms, such as night-scented stocks and sweet peas, or lavender and lemon balm. If the border is backed by a wall or fence, include fragrant climbers too. For winter fragrance, the sweet-smelling flowers of *Daphne odora* 'Aureo-marginata' and Christmas box (*Sarcococca*) are among the best. Not only will these varieties look wonderful together, but their fragrances combine in a heady perfume that will carry halfway around the garden.

A riot of color
Here, an exuberant diversity of plants and colors comes together in an informal grouping that looks more like a happy accident than a predetermined design. In reality, it takes just as much planning to create a successful combination in this style as it does to produce a traditional formal bed.

Restrained palette
Sticking to a single color can create harmonious plantings with an air of calm tranquility. However, as this lovely example illustrates, what we might consider a white border is in fact made up of several complementary soft grays and shades of green, with touches of yellow and green-tinged white in addition to the truly pure white blooms. The planting includes white hydrangeas, Convolvulus cneorum, *and sculptural calla lilies* (Zantedeschia aethiopica). *The warm, terracotta-colored brick edging emphasizes the cool colors of the border.*

COLOR CONTRASTS
Different color combinations can be fun, but they can also be hard to handle. For a harmonious scheme, try planting E*uphorbia amygdaloides* 'Rubra' with its red-purple foliage to contrast with the pink flowers of astilbe. Alternatively, make the most of clashing color contrasts, perhaps growing yellow tulips with bright red ones. A favorite combination of mine is the bright pink *Geranium psilostemon* with *Lavatera trimestris* 'Mont Blanc', which is pure white.

LIMITED COLOR RANGE
Creating designs using only a restricted range of colors can produce lovely displays, varying in temperament from icy cool whites and silvers through to fiery hot, roaring reds and oranges. A limited color scheme can also be used to make a definite design statement – perhaps starkly modern or, like the famous white garden at Sissinghurst in England, with a twist on traditional style.

If you are developing a limited color scheme in an existing border, you will need to see one full year through to find out exactly what colors are already contained within the border, and which plants are worth keeping. Even in a brand-new bed it may be preferable to build up your scheme gradually. This allows you to reassess the overall effect regularly and remove any plants that are not fitting as planned.

You need not overly restrict the colors you choose: mix deep yellows with orange, and maybe even red or plant pale blue with white or silvery gray. Remember also the part that foliage color may play. Dark or light bright greens, silvery grays, and purple hues can all be used either as part of the color scheme or as a unifying (and sometimes calming) backdrop.

Foliage effects
This beautiful design creates a rich tapestry of color in which the few flowering plants are of secondary importance to a wonderful array of foliage. The burgundy and yellowy greens are provided by a range of Japanese maples; Solomon's seal (Polygonatum) with its delicate, unobtrusive flowers stands out against the burgundy backdrop.

Architectural form
The blue-green, ridged leaves of a Hosta sieboldiana contrast boldly with a New Zealand flax (Phormium tenax).

FOLIAGE AND PLANT FORM

There are so many flowering plants to choose from that it can be easy to overlook the impact that foliage may have in its own right. Yet from feathery ferns to the bold spikes of a yucca or the monster leaves of marsh-loving Gunnera manicata, there is massive variety in leaf shape and texture and in the effects they can create.

Place irises, Sisyrinchium striatum, and yuccas to form strong focal points, their sharp, pointed leaves set off by a foil of simple foliage. Elsewhere use dicentras and polemoniums for a prettier effect.

Textures range from furry stachys leaves to more solid hens and chicks and sedums, and foliage colors can be exciting, too. The euphorbia family, for example, produces bracts (leafy "flowers") in a range of arresting colors from sharp lime green to rich oranges and reds. There are rose-tinted epimediums, black ornamental grasses (Ophiopogon planiscapus 'Nigrescens'), and a wide range of variegated and silver-leaved plants to choose from.

Plant form also has an important role in border designs. Solidly shaped plants such as the neat-domed Buxus microphylla 'Green Pillow' or the giant thistle (Onopordum acanthium) clearly have strong architectural impact. Yet soft, hazy nigella and gypsophila have a part to play as well.

SEASONAL EFFECTS

As you plan, consider what the border will look like at various times of year – you may prefer to concentrate on summer color, but it takes only a couple of autumn or winter interest plants to brighten up the border for the rest of the year.

Select herbaceous perennials with interesting seedheads, such as rudbeckias, that can contribute structure through the autumn and winter. If you plant spring-flowering bulbs alongside, their early display will be on the wane as new perennial shoots emerge and disguise the yellowing bulb foliage.

There are also a number of plants that are positively at their best in the winter months. Shrubs with colored stems, including dogwoods and willows, and evergreen shrubs and perennials have an austere beauty. There are even some shrubs – witch hazel, for example – that flower in winter. Closer to ground level, evergreens such as Ajuga reptans 'Atropurpurea', with its bronze-purple leaves and promise of blue flower spikes in spring, brighten the otherwise bare soil.

Winter wonderland
Plant dogwoods for the magnificent color of their glowing, fiery red winter stems.

Bright and beautiful spring color
Celebrate the start of a new gardening year with a cheerful mixture of spring flowers. Here daffodils and two varieties of tulips combine with forget-me-nots and the jolly pink pompons of English daisies.

Planting in the Border

Before you buy anything to plant in your border, stop and think: will the plant fit in where you picture planting it in terms of size, shape, season of interest, and color? Does the site have suitable pH, soil texture, and exposure? Will the fully-grown plant swamp its neighbors? When you are satisfied that you have the right plant, prepare its new home well and plant as soon as possible after buying. Your new addition may look tiny in the border, but don't be tempted to overplant – keep to the correct spacing, and fill gaps with annuals that will provide you with a colorful display in the short term without jeopardizing the long-term success of the border. Water regularly until the plant is established and continue to care for it as needed, and it will look good for years to come. Woody plants are covered on these two pages and non-woody ones (including bulbs) on the next two.

Planting a Container-grown Shrub

Container-grown shrubs can be planted during most of the year, provided that the ground is not frozen, waterlogged, or extremely dry, but they are more likely to establish well if they are planted in autumn or spring. Prepare a planting hole about twice the diameter of the root ball, larger if you are planting in clay soil. The hole must also be deep enough so that the top of the soil mix in the container is level with the soil surface once planted. Incorporate plenty of organic matter or soil mix into the hole, and add a complete fertilizer at a rate of 2oz/sq yd (70g/sq m).

Before planting, water the root ball well – this ensures that the soil mix is thoroughly moist, even in the center. Tease out the roots or loosen the root ball a little when planting. A slightly potbound plant – one that has grown too large for its container – will still grow reasonably well if you tease out its roots and prune out any that are large and coiling around the outside of the root ball. Give the whole area a thorough watering after planting and apply a 2–3in (5–7cm) layer of mulch

You Will Need
•Spade •Fork •Soil mix or organic matter •Fertilizer •Plant •Stake •Pruners •Watering can •Mulch

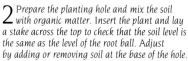

to an area just wider than the spread of the roots, keeping it well clear of the stem. Continue to water the shrub regularly, especially in its first year. For more details on mulching, *see p.46*.

Preparing the Planting Hole

Loosen the soil at the base and sides of the hole. Mix in organic matter to avoid a major change in texture between the soil around the plant and the planting hole, thus helping roots to spread.

Loosening the sides of the hole
Dig the hole deep and wide enough to suit the size of the root ball. Use a fork to roughen the sides of the hole.

1 *Support the plant in one hand, carefully holding the stems between your fingers, and remove the pot with the other hand using a firm, twisting movement if it does not come away readily. Tease out a few roots from the root ball.*

2 *Prepare the planting hole and mix the soil with organic matter. Insert the plant and lay a stake across the top to check that the soil level is the same as the level of the root ball. Adjust by adding or removing soil at the base of the hole.*

3 Backfill the hole with the remaining soil and organic matter mixture, firming it gently as you go until the soil is in contact with the roots and there are no large air spaces. Fill the hole level with the top of the plant's soil mix, then cover with a thin layer of soil mixture to reduce moisture loss.

4 Firm the plant into the hole, using your heel for larger shrubs or your hands for smaller ones, so that the soil is firmly in place but not compacted. Cut out any unhealthy or crossing stems to an outward-growing bud, being careful to maintain a well-balanced shape. Water, and apply a mulch.

PLANTING A BARE-ROOT ROSE

Roses establish best if they are planted at the end of autumn or, in areas with cold winters, in early spring. It is important to plant as soon as possible after buying – most suppliers offer roses in late autumn and spring, so it is not too difficult to tie in your purchasing and planting times.

Before planting, check that the roots have not dried out and, if necessary, soak them in a bucket of water for a couple of hours. This will make the roots easier to spread out in the planting hole. Remove any that are badly damaged, withered, diseased, or dead. If any roots are much longer and thicker than the rest, prune these back by about one-third.

Prepare the planting hole as described for planting a container-grown shrub. Check that the graft union is placed at the correct depth (one inch above the soil surface in the South, and an inch or two below in the North) before backfilling with the planting mixture. Water well, then apply a mulch to an area just larger than the planting hole.

Remove weak or crossing shoots before planting.

1 Before planting, use a sharp pair of pruners to cut out all straggly, crossing, diseased, damaged, or dead stems, ensuring that those remaining form a shape that is evenly balanced.

2 Hold the rose in the center of the hole with its roots well spread, and lay a stake across the hole to gauge the correct planting depth for your area (see left). Backfill with soil and firm well.

HEELING IN
If the ground is too wet or cold to plant immediately, heel in your new plants temporarily by planting them in a trench in a spare piece of ground. This keeps the roots moist and protected.

PLANTING AND STAKING A TREE

You may need to stake a large tree or shrub to keep it firmly in the ground and prevent windrock – this is best done at planting. A short stake is usually better than a longer one since it lets the tree move slightly in the wind so the trunk thickens well. Trees with very flexible stems may need a long stake.

Plant a tree as for a shrub, but drive the stake into the planting hole first. In windy areas, stake the tree on the windward side to prevent it from being blown too much in one direction. Once the tree has an adequate root system (usually after about two years), remove the stake. For trees with a long stake, saw off a portion each year, removing it entirely in the third year.

1 Drive a single stake into the hole just off center. Lay the pot on its side and slide it away from the root system. Spread out the roots to encourage them to grow into the planting mixture and so that it is easy to place the root ball close to the stake.

2 Put the tree in the planting hole. Check that the level is correct using a stake laid across the top of the hole. Keep the trunk close to the stake and spread out the roots evenly. Backfill, firming as you fill the hole. Water in well.

STAKING METHODS

Stakes can be used vertically or angled; angled ones can be added after planting. Use a buckle-and-spacer tie with the buckle away from the trunk to prevent chafing.

Buckle-and-spacer tree tie

Angled stake

PLANTING A BALLED-AND-BURLAPPED TREE

Balled-and-burlapped trees can be planted in a similar way to container-grown trees, ideally in autumn or, failing this, spring. Balled-and-burlapped trees have fewer fine, fibrous roots than container-grown ones, so good, moist, and warm soil conditions are vital for success. Make a planting hole twice as wide as the root ball, larger if planting in clay. Place the tree in the hole, adjusting the depth if necessary, and remove the burlap or other wrapping. If you need a stake, drive it in before backfilling. Firm the soil around the tree in stages, checking the depth as you go. Water well and apply a 2–3in (5–7cm) mulch, keeping it clear of the tree's trunk.

PLANTING PERENNIALS

The techniques needed for planting perennials are straightforward and vary little from plant to plant, so you can safely use the same basic method for all kinds of perennial. They can be planted during much of the year, but it is best to avoid planting during periods of extreme weather such as drought, waterlogging, or severe cold.

Ensure that the plant is suitable for the spot you have in mind by checking what sort of soil the plant prefers and how much sun or shade it needs. All soils are improved by adding well-rotted organic matter, such as manure or compost, which helps make light soils more water retentive, and lightens heavier soils. If your soil is very poor, add fertilizer. Incorporate all of the above into the soil dug out from the planting hole (see "Planting a Container-grown Shrub," p.42).

Before removing the pot, water the plant well or plunge the pot in water and allow it to soak for at least 20 minutes. If the roots are tightly congested, the plant is pot-bound; gently uncoil any girdling roots and spread them out. Check also that there are no weeds growing in the soil mix around the crown of the plant. After planting, water regularly until the plant is well established.

Root ball

1 To remove the plant, invert the pot and tap or strike the base, using either your hand or a trowel. You should then be able to slide the root ball out of the pot quickly and easily.

2 Holding the plant firmly in one hand, tease out a few roots around the root ball. Examine the roots for any that are dead, damaged, soft, or rotting, and cut these back to healthy parts.

3 Put the plant into the planting hole, and check that it is at the correct depth. Fill in with soil mixed with compost or fertilizer. Firm gently, level the soil surface, and water in.

PLANTING DEPTHS

Most perennials need to be planted so that the top of the soil mix in their pots is at the soil surface. Others prefer to be planted at a slightly higher or lower depth than the soil level in their pots – it depends on whether they need well-drained or deep, moist conditions.

Crown set level with the soil

Crown set just above soil level

Crown set just below soil level

Crown set much lower than soil level

Shallow planting
This is used for perennials that need plenty of moisture at their roots. The crown is set 1in (2.5cm) below soil level.

Deep planting
This is used for perennials with tuberous roots, to prevent them from drying out. The crown is set 4in (10cm) below soil level.

Raised planting
This is used for plants that rot at the crown, and variegated plants with a tendency to revert back to green. The crown is set higher than normal.

AFTERCARE

For the first year after planting, good conditions are essential so that the plant grows well. Always water thoroughly, and prevent moisture from being lost in hot weather by shading the plant as necessary.

A layer of mulch also helps to retain moisture around the roots, where it is most needed (see p.46), as well as deterring the growth of weeds. Individual plants that are tall, thin-stemmed, or in an exposed position may need to be given some additional support by staking or tying.

Shading
In hot weather, the drying effects of the sun, especially when combined with wind, may cause moisture stress. Reduce this by erecting a small, temporary tent made of netting supported on sticks.

Staking
For tall, multistemmed plants, use ready-made link stakes. These can be raised as the plant grows.

Staking a single stem
Tall or willowy, single-stemmed plants usually need extra support – tie the plant carefully to a stake.

PLANTING ANNUALS

Annuals can be planted from midspring onward. For half-hardy annuals, ensure that the plants are hardened off and all danger of frost is past before planting out. Check that your site is suitable – many annuals flourish only in a sunny spot and will become leggy and fail to flower well if planted in shade.

Prepare the soil by digging, mixing in fertilizer, then leveling off – annuals need good conditions throughout their short lives if they are to grow and flower well. Water the soil mix before attempting to remove the plants from their containers since this will minimize root damage. If the plants are in strips or trays rather than individual pots or plugs, separate them by pulling them apart carefully. Handle the plants gently by their leaves or root balls, taking care not to crush the stems. Plant at the recommended spacing – annuals grow quickly so will soon fill any gaps. Water to keep the plants just moist, and pinch out any that become leggy to encourage a more compact shape.

RETAINING MOISTURE

Avoid planting annuals during the hottest part of the day, and water them well after planting. If you are planting in a very dry spot, make a small basin around the base of each plant so that water is collected around the roots of the plant where it is most needed.

Planting out
Water the plants thoroughly, remove from their containers, and plant out at the suggested spacing and depth, firming the soil around the roots. Water in using a watering can.

PLANTING BULBS

Bulbs are generally best planted as soon as you buy them, since they are likely to deteriorate unless stored under ideal conditions. Individual types of bulbs are usually available over a period of several weeks, so you can time your buying to an extent to avoid planting during very wet weather or when the soil is extremely dry. A few bulbs, such as snowdrops, are usually planted "in the green," with a full complement of foliage. These are sold in this state and should also be planted as soon as they arrive. Most bulbs originate from warm, dry climates and so prefer a well-drained and warm site. Select bulbs that are suitable for your site, and plant them at the correct depth.

POTGROWN BULBS

Bulbs that have been flowering indoors as pot plants can be planted out after they finish flowering, although it's best to allow the leaves to die down first. If planting them in leaf, make the planting hole large enough to hold the entire root mass without disturbing it.

Planting depths

The planting depth should be given on the package but, as a general guide, bulbs are usually planted at 3 times their height; where winters are very cold, they need to be planted more deeply.

Bulb planted at 3 times its height

Bulb planted at 3–5 times its height

Wet conditions

Improve drainage in a heavy soil by digging in 2 buckets of grit per sq yd (sq m). A 1in (2.5cm) layer of grit in the base of the hole also improves drainage.

Layer of grit beneath bulb

Dry conditions

If planting conditions are very dry, the addition of a little compost to the base of the planting hole will help to retain moisture around the newly planted bulbs.

Compost

Planting out
Bulbs can be planted individually, but most look far more attractive and much less regimented if they are planted in random groups. To save time and effort, several bulbs can be planted together in the same large hole.

PLANTING BULBS IN A BASKET

If you have a small garden, or if you want to avoid having yellowing bulb foliage in the border, plant your bulbs in a basket so they can easily be lifted out after flowering. Pond baskets are ideal. Bury the basket so that its rim is below soil level, and the bulbs at the planting depth they need. Most roots will stay within the basket, making it easy to remove. For details on lifting after flowering, see p.47.

1 Fill the basket about half full with a soil-based mix or garden soil, and nestle the bulbs gently into the soil with their growing points upward.

2 Top up the basket with soil mix or soil, filling it right up to the brim, and then lower it into a prepared hole so that the bulbs are at the correct depth. Cover with garden soil, firm, and level the surface.

LOOKING AFTER BORDER PLANTS

Planting is something most of us enjoy, and a flourishing new plant is an obvious sign of success, but sometimes it is easy to forget the most important part of gardening – maintenance and aftercare. The first year or so is the critical period when the plant becomes well established; during this time all your care and attention should encourage the plant to increase in size and perform to perfection. Every plant has an optimum size –

after this point it may be necessary to divide it (*see* pp.50–51). Some aftercare jobs, such as mulching, watering, and feeding, covered on these two pages, should be done as needed throughout much of the year; others, such as pruning and deadheading, covered on pp.48–9, may need to be carried out at specific times. Not all plants need regular pruning, but most still benefit from deadheading and the removal of dead, diseased, or overcrowded branches.

MULCHING

Putting a good layer of summer mulch around individual plants or over an entire border saves watering and weeding later on and improves growing conditions. A 2–3in (5–7cm) deep layer restricts or even eliminates the light reaching the soil surface; even if weeds germinate in these conditions, many will not be able to grow through the layer of mulch. Summer mulches also reduce the evaporation of moisture from the soil, and most are easily penetrated by water.

Once you have mulched at planting, the best times to mulch again are in autumn (for winter protection) or spring when the soil is moist. Renew or add summer mulch when it starts to degrade; remove winter mulches before plants begin to grow in spring. Avoid strongly alkaline or acidic materials that may alter soil conditions.

Year-round mulching
Mulch in summer to deal with drought and weeds, and in winter to protect from cold damage.

Mulch beyond the spread of the roots – about the same area as the spread of the top-growth.

2–3in (5–7cm) deep layer of mulch

Keep the area around plant stems free of mulch to avoid rotting.

USING SHEET MULCHES

For large areas or around groundcover plants, use black landscape fabric or plastic sheeting as a mulch. Landscape fabric allows water to penetrate. Disguise with a layer of another mulching material.

Laying a sheet mulch
Weed thoroughly, then lay the sheeting over the soil, anchoring it at the edges. Use a knife to cut cross-shaped slits through which to plant.

WHICH MULCH?

• Well-rotted manure feeds the plant without much effect on soil acidity.
• Mushroom compost is alkaline, so is unsuitable for mulching lime-hating plants.
• Coarse grit does not degrade or break down, but is expensive.
• Bark chips should be partially rotted before use; they may be slightly acidic.
• Commercial mulches vary in composition, often depending on local materials.
• Cocoa shells are light-weight, but stable once wet; they are costly and slightly acidic.
• Good winter mulches include oak leaves, straw, and pine boughs.

Manure

Coarse grit

Commercial mulch

Cocoa-shell mulch

WATERING

Without water, plants suffer moisture stress, and many soon wilt and die. Larger plants with wide and deeply penetrating root systems, such as established shrubs and trees, can cope better with

lower moisture levels than plants with shallow roots, such as annuals. Always water young plants and those needing more regular watering first. A thorough watering is better than frequent, shallow watering.

Correct watering
For very dry soil, water gently, leave, then water again. A plastic tube inserted near the roots at planting will carry water directly to the roots.

Incorrect watering
Never direct a strong jet of water at the base of a plant – it will wash the soil away from the roots, leaving them exposed and liable to dry out.

FEEDING

Plants need a balanced diet if they are to grow and develop well. Although they obtain most of their food from the soil and by photosynthesis, they almost always benefit from some extra feeding. Most fertilizers are best applied when the plant is growing actively; feeding outside this period may promote soft growth that is easily damaged in cold weather.

The precise makeup of fertilizers varies: those with high nitrogen levels promote foliage production; those with a high proportion of phosphorus encourage flowering and fruiting; and those with high potassium levels encourage healthy roots and hardening of growth. Some fertilizers are especially for use on acid-loving or lime-hating plants. For more details about fertilizer content, *see* p.27.

Fertilizers are available in several different forms (*see* right); whichever type you choose, make sure you apply it at the rate and frequency suggested by the manufacturer, avoiding hot, dry conditions, and heavy rain.

FOLIAR FERTILIZERS
Available as powders or liquids, these are diluted and then sprayed onto the foliage; any liquid that runs off is taken up by the roots. Avoid applying in direct sunlight to prevent scorching.

GRANULAR FERTILIZERS
These are sprinkled around individual plants or over the whole border. Avoid scattering them directly on a plant since the leaves may be scorched.

LIQUID FERTILIZER
Diluted before use, liquid fertilizer is applied to the root area. Since the fertilizer is already in a soluble form, it is taken up rapidly by the roots.

FERTILIZER STICKS
These slowly disintegrate when inserted around the root area, releasing the fertilizer.

PELLETED ANIMAL MANURE
This contains natural food materials and is sprinkled around the plant.

SLOW-RELEASE FERTILIZER GRANULES
These contain fertilizer within a resinlike shell; they are easily incorporated into the soil at planting. The fertilizer is released over several months.

LOOKING AFTER BULBS

Bulbs are generally easy to look after, but a few simple measures ensure they flower well from year to year. Even though most bulbs prefer a freely draining soil, watering is essential for healthy growth. Regular feeding is also needed to ensure that the bulbs have stored sufficient nutrients to flower well the following year. Since the leaves are needed for energy production, allow them to die down naturally after flowering rather than cutting them back. After several years, bulb clumps may become congested and flower less well; they then need dividing (*see* p.51).

The majority of bulbs and tubers can be left in the garden over the winter without suffering any damage. However, a number of more tender specimens or those prone to rotting in cold, wet conditions need to be lifted, cleaned off, and then transferred to a cool but frost-free place to overwinter. Tuberous begonias, freesias, cannas, caladiums, tuberoses, dahlias, callas, gladioli, and other summer-flowering bulbs all benefit from this treatment (*see* right).

BLIND BULBS
If bulbs are not well maintained, then a condition known as blindness is likely to develop. In a blind bulb, the flower bud either fails to form or is not able to open and develop properly. Treat by feeding and watering the bulb well and it should recover within a year or two.

1 *Once the foliage has died down, lift the tubers. Discard any that are damaged or diseased. Shake off loose soil and cut back old foliage or stems using a knife. Dust cut surfaces with sulfur to discourage fungi.*

2 *Pack the tubers loosely into trays of fine bark chips and store in a cool but frost-free and well-ventilated spot. Never expose them to temperature extremes.*

LIFTING BULBS IN BASKETS

If you plant bulbs in a basket (*see* p.45), they can easily be lifted out of the flower bed once flowering is over. This avoids the problem of having unsightly, dying bulb foliage in a prominent place, spoiling the appearance of a border. Use a garden fork or spade to lever the basket out of the ground, taking care not to disturb the surrounding plants.

Alternatively, surround the bulbs with plants that emerge slightly later in the season and spread their leaves in time to disguise the yellowing bulb foliage.

Caring for bulbs after flowering
Lift the bulbs and replant in a less visible spot. Alternatively, leave the basket in a bright place so that the leaves can die down naturally.

DEADHEADS AND SEEDHEADS

Deadheading – removing dead flowerheads – neatens plants up and encourages new buds and sometimes a second flush of blooms. Deadhead annuals, some perennials, and roses to keep them flowering.

A few perennials, such as rudbeckias and sedums, have attractive seedheads; leave these on to add interest to the border in autumn and winter. Also leave the seedheads to ripen if you want to collect the

seeds or allow the plant to self-seed. This gives you more plants for free. These will either be true to type (the same as the parent plant), or sometimes different-looking plants of the same species.

Ripe seedhead splitting open to release seeds.

Seed-head still ripening

Hollyhock seedheads

Deadheading a rose
As soon as the bloom has faded, use sharp pruners to cut back the stem to a strong shoot or to an outward-facing bud lower down.

Deadheading a perennial
Cut back the old flowering stem. On some perennials, such as foxgloves, phlox, and lupines, sideshoots may then flower or a new stem develop.

Saving seed
On a dry day, tip the ripe seed into an envelope, label, then store in a cool, dry place. Alternatively, shake the seedheads over the ground.

BASIC SHRUB PRUNING

Regular pruning is essential for many shrubs to encourage them to flower and to keep the plant to a compact and manageable shape and size. By following a few simple rules, you can tackle your shrubs with confidence. The timing and amount of pruning varies, depending on when the shrub flowers and the age of the flower-producing stems. If you are unsure of your shrub's flowering habit, consult a nursery or a reference book.

Many shrubs flower in spring and early summer, producing

their flowers on the previous year's wood or on shoots growing directly from it. When pruning these, you must take care to leave the previous year's growth – otherwise you will have no flowers! To avoid cutting out this older wood, it is easiest therefore to prune right after flowering. Weigela is a good example of this group of shrubs – pruning guidelines are given below.

Other shrubs produce their flowers on the current season's wood. Prune these back in late winter or early spring

to encourage them to produce new stems that will flower later in the year. Cut back the previous year's stems to within two to four buds of the older wood. For *Buddleia davidii*, cut back to varying lengths; this will encourage flowering at different heights.

Evergreens and a few other shrubs, such as corylopsis, chimonanthus, and witch hazel, simply need neatening up after flowering – do this by removing any dead, diseased, and crowded stems, cutting back to healthy wood.

1 *Use a good, sharp pair of pruners to cut any dead, diseased, damaged, or dying wood back to healthy growth. If in doubt, always remove more, rather than leaving unhealthy wood.*

2 *Remove up to one-fifth of the older wood, pruning it back to within 2–3in (5–8cm) of ground level. Remove the stems evenly over the whole shrub to maintain an attractive and well-balanced shape.*

3 *Prune out any crossing, spindly, or weak growths to just above ground level. By removing unwanted stems you will ensure that all water and nutrients go straight into the productive, healthy growth.*

WHEN TO PRUNE SHRUBS

PRUNE AFTER FLOWERING
Buddleia alternifolia ○
Flowering quinces
   (Chaenomeles) ○
Cotoneasters ●○
Deutzias ○
Exochordas ○
Forsythias ○
Kerrias ○
Magnolias (M. x soulangeana,
   M. stellata) ○
Mock orange (Philadelphus) ○
Photinias ●○
Rhododendrons
   and azaleas ●○ᵉᴴ
Flowering currant (Ribes
   sanguineum) ○
Spiraea 'Arguta', S. prunifolia,
   S. thunbergii ○
Lilacs (Syringa) ○
Weigelas ○

PRUNE IN WINTER OR EARLY SPRING
Abelia x grandiflora ●
Buddleia davidii ○
Caryopteris ○
Ceanothus [some] ●○
Ceratostigmas ○
Fuchsias ○ [many ❄]
Hibiscus ○
Hydrangeas [some] ○
Perovskias ○
Spiraea douglasii,
   S. japonica ○

PRUNING ROSES

Most rose pruning is carried out in late winter when the rose is dormant. Always use a sharp pair of pruners and wear long sleeves and gloves. Cut to an outward-facing bud to encourage an upward and outward growth habit, and to prevent the center from becoming overcrowded. Make each cut at an angle, sloping down away from the bud, leaving a clean edge. Remove any dead, dying, diseased, spindly, or crossing stems, cutting back into healthy, firm-textured wood – identified by its white, not brown, pith. Apply a layer of fertilizer and mulch to promote new, healthy growth.

YOU WILL NEED

- Thick gloves
- Pruners
- Fertilizer • Mulch
- Garden fork

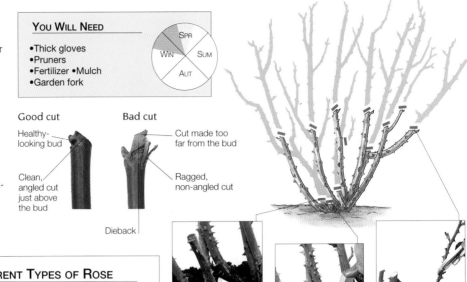

Good cut
Healthy-looking bud
Clean, angled cut just above the bud

Bad cut
Cut made too far from the bud
Ragged, non-angled cut
Dieback

POOR GROWTH
Remove all weak and spindly growth and diseased, damaged, or dead wood, which may spread infection or continue to die back.

CROSSING BRANCHES
Prune out any crossing or overcrowded branches to promote good air circulation.

WHERE TO CUT
Cut back to a strong, healthy bud that points in whichever direction you want the new growth to develop.

PRUNING DIFFERENT TYPES OF ROSE

Different types of rose have specific pruning needs, in addition to the general instructions above, to keep them healthy and flowering well. On hybrid teas, prune shoots back to 8–10in (20–25cm) from ground level. On floribundas, prune sideshoots back by between one- and two-thirds, and cut main stems back to 12–16in (30–40cm) from ground level. On established shrub and old garden roses, cut one or two of the oldest stems back to the base every year. On standard tree roses, cut back sideshoots by about two-thirds. For pruning climbers and ramblers, see p.78.

HARD PRUNING

Sometimes known as coppicing, this is one of the most severe forms of pruning, and is done in spring before any new growth appears. It is only appropriate for certain shrubs. Hard pruning is not necessary for the health of the plant, but is mainly done to stimulate the growth of vigorous and colorful winter stems on shrubs such as many dogwoods (including *Cornus alba* cultivars and *C. stolonifera* cultivars) and some willows (*Salix alba* 'Britzensis' and *S. daphnoides*). The young stems of these shrubs, which shoot from the base of the plant, have a much brighter color than older branches. Hard pruning also promotes a display of large flowers on other shrubs, including some hydrangeas (*Hydrangea paniculata* 'Tardiva' and *H. p.* 'Grandiflora').

Apply an appropriate general-purpose fertilizer after pruning to feed the plant and encourage a mass of new shoots, and then apply a thick layer of mulch: this will help to conserve moisture and deter the growth of any weeds.

Hard pruning a dogwood
Cut the stems back to a bud or pair of buds so that only 2–3in (5–8cm) of growth remains. Shoots will be produced from the base in spring and summer, and their vibrant color will be clearly seen the following winter.

CUTTING OFF A BRANCH

Dead, diseased, or obstructing branches may need to be removed from trees. For large branches, seek the help of a tree surgeon. For small branches, use the technique of undercutting to reduce any tearing of the branch as it falls; this involves removing the bulk of the branch first, then the branch stub. Avoid cutting into the branch collar (the ridge where the branch meets the trunk) because it contains the substances needed to heal the cut.

SECOND CUT
Cut slightly beyond the first cut to remove the bulk of the branch.

Branch collar

FIRST CUT
Cut upward toward the center of the branch, about 12in (30cm) from the trunk.

THIRD CUT
Cut about halfway through the branch close to the branch collar.

FINAL CUT
Remove the stub from above to meet the third cut.

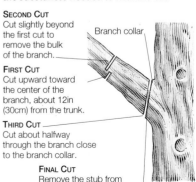

DIVIDING PLANTS

Raising your own plants can be an extremely satisfying process. Although plant propagation techniques are all too often seen as complex and only for experienced gardeners, this is not so. In fact, most plants reproduce themselves easily in their natural environment, and propagation in the garden usually takes advantage of these natural ways of increasing. Dividing plants is one of the simplest and cheapest ways of stocking your border,

and enables you to produce several vigorous, new plants from one established clump. It is an easy method of propagating many fibrous-rooted plants as well as bulbs and rhizomes – it also allows you to rejuvenate an old clump by cutting away dead or weak areas and removing any weeds growing through the roots. For other propagation methods, *see* "Taking Cuttings and Sowing Seed," pp.52–3, and "Increasing Your Stock of Climbers," p.81.

DIVIDING PERENNIALS

Division is best suited to perennials that produce shoots from the base or have spreading root systems. Many of these perennials die out in the center after a few years, but the younger and healthier outer areas can be used to make new plants. Most plants should be divided in mid-autumn and midspring, but not during extreme weather conditions such as drought or cold. As a general rule, divide

spring-blooming plants in autumn and autumn-blooming plants in spring; divide summer bloomers in spring or autumn.

Clear away enough soil so that you can see where to divide the clump and which parts to discard. For dormant plants, gently wash the clump so that the new growth shows up even more clearly. Make each division carefully so that every section will form a healthy, new plant. Replant the divisions as soon as possible so the roots do not dry out.

1 Carefully lift the plant by easing out the roots with a fork. This plant is dying in the center – the young, healthy outer parts will provide several vigorous, new plants.

2 *Tease apart fine-rooted perennials by hand. The clumps are often easy to see, but if in doubt, feel with your fingers, too. Try to minimize root damage and keep teasing apart the clump until you are left with small plants, each with healthy, fibrous roots and vigorous top-growth.*

Gently tease the clump apart.

Divide into separate plants.

3 *Replant the divided sections as soon as possible to prevent them from drying out. If the old top-growth is extensive, cut it back slightly to reduce moisture loss from the leaves. Replant at the same depth as before, refirm the soil, and water in well.*

OTHER METHODS OF DIVIDING PERENNIALS

Tough or fleshy-rooted plants can be divided into sections with a spade, cutting down through the roots. Some buds will be cut up in the process, but this is unavoidable. Use a sharp knife to neaten up each new plant, removing crushed or damaged buds. Small, fibrous-rooted perennials can be divided using two hand forks back to back.

Dividing with hand forks
Carefully insert the forks back to back to separate the roots. Ease the forks apart slowly and gently.

Dividing with a spade
Slice the clump into sections. Each plant must include several buds.

DIVIDING RHIZOMES

Rhizomatous plants, such as bergenias and many irises, have thick, often fleshy, rhizomes that are extremely easy to divide. Most plants that are divided in autumn or spring will flower during their next usual bloom season. Using a fork, carefully lever out the clump, Divide the clump by pulling the rhizomes apart. With a sharp knife, cut them into several sections, each with at least one plump, healthy-looking bud. Some rhizomes, such as irises, need to be replanted close to the soil surface; others, such as bergenias, should be planted so that the rhizomes are buried and the top-growth remains above ground.

YOU WILL NEED

- Sharp knife
- Trowel
- Watering can

(seasonal wheel: SPR, SUM, AUT, WIN)

1 *Shake the clump so that excess soil falls away. The individual rhizomes should now be easy to see. Grip the clump firmly and carefully pull it apart into sections that are easy to handle. If the clump is very congested, use a knife to cut through and separate the rhizomes.*

PLANTS THAT ARE EASY TO DIVIDE

PERENNIALS
Achilleas ❧
Michaelmas daisies (*Aster*) ❧
Astrantias ❧
Tickseeds (*Coreopsis*) ❧
Crambe cordifolia ❧
Dicentras ❧
Leopard's bane
   (*Doronicum*) ❧
Helianthus ❧
Daylilies (*Hemerocallis*) ❧
Hostas ❧
Gayfeathers (*Liatris*) ❧
Lychnis ❧
Loosestrifes (*Lysimachia*) ❧
Ophiopogons ❧ [some ❋]
Phlox ❧
Obedient plants
   (*Physostegia*) ❧
Polemoniums ❧
Primroses (*Primula*) [some] ❧
Lungworts (*Pulmonaria*) ❧
Scabious (*Scabiosa*) ❧
Stonecrops (*Sedum*) ❧
Goldenrods (*Solidago*) ❧
Comfrey (*Symphytum*) ❧
Meadow rue (*Thalictrum*) ❧
Veronicas ❧

RHIZOMES
Anemone hupehensis ❧
Bergenias ❧
Irises ❧

BULBS
Alliums ❧
Crocuses ❧
Snowdrops (*Galanthus*) ❧
Gladioli ❧ [some ❋]
Hyacinths ❧
Lilies (*Lilium*) ❧
Grape hyacinths (*Muscari*) ❧
Daffodils (*Narcissus*) ❧
Tulips (*Tulipa*) ❧

2 *Discard old, shriveled, or diseased rhizomes. Select plump, healthy ones, each with at least one bud, and trim off any damaged ends.*

3 *Trim long roots by about one-third. For irises, cut back the foliage to about 6in (15cm) to decrease the risk of wind topple.*

4 *Plant the sections 5in (12cm) apart with buds and foliage upright and the rhizomes partly exposed. Firm well and water in.*

DIVIDING OVERCROWDED BULBS

Most bulbs produce offsets around the base of the parent bulb; as these develop they become overcrowded and do not receive enough nutrients to flower well. These offsets can all be separated and replanted, correctly spaced, to give you a new supply of healthy bulbs. Daffodils and snowdrops need dividing every few years, other bulbs less frequently. Most bulbs are best divided when their foliage is dying back, although snowdrops should be divided in full leaf.

1 *Loosen the soil around the clump, then lever it out. Firmly pull away the individual bulbs by hand, discarding any that are damaged, soft, or dried out.*

BULB TUNIC
Remove loose outer layers, but leave most of the bulb tunic intact.

2 *Divide large offsets or pairs of bulbs by pulling them apart. Remove the loose outer layers of the tunic. Replant healthy bulbs immediately.*

TAKING CUTTINGS AND SOWING SEED

Taking cuttings from friends' or your own plants and sowing seed are easy ways to increase the range of plants in your garden. There are three main types of cutting: softwood cuttings, taken from green, unripe shoots; semiripe cuttings, taken from slightly tougher shoots; and hardwood cuttings, taken from ripe shoots. Softwood cuttings are generally used for propagating perennials and most shrubs, and semiripe and hardwood cuttings

for trees, shrubs, and roses. Take cuttings from non-flowering sideshoots since these usually root more readily than those from the main stem, and choose cutting material that is not wilting or diseased – there is no point in propagating problems.

Sowing seed, indoors or out, produces lots of new plants with very little trouble – though some seeds germinate more readily than others. This is an ideal way to raise annuals and many wildflowers.

SOFTWOOD CUTTINGS

Softwood cuttings are taken in spring from the soft growth at the top of the stem. These cuttings are usually an inch or two long, depending on the plant. Stem-tip cuttings (see below) are a type of softwood cutting consisting of the very small tip of a stem.

Some softwood cuttings, such as fuchsia and coleus, will root in water. Others, such as geraniums and impatiens, should be inserted directly into soil mix. For the best cutting material, always choose strong, healthy, nonflowering sideshoots, avoiding any that are excessively soft, leggy, or diseased.

YOU WILL NEED

- Knife •Wire netting
- Jar •Small pots
- Multipurpose
soil mix •Watering
can or mister •Dibble

1 Use a sharp knife to take a 3–5in (7–12cm) cutting, making the cut just below a leaf node. Remove the lowest pair of leaves.

KEEPING CUTTINGS HEALTHY
Mist cuttings regularly to promote rooting and stop leaves from wilting. Promote air circulation around cuttings to discourage rotting.

2 Bend a piece of wire netting over the top of a glass jar to hold the cuttings in place, and fill the jar with clean water. Place several cuttings in the water. Put the jar in a well-lit spot out of direct sunlight, and top up the water level as necessary.

3 When several healthy roots have developed, remove the young plants, and pot them individually into small pots filled with multipurpose soil mix. Water them in well. Grow on until they are large and sturdy enough to plant in their final position.

EASY CUTTINGS

SOFTWOOD CUTTINGS
Asters ☘◎
Coleus ☘❋◊↡
Fuchsias △ [many ❋] ◎◊
Hydrangeas △☘◎
Impatiens ❋☘ [some ❋]
　◎◊↡
Geraniums (Pelargonium)
　☘❋◎↡
Sage (Salvia) ☘ [many ❋]
　◎↡

SEMIRIPE CUTTINGS
Berberis △▲◎
Camellias ▲◎
Deutzias △◎
Forsythias △◎
Hibiscus △ [some ❋] ◎
Hollies (Ilex) ▲◎
Azaleas (Rhododendron)
　△▲◎
Viburnums △▲◎

KEY
◎ put in soil mix
◊ put in water
↡ stem-tip

STEM-TIP CUTTINGS

These are useful for preserving stocks of plants that are not fully hardy. Take them during the growing season, trimming to 2–3in (5–7cm) with a straight cut below a node. Remove the lower leaves and plant into soil mix.

Leaf node

Planting cuttings
Insert a few cuttings into a pot of soil mix, spacing them out well. Firm in and water, then cover with a clear plastic bag to reduce moisture loss. Pot rooted cuttings into 4in (10cm) pots.

SEMIRIPE CUTTINGS

Take semiripe cuttings from stems of the current year's growth, during early to midsummer. Choose healthy sideshoots that are soft at the top and just hard at the base, and cut them from the plant above a node. Cut out any very soft growth at the tip and remove the lower leaves. Several cuttings can often be made from one stem.

YOU WILL NEED

- Knife • Hormone rooting powder • Dibble
- Multipurpose soil mix
- Pots

1 Trim a healthy and undamaged stem into several cuttings, each about 3–6in (7–15cm) long, and sever each just below a node. To stimulate good root growth, carefully slice away a strip of bark about 1–1½in (2.5–4cm) long on one side of the base of the cutting.

2 Dip the cutting in hormone rooting powder. Insert it into multipurpose soil mix in a cold frame, pot, or propagator.

3 When the cuttings are well rooted, transfer them into individual pots. Harden them off before planting out.

HARDWOOD CUTTINGS

Euonymus, forsythias, kerrias, willows, and philadelphus root easily from hardwood cuttings. Take 8in (20cm) cuttings, making angled cuts at the top and straight ones at the base so you can plant them the right way up. They should root in six to twelve months.

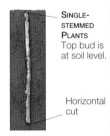

Angled cut

MULTI-STEMMED PLANTS Cutting protrudes 1–1½in (2.5–3cm) above the soil surface.

SINGLE-STEMMED PLANTS Top bud is at soil level.

Horizontal cut

Planting the cuttings

Insert the cuttings in a trench outside or in deep pots. If your soil is heavy, add gravel or compost. Space cuttings 4–6in (10–15cm) apart.

SOWING IN A TRAY

You can grow just about anything from seed. Start with seeds that are easy to germinate, such as zinnias and marigolds, and then move on to those that need more precise conditions. Seeds of half-hardy plants or those with more particular needs should be sown in a tray and raised in a controlled environment before planting out. The time of sowing depends on the seed type. Most annuals need to be sown in late winter or early spring, but always check the packet for details of when to sow and any special needs. Most seeds,

YOU WILL NEED

- Tray • Multipurpose or seed soil mix • Block of wood • Seeds • Paper
- Glass • Dibble • Pots

especially those that are sensitive to temperature and humidity changes, should be covered with a sheet of glass to give them additional protection.

1 Fill the seed tray with sieved, dry multipurpose or seed soil mix. Level the soil mix with a block of wood and firm to about ½in (1cm) below the rim. Water and leave for 30 minutes.

2 Sprinkle the seed using a paper fold. Cover with a fine layer of soil mix or perlite, then place glass over the tray (below).

3 When the seedlings are large enough to handle, prick them out. Always hold them by the seed leaves (the lowest ones), never by the stem or true leaves. Discard any weak or damaged ones, and plant the rest into pots or trays. Grow on and harden off the seedlings before planting out.

SOWING IN THE BORDER

The seeds of many plants can be sown directly where they are required to flower by scattering thinly onto the soil – this method is known as broadcast sowing. Sweet alyssum, amaranthus, candytuft, cornflowers, toadflax, poppies, and Virginia stocks are all easy to grow in this way, and many wildflower seeds also flourish if broadcast straight into the border. Before sowing, use sand to mark out where to scatter the seed, and label each area clearly afterward.

1 Prepare the soil so that it is finely raked, moist, and weed-free. Sprinkle an outline with sand to mark where to sow, then scatter the seed thinly onto the surface.

2 Lightly rake the soil over the area to cover the seed. Keep the ground just moist at all times, weeding as necessary. Thin the seedlings to the spacing indicated on the packet.

·4·
LAWNS

*At the heart of almost every garden is an area of grass. This
may be a green velvet sward of manicured perfection, or
perhaps a clover-studded arena for family rough-and-tumble.
In this chapter you will find advice on choosing a style and
shape of lawn to suit your garden and your needs. A well-
planned and tended lawn is a unique combination
of the functional and the ornamental, reflecting its
glory onto the rest of the garden.*

CREATING A GREEN CARPET

A green oasis, children's playground, or visual link between disparate areas of a design – a lawn can be any or all of these things. While some people can become positively obsessive about tending their piece of turf, and would probably be happiest with a boundary-to-boundary lawn, even the most lawnmower-shy usually find it necessary to include at least one area of grass in a garden design.

CHOOSING A LAWN STYLE

Optimum lawn size is determined by the overall size of the garden, and how prominent or practical a feature it is to be. The style of the lawn will be decided by its shape, the mix of grasses that it is planted with, and how carefully it is maintained.

A formal high-quality lawn is usually sown with fine, ornamental grasses, and is laid in a symmetrical or straight-edged shape. This traditional lawn style takes a great deal of time and effort to maintain, with frequent mowing, so to earn its keep should form the focal point of the garden.

At the opposite end of the scale is the utility lawn. Functional rather than decorative, it is made up of a tough blend of grasses in which rye predominates. This type of lawn is the perfect choice for a family garden, where it will withstand regular hard use and need minimal care. It should be large enough to accommodate ball games, and perhaps a swing or slide.

An informal lawn is a compromise between the two extremes, sown with a blend of ornamental and utility grasses. It looks attractive but not perfect, requires a certain amount of maintenance, and may have bulbs or wildflowers planted into it.

Formal precision
This glorious, weed-free lawn shows the level of perfection it is possible to attain with a fine blend of ornamental grasses. Maintaining such high standards is, however, a real labor of love – the frequent mowing, feeding, and edging required can be extremely time-consuming.

PUTTING PLANS INTO PRACTICE

Whether you are starting a garden design from scratch or adapting an existing layout, you should give as much thought to the size, position, and planting of the lawn as you would to the creation of an ornamental flower bed.

The shape of a lawn is determined partly by the proportions of the garden, and partly by your choice of lawn style. The style you choose will influence whether you decide to lay sod or to grow the lawn from seed – formal lawns are usually laid from high-quality sod – though price and convenience also play a part. Whether you decide on sod or seed, it is important to select varieties best suited to the position and function of the lawn. Not only should you choose a grass that will withstand the use it is likely to receive but, if your lawn is in shade, you need to select a special seed mix for shady places. Always sow or sod on well-prepared ground to get your new lawn off to the best start. For full details on sowing and sodding, *see* pp.56–8.

If your garden already has a lawn, it may well need some renovation work (*see* pp.64–5). However, even if the basic condition is fine, you may want to alter the appearance by planting with bulbs or changing the whole shape and size of the area (*see* pp.62–3).

Carefully recutting edges will instantly improve the look of the lawn. Either follow the existing outline or subtly reshape it. Choose straight lines and sharp angles for a formal effect, or use curves to create a relaxed design – but don't get too carried away if you decide on the latter, since tight curves are difficult to maintain.

MAKING MAINTENANCE EASIER

Apart from selecting the right grass type for your site, the best way to save time on aftercare is to install a mowing strip or edging. These make the edges of the lawn easier to mow and prevent them from encroaching on the surrounding beds. Follow the aftercare program outlined on pp.59–61. It takes a lot more effort to restore a neglected lawn than to keep it in good shape from the start.

A shady lawn
Nowhere is it more important to select a suitable mixture of grass seed than in a shady area. This lawn is the picture of health, thanks to a combination of careful planning, correct choice of grass seed, and regular maintenance.

SOWING AND SODDING YOUR LAWN

Your lawn will look better and last longer if you prepare the site well, so before you start sowing or sodding, clear away all weeds and debris, and firm and level the soil. There is a wide choice of types of grass seed and sod – choose the one most suitable for your site and the amount of use the lawn will get. Sowing is easy and inexpensive, although you will have to wait for about three weeks for the grass seedlings to emerge, and up to ten weeks before cutting and using your new lawn. Sodding is more expensive than sowing, but provided you look after the newly laid lawn, it will become usable more quickly – usually within two months. It is less likely than a seeded lawn to be damaged or uprooted early on. If you are going to lay an edging around the lawn, it is easier to do this at the same time as sowing or sodding. A range of edgings can be bought at local garden centers.

PREPARING THE SITE

The aim when preparing for a new lawn is to create a completely clear, level surface. Avoid doing this too far ahead: weeds may regrow and need to be treated again.

CLEARING

Remove all debris, weeds, and the remains of any old grassy areas or lawn. Kill off or dig out perennial weeds when they are growing actively but before they have started to set seed. Digging is usually not enough to get rid of these weeds since if their taproots or rhizomes are broken, any small pieces left in the soil will form new plants. An easier solution is to spray the whole area with a systemic weedkiller containing glyphosate, which is carried down to the plants' roots or rhizomes. The weedkiller is inactivated on contact with the soil, making it safe to sow or sod after clearance. When the top-growth of the weeds has died back, rake it off, then dig over the site. The ideal soil for a lawn is a light loam that drains freely and does not easily become compacted or waterlogged. Add well-rotted organic matter to soil that is sandy and light, and horticultural sand if it is too heavy. In wet conditions, you may need to lay a drainage system – for this you will need to seek professional advice.

LEVELING

If your garden has a good depth of topsoil and is fairly level, rake over the area, judging the levels by eye, add fertilizer, and firm down. For more systematic leveling, see "Accurate Leveling," below.

1 Firm the whole area by treading over it evenly – it may take several attempts to firm it well. Pay particular attention to the edges. Mark some pegs, each at the same distance from the top.

2 Drive in the pegs: for sowing, the marks should be at the required level of the lawn; for sodding, push the pegs ¾in (2cm) lower. If the lawn is next to paving, keep the marks level with the paving surface.

3 Add a parallel row of identically marked pegs, check they are level with the first row and each other, and adjust them if necessary.

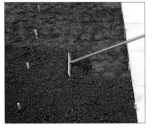

4 Rake the soil to the level of the marks on the pegs. When the site is level, remove the pegs, firm the soil again, then add a granular lawn fertilizer and rake it in carefully, keeping the soil level.

ACCURATE LEVELING

The method explained above is suitable for most sites, but to achieve an extremely accurate level, make a more closely spaced grid of marked pegs, driving them in at up to 3ft (1m) intervals across the site. Lay a board on the top of each set of pegs in turn. Put a level on the board to check the evenness; adjust as necessary before repeating over the entire area.

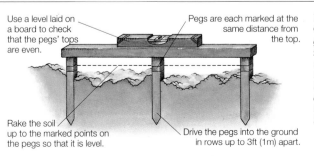

Use a level laid on a board to check that the pegs' tops are even.

Pegs are each marked at the same distance from the top.

Rake the soil up to the marked points on the pegs so that it is level.

Drive the pegs into the ground in rows up to 3ft (1m) apart.

Leveling the soil
Once you have created an accurate grid of pegs on the firmed lawn surface, rake up the soil to the marked point on each peg, adding more to fill in any hollows and leveling off any bumps. Remove all the pegs and firm the soil again, then rake in a lawn fertilizer before starting to sow or sod.

HOW TO SHAPE THE LAWN

The edge you create when sowing your lawn – whether it is curved or straight – should be clean and well defined, and follow the planned line. Mark it out before you start sowing to prevent any seed from straying out and spoiling the sharp edge.

For marking a straight edge before sowing lawn seed you will need a large piece of plastic sheeting, and for a curved edge a number of pegs and some string. For marking out an edge on newly laid turf or on an existing lawn, *see* "Shaping a Sod Lawn," p.58.

Straight edge

Lay down a piece of plastic sheeting so that its edge is positioned where you want the straight line of the lawn edge to be. Sow grass seed right up to and over the sheeting, keeping the area beneath free from seed.

Curved edge

To mark out a curved edge, drive a peg into the ground, tie string to it, pull it taut, and use a stick attached to the free end of the string as your marker. Score the line of the curve into the soil as a clear guide for where to sow.

MARKING OUT AN IRREGULAR LAWN

For lawns that are a combination of curves and straight edges, lay some string or a length of hose in the shape you want, and use that as a guide when sowing or sodding.

SOWING A LAWN

Sow lawn seed in warm, moist conditions so that the seed germinates rapidly and the young grasses establish quickly.

WHICH SEED MIXTURE?

There are different seed mixtures available for creating different types of lawns – from a very fine putting-green lawn, to a hard-wearing utility lawn, or a lawn for a shady site. For more details about grass types, *see* "Creating a Green Carpet," p.55. Before sowing, shake the package well so that the different types of seed are well mixed; otherwise, the various grass types will grow unevenly, giving a patchy effect.

SOWING RATES

The rate at which you apply the seed varies with the mixture you choose, so always check on the package. To calculate how much seed to buy, just multiply the size of the lawn area by the rate on the package. Always stick to the recommended rates – sowing too thinly lets weeds invade and produces a lawn that looks thin and establishes slowly, while sowing too thickly creates a damp, humid microclimate among the seedlings, in which grass diseases thrive. For a really large area of lawn, it may be worth borrowing or renting a machine, but hand-sowing is suitable for most gardens.

2 *Using pots, mark out a test area of 1 sq yd (1 sq m). Weigh out the quantity of seed needed for this area and scatter evenly from the pot. Use as a guide to the sowing density for the rest of the lawn.*

Seed scatters from holes in the base of the flower pot.

1 *An easy way to make sure you sow evenly is to use a small plastic flower pot as a shaker. Choose a clean pot with several small holes around the base. When you shake the pot, the seed will scatter from the holes onto the ground.*

3 *When you have sown the lawn, lightly rake a thin layer of soil over the seed. Water regularly with a fine sprinkler. The lawn is ready for its first cut when the seedlings are about 2in (5cm) high.*

MAINTAINING A CRISP EDGE

A neat edge to a lawn makes it look well cared for. Laying specially made edging before you start to sow or sod keeps the edge from breaking up and saves time with the edging shears. Choose from corrugated plastic or metal edging strips that you bury before sowing or sodding and that are invisible once the grass is growing strongly; alternatively, lay a brick mowing strip. For this, the surfaces of the bricks need to be only just above the soil level to contain the grass without interfering with mowing.

Top of edging is just above soil surface

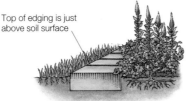

Mowing strip

Brick mowing strips around the edges look attractive and prevent the grass from spreading.

Edging buried to prevent the lawn and the border from encroaching on each other

Buried edging

Corrugated metal or plastic edging protrudes just above soil level; it can be laid into established lawns.

SODDING YOUR LAWN

Always buy good-quality sod from a reputable supplier. Choose your sod carefully to suit your site and in anticipation of the amount of wear it is likely to receive. Cheaper sod may contain weeds, pests, diseases, too much thatch, or a poor mixture of grasses and is often not a good investment since it may need a lot of time, energy, and money spent on it before it starts to grow as it should.

STORING SOD

Whenever possible, lay the sod within a day or two of buying, since if you are not able to do this, the grass will go yellow and the soil and roots start to dry out. If you do need to store the sod for more than a day or two, unroll it as soon as it is delivered and lay it out, grass upward, on paving or plastic sheeting in a shady spot.

Regular watering should keep the sod in reasonable condition (for a few weeks) until you are able to lay it.

WHEN TO LAY SOD?

Sod can be laid at almost any time of year, but try to avoid very dry or very wet spells and prolonged periods of high or low temperatures. Choose a time when the soil is moist, so that the grasses root well, but not too wet, or the roots may rot off. An ideal time is when rain is forecast, since the newly laid sod will then be watered in well without any effort on your part.

CREATING AN EVEN LAWN

To produce the best result, it is well worth taking the time to prepare the site well (see p.56). Lay the sod close together, without allowing the edges to overlap. The

joints in each row should be staggered, like the bricks in a brick wall; this will give an even finish.

When you are laying rows of sod, if you need a small piece to complete the row, add it in the middle rather than at the end where it may dry out or be dislodged. For a curved lawn, lay the sod so that it overlaps the lawn edge, then cut it to shape (see below) – sod cut before being laid rarely sits right or holds together well.

1 Sod is delivered either rolled or stacked flat. If possible, avoid leaving it rolled up for more than a couple of days at a time, since it will quickly dry out and the grass will turn yellow, making the lawn hard to establish.

2 Starting at one side, lay the first row of sod along a straight edge. Roll out each piece so that it just touches the next. To lay the next row, kneel on a board to avoid damaging sod just laid. Stagger the joints to give an even finish.

3 When the whole area is laid, use the back of a rake or a light roller to firm down the sod and exclude any air pockets. If necessary, brush in a sandy top-dressing to fill in any gaps. Keep the sod moist so that it roots quickly.

SHAPING A SOD LAWN

To achieve a flowing, clear-cut curve on a new lawn, mark out the curve on the sod using a peg and string with a small guiding funnel of sand tied at the end. Cut along the marked line with a half-moon edger.

To mark out a straight edge, use two pegs with string drawn taut between them. Line up a board with the string and slice through the sod against the edge of the board, moving the board along as you go.

1 Using a peg and string with a funnel of sand attached, pull the string taut, and dribble the sand on the sod to mark out the desired curve.

2 Use a half-moon edger to cut along the curve marked out by the sand. Stand directly above the edger to achieve the most accurate cut.

SPRIGS AND PLUGS

Sprigs are grass stolons or rhizomes; plugs are small pieces of sod. Both are often used to establish a lawn in warm areas using warm-season grasses or cool-season bentgrass. Prepare the area (see p.56) and, toward the end of spring or in early summer, plant plugs at intervals or scatter sprigs; then apply a top-dressing (see p.61). Keep well watered, and in two months the grasses should have rooted and grown together to create a smooth, even lawn.

Small plugs planted 6–12in (15–30cm) apart.

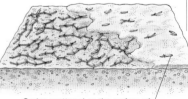

Sprigs scattered on the surface of the soil and covered with top-dressing.

LOOKING AFTER YOUR LAWN

Whether your lawn is one you have recently sown or laid yourself, or is older and long-established, it will need some routine maintenance to keep it in good condition. The amount of time this will take varies, depending on how well the grass is growing and on the type and standard of lawn you want. Mowing and watering need to be done quite regularly, though weather conditions will determine how often. Other tasks need to be carried out occasionally; these include fertilizing, top-dressing, aerating, and scarifying. Only a few hand tools are needed for most lawncare tasks, as well as, of course, a lawnmower, but if the area is large it may be worth borrowing or renting power or mechanical tools for jobs such as scarifying and fertilizing. To deal with a lawn in very poor condition, and for more specific information about lawn weeds, *see* "Renovating Your Lawn," p.64.

MOWING

To keep your lawn looking healthy and feeling good underfoot, regular mowing is essential. A well-mown lawn will stay in good condition and grow to become dense and less prone to invasion by weeds and moss.

The type of mower you choose will determine the quality of the cut you give your lawn – for most gardeners a cylinder or rotary mower is fine. A rotary mower gives a slightly lower-quality cut, but unless you want a perfect lawn, it is adequate. If you want a traditional lawn with stripes, choose a cylinder mower that has a roller attachment.

WHEN TO MOW?

Grass grows most rapidly during mild or cool weather, especially when the ground is moist, so spring and autumn are the times when frequent mowing is a necessity.

During the hottest part of the summer, and in periods of very dry weather, try to avoid mowing altogether, or mow less frequently and with the blades set higher. If the grass and ground are very wet or waterlogged, mowing should be delayed too, since it will encourage compaction and the wet clippings may clog up the mower. Similarly, in frosty or freezing conditions, the grass will be damaged and diseases encouraged by mowing. If possible, mow a lawn as soon as it needs it – if you allow the grass to get too long and then cut it too short, it will look patchy and brownish green and is more likely to be troubled by weeds and moss later on.

REMOVING GRASS CLIPPINGS
Rake away clippings promptly, or the grass beneath may die. Mix clippings with other organic matter, such as woody prunings, before adding to the compost.

HOW HIGH TO CUT?

The right height of cut depends on the time of year – cut the lawn more frequently in spring and autumn than in summer, unless conditions are very dry, since it grows faster in cooler weather.

UTILITY LAWN
Cut a utility lawn to a height of 1–2in (2.5–5cm) once a week.

FINE LAWN
Cut a fine lawn as low as ½in (1cm) up to two or three times a week.

EDGING

Neatly trimmed edges around a lawn are as important as the lawn itself – however well-maintained, fed, watered, and weeded a lawn is, unless the edges are well defined, the effect will be spoiled.

For the neatest cut, use a pair of long-handled edging shears, but remember that the blades must be kept vertical at all times to make a clean line along the edge. If you own a nylon-line trimmer with an adjustable head you could use this as an alternative – it will certainly speed up the job, although it sometimes leaves a slightly ragged edge. If you have a very large area of lawn, or one with a lot of complicated edges, it may be worth your while to periodically rent a mechanical edger.

Once the lawn edges have become worn and have started to collapse, or are very irregular and neglected, it is almost impossible to neaten them up with either edging shears or a nylon-line trimmer. Instead you should recut the edges using a half-moon edger, cutting against a board to achieve a straight line (*see* below). Even on lawns that look relatively neat, it is still well worth taking the time to do this once or twice a year, since it will maintain the edges in good condition. Good times to edge are in spring and autumn.

Trimming the edge
When the grass has been mown the edge is clearly visible, so edging is easier and more accurate. Use long-handled edging shears held vertically to remove all the grass overhanging the edge. Alternatively, you can use a nylon-line trimmer with an adjustable head.

Reshaping the edge
Using a well-sharpened half-moon edger held firmly and vertically, cut straight down along the edge of a board to neaten up any irregular edges.

FEEDING

Most lawns manage to survive with little if any feeding but, for lush, green grass, a well-planned feeding program is essential. Organic and manufactured lawn fertilizers are available in granular and liquid forms. Choose a granular fertilizer that includes both slow- and fast-release fertilizers for long-term benefit.

Feed lawns in spring or early summer with high-nitrogen fertilizer to stimulate new growth. In early autumn after scarifying and aerating, feed with a balanced fertilizer containing nitrogen, phosphorus, potassium, and iron – too much nitrogen late in the year encourages soft new growth that is prone to frost and fungal attack. Check manufacturers' instructions for rates. Soil type, weather conditions, and grass type will also affect the rate and frequency of application: for sandy, free-draining soil, apply fertilizer at a higher rate; for heavier soils, only a lower level of feeding is needed. Overfeeding can scorch grass.

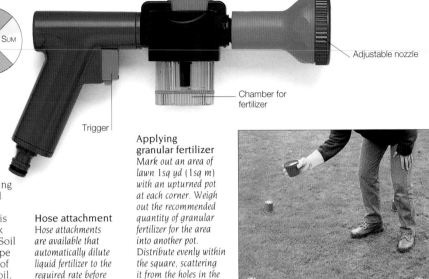

Adjustable nozzle

Chamber for fertilizer

Trigger

Hose attachment
Hose attachments are available that automatically dilute liquid fertilizer to the required rate before releasing it. Alternatively, use a watering can.

Applying granular fertilizer
Mark out an area of lawn 1sq yd (1sq m) with an upturned pot at each corner. Weigh out the recommended quantity of granular fertilizer for the area into another pot. Distribute evenly within the square, scattering it from the holes in the pot. Use this as a guide for the rest of the lawn. Water thoroughly.

AERATING

The soil under a lawn easily becomes compacted; the lawn then deteriorates in very dry or wet weather and moss may develop. Aerating a lawn makes it less compacted and encourages healthy growth. Most lawns need aerating every two or three years, but you may have to deal annually with areas where the lawn receives heavy use. Autumn, after mowing, is the best time for aerating since the grass can grow strongly before winter. A garden fork is ideal for small areas. For large-scale aeration, it is easiest to use a hollow-tined aerator – a fork that removes cores or plugs of grass and soil. Afterward, top-dress the lawn to improve aeration and drainage.

Advantages of aeration
The semipermanent channels created by aeration make it easier for moisture, air, and fertilizer to reach the roots of the grass, deterring moss.

When filled with top-dressing, this will form a semipermanent drainage channel.

Core of soil removed to leave channel.

With less compaction, the soil drains more freely and moss is less likely to develop.

Soil adjacent to channel can expand slightly; this reduces the likelihood of compaction.

Spiking with a fork
To aerate smaller lawns or localized areas of compaction, use a garden fork. Drive the fork into the soil and gently ease it back and forth to enlarge the holes. Repeat at intervals of 4–6in (10–15cm) over the whole area to be spiked. Top-dress the area afterward.

Hollow tining
Push the hollow-tined aerator vertically into the soil, then pull it out again. The tines remove small cores of soil and grass at 4in (10cm) intervals across the lawn. Do this evenly over the whole area. Sweep up the extracted cores and then brush a top-dressing mixture into the holes.

SCARIFYING

Scarifying is the removal of the living and dead organic debris, known as thatch, that builds up at the base of the grass stems. A buildup of thatch prevents good air circulation and smothers the grass, preventing water and fertilizers from reaching the roots quickly. This causes the grass to dry out, decline in quality, and be more prone to diseases.

On all but the largest lawns, scarifying can be done by hand using a spring-tined rake to pull the thatch out from among the grasses. It is best done in autumn when the soil is just moist; kill off any moss beforehand, or it will be spread to new areas. Lawns look far worse after scarification than before you started work – the benefits will not be seen until spring when plenty of healthy, new grass is produced. If there is a heavy buildup of thatch on your lawn, you might need to rent a mechanical or power scarifier.

Scarifying grass
Using a spring-tined rake, vigorously rake the lawn, making sure that the tines reach down to the soil surface. New grass will soon fill out the thinned areas.

MAINTENANCE CHECKLIST

SPRING
- Start mowing when the grass has greened up and started to grow again after the winter.
- Apply spring fertilizer.
- Water if necessary.
- Apply crabgrass killer when forsythia blooms.
- Apply broadleaf weedkiller.

SUMMER
- Continue mowing as needed.
- In very dry conditions mow less often.
- Trim the lawn edges with shears after mowing to keep it looking neat. If the edges are very ragged, recut them with a half-moon edger, cutting along the edge of a board.
- Water as needed to prevent the grass from drying out.

AUTUMN
- Sod or sow any new areas and repair any bare patches.
- Continue to mow, but less frequently.
- Apply autumn fertilizer.
- Apply mosskiller if necessary.
- Aerate the whole lawn every few years, and compacted areas every year.
- Scarify.
- Top-dress.
- Rake fallen leaves off grass regularly.

WINTER
- Mow only if essential (milder areas).
- Service lawnmower.
- Avoid walking on the lawn in frosty or waterlogged conditions since this damages the grass and compacts the soil underneath.

TOP-DRESSING

Applying a top-dressing to your lawn improves the texture of the soil. If the area has just been hollow-tine aerated, the top-dressing makes an excellent filling for the holes since its sandy, open texture creates semipermanent channels for better drainage and aeration.

Buy top-dressing ready-mixed, or make it yourself using a mixture of loam, horticultural (not builders') sand, and well-rotted organic matter, such as sieved leafmold. The usual rate for applying top-dressing is 2–3lb/sq yd (1–1.5kg/sq m); if the lawn has just been scarified and hollow-tine aerated or if it has any small irregularities, use a higher rate of about 6½1b/sq yd (3kg/sq m), but be careful not to smother finer grasses.

Ingredients for lawn top-dressing

6 parts medium-fine or sharp sand

3 parts sieved, good-quality loam

1 part well-rotted organic matter

Applying top-dressing
Top-dressing is best applied on a dry, autumn day. Distribute the top-dressing over the lawn with a spade or shovel. Brush or work it in gradually and evenly over the whole surface with a broom or the back of a rake.

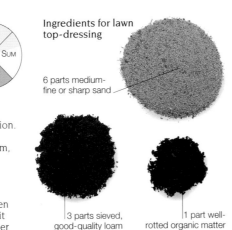

TRANSFORMING YOUR LAWN

An easy way to achieve a radical new look for your garden is to change the shape of your lawn – a rectangle or square of grass can look dull and predictable in many situations. You can alter your lawn to make a clean, geometric shape that is the focus of the garden, or soften its edges into gentle, sweeping curves. If you have a large lawn, a practical way of providing more planting space is to add one or two island beds. To modify the shape of your lawn you do not usually need to buy extra sod – in fact, for a seamless appearance once the lawn is reestablished, it is much better to reuse old sod rather than trying to match new pieces. It is quite straightforward to move sections from one place to another. Planting bulbs that will naturalize is a simple and effective way of livening up a bare expanse of grass; most will quickly increase in number and reappear year after year.

LIFTING SOD

You can lift and relay sod at any time of year, provided the weather conditions are not extreme. The whole process is easier if the soil is moist since this will encourage the sod to root quickly in its new position. Be sure to cut the sod to the same width and depth so the pieces fit together neatly when relaid. As you work, stack the sod, laying the pieces soil to soil and grass to grass. Relay the sod as soon as possible to prevent the soil from drying out and the grass being deprived of sufficient light. For how to lay sod, and for details of how to cut a curved edge accurately on a newly laid sod lawn, *see* p.58.

YOU WILL NEED

- Stake • Board
- Half-moon edger
- Spade

1 Cut the sod to be moved into sections that will be easy to handle: straight-edged strips are the easiest both to cut and to lay again. Drive 2 markers into the sod about 18in (45cm) apart and 12in (30cm) from the edge of the sod, and lay a board against them. Stand on the board and cut neatly along its edge with a half-moon edger.

2 Divide each strip into pieces about 18in (45cm) long. Insert the blade of the spade carefully under each piece to remove at least 1in (2.5cm) of soil and roots. Trim the base of the pieces so that they are all the same depth and can be evenly laid. Stack the pieces carefully and relay them as soon as possible before they start to dry out.

DIFFERENT LAWN SHAPES

When changing the shape of your lawn, remember that, although curves give an informal effect, they are harder to mow than straight edges.

Once you have altered the lawn, you will have to adjust the adjacent borders, which might involve lifting and moving a few plants.

Curved edges
A lawn with curved edges will make your garden less regimented. If the curves are wide, they should be easy to maintain.

Straight edges
A formal lawn gives an air of classical elegance, but edges and lawn must be kept in excellent condition to maintain the effect.

Dividing a lawn
A path dividing a square or circular lawn into two sections breaks up a large expanse of lawn, and often makes a long garden look wider.

Island beds
An island bed of any size or shape adds interest and breaks up the monotony of a large lawn. The surplus sod can be laid to change the shape at the edges.

PLANTING BULBS IN A LAWN

Bulbs bursting through the grass in spring is one of the most cheerful sights in the garden. Bulbs are easy to plant and many naturalize well, returning in increasing numbers each year. Both large and small ones are suitable for planting together in large groups, and look best arranged at random to create informal drifts of color. Cutting the grass as short as possible before planting bulbs makes the job much easier.

MOWING AROUND BULBS

Aim to leave the area around the bulbs unmown for at least six weeks after flowering since this allows the leaves to die down naturally, ensuring that the bulbs will flower better in the future. If the grass is a prominent feature in the garden and needs to be mown quite early in spring, then choose early-flowering bulbs; if it is unobtrusive and mowing can be left until later in the year, then select later-flowering bulbs. Large bulbs, such as daffodils, are especially well suited to

growing in rough grass since the lush greenery will hide their yellowing foliage.

Bulbs that have become naturalized in lawns will need to be fed with a balanced fertilizer every year to ensure that they continue to grow and flower well. If the bulb clumps become overcrowded they may need to be divided (see p.51).

1 *Choose the area you wish to plant and scatter the bulbs over the surface to achieve a natural, random effect. Check that each is at least its own width apart from the adjacent bulb, and thin them out if necessary.*

2 *Check how deeply the bulbs need to be planted, and use a bulb planter to remove a core of sod and soil to that depth. Planting can be done using a trowel, but a bulb planter makes a neater job.*

3 *Mix some of the soil from the core with a pinch of high-phosphate fertilizer and scatter it in the base of the hole. Plant the bulb with its growing point facing upward.*

4 *Crumble the soil from the base of the core over the bulb, and then replace the remainder including the circle of sod. Gently firm down the core and water in well.*

PLANTING SMALL BULBS

For planting small bulbs in a lawn, by far the easiest method is to cut and peel back the sod carefully, enabling you to plant several bulbs at once – this is much simpler than making individual holes, and the bulbs will soon form an attractive clump. Make sure you fork over the soil underneath since it may be compacted; this also helps the bulbs to root more easily. After replacing the sod over the bulbs, tamp it down evenly, either by hand or using the back of a rake.

Planting crocuses
Add some fertilizer to the soil beneath the sod. Plant the bulbs at least 1in (2.5cm) apart, growing points uppermost. Loosen the soil on the sod, fold down, firm, and water.

Crocuses in grass

RENOVATING YOUR LAWN

A lawn that is not entirely flat, with one or two damaged patches or edges, and a few weeds, does not necessarily need replacing. If, after inspection, you feel that the grass is winning out over the weeds, you can probably restore it to health. But if most of the "lawn" consists of weeds, moss, and lichens, and the remaining grass is patchy, it probably needs replacing. Renovation is best done in spring and autumn when grasses will grow quickly and fill in the bare spaces left after removing weeds. If you need to resow or resod, use the same seed mixture or sod type as the original to avoid a patchy effect. By the end of summer, new and existing grass should be established. Keep your lawn looking good by following an annual care routine (see "Looking After Your Lawn," pp.59–61).

LEVELING A HUMP OR HOLLOW

On an informal lawn – one in a cottage garden or a play area, for example – a few small humps and hollows will not look out of place. For a more formal lawn, it is simple to correct uneven areas. Small hollows can easily be leveled by careful top-dressing. If the surface is very uneven, this may not solve the problem since too much top-dressing will only smother the grasses underneath. Instead, you may be able to peel back the sod, add or remove soil, and fold down the sod again. For large areas, rather than peeling back the sod, lift it from the uneven area (see "Lifting Sod," p.62). Level the soil underneath, add sandy topsoil if necessary, then replace the sod. Top-dress the area and water it regularly until the sod is established.

YOU WILL NEED

- Half-moon edger • Hand fork
- Trowel • Sandy topsoil
- Watering can
  or sprinkler • Sandy
  top-dressing

SPR WIN SUM AUT

1 With a half-moon edger, cut a deep cross through the center of the hollow, slicing beneath the roots and beyond the problem area. Peel back the sod sections, and fold over to expose the soil beneath.

2 Fork over the soil lightly with a hand fork. To fill a hollow, add some sandy topsoil, a little at a time, until you have restored the correct level. If the soil forms a hump underneath the sod, remove as much as you need to. Firm down the remaining soil evenly over the area so that it is completely level with the surrounding lawn.

Leveling with top-dressing

You can level slight hollows in the lawn with a sandy top-dressing. The grass in the hollow will grow through and then root into the top-dressing.

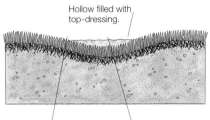

Hollow filled with top-dressing.

Grass grows through the top-dressing.

Level raised to the same height as the surrounding soil.

3 Carefully fold down the sections of sod. Firm gently and recheck the level – peel back again and add or remove more soil if necessary. When the level is correct, firm thoroughly, add top-dressing, and water well.

REPAIRING DAMAGE

Cut out a damaged edge and then rotate the sod so the edge faces inward. Top up the bare area with sandy soil and reseed. Within lawns, cut around and remove the whole damaged section. Add topsoil, firm, and fit a new piece of sod.

1 Cut out a square or rectangular piece of sod around the damaged edge. Rotate and replace the sod so that the damaged area faces inward, toward the lawn. Firm well.

2 Add a sandy soil mixture to the soil in the damaged area to bring it back to the original level, then reseed with a suitable mixture and keep the area well watered.

DEALING WITH LAWN WEEDS

Even the best-maintained lawn will develop some weed problems – weed seeds are often blown onto the lawn or brought in by birds or animals. In the right conditions, the seeds soon germinate and the weeds then spread and even flower and set seed, benefiting from the regular lawn feedings. Many weeds are able to thrive despite fairly close mowing.

USING WEEDKILLERS

If your aim is to own a weed-free lawn, remove or treat weeds as they appear, before they spread. If you have a variety of small lawn weeds,

a weedkiller is usually the best solution. Lawn weedkillers are selective in their action so that they do not harm lawn grasses; most work by translocation, meaning that they reach the roots, which are the most persistent part of many weeds.

Weedkillers should usually be applied in spring or summer, shortly after or while fertilizing – the fertilizer stimulates the grasses to grow strongly and cover the areas left once the weeds have been killed. Follow the instructions on the weedkiller package precisely. Many weeds are initially resistant to weedkillers

– these may need a second application later in the season if they grow back.

REMOVING LARGE WEEDS

Some large weeds may be effectively treated with weedkiller – if there are only a few, apply weedkiller directly to each weed. Alternatively, or for weeds that are hard to control with weedkillers, dig out each weed by hand. Remove every bit of the roots to prevent the weed from regenerating. You will be left with a small hole in the lawn – press down the soil slightly so that the top of the hole is less obvious.

GRASS UNDER TREES

In the shade cast by a tree, grass often becomes patchy – in addition to the lack of light, the soil is often dry. To avoid bare areas, remove the grass, then resow or resod; choose a seed mixture or sod formulated especially for shady areas. In dense shade, even a special grass mixture may not survive; instead, plant some shade-tolerant perennials and bulbs (see "Plants for Different Microclimates," p.23).

Removing a dandelion
Keep the knife blade almost vertical and cut downward right next to the base of the weed, repeating this in a circle all the way around. Lever the knife back and forth very gently, then pull out the weed, making sure that you do not leave any root in the lawn. Firm down the soil carefully.

CONTROLLING LAWN MOSS

Several different sorts of moss may appear on a lawn – each of them indicates that the lawn itself is in a poor state and that you need to improve the growing conditions as well as take steps to control the moss. Moss develops where there is little aeration (often due to compaction or heavy soil), dieback of grass roots (caused by waterlogged conditions, drought, or compaction), shade, or low soil fertility.

To treat it, use a commercial mosskiller, following the instructions. Once the moss is dead, rake it out – removing it when still living could spread the problem. Aerate the lawn regularly (see p.60) and brush in a top-dressing. Follow a maintenance program (see "Maintenance Checklist", p.61) to encourage the grass to grow strongly. This will also ensure it is less prone to invasion by moss in the future.

Yarrow
Has finely divided, feathery foliage and flat, white flowerheads, which are borne in the summer.

Common mouse-ear chickweed
Has a creeping habit and tiny, white, starlike flowers in early summer.

Broad-leaved plantain
A rosette-forming plant with prominent flowerheads, followed by brownish green seedheads.

Self-heal
Leaves have a purplish brown tinge, and purple flowers are borne in summer. Spreads by runners.

Creeping buttercup
Leaves have white markings and are linked by runners. Bright yellow flowers are borne in summer.

Lesser yellow trefoil
Typically mat-forming, has small, pale yellow flowers borne on upright stems, and tiny, cloverlike leaves.

Common white clover
Has three-sectioned leaves and creamy white flowerheads in summer. Sometimes considered worthwhile.

Slender speedwell
Bright blue, long-stemmed flowers are borne in spring. Has creeping stems and tiny leaves.

·5·
BOUNDARIES
AND SCREENS

*Boundaries need not be merely functional – walls, fences,
and even hedges can all be transformed with climbers. Within
the garden, screens and arches allow you to extend the vertical
planting to new heights. This chapter introduces the rewards
of gardening in three dimensions.*

ADDING HEIGHT TO YOUR GARDEN

A boundary can be anything from a sturdily built brick wall to a fence, hedge, or fairly informal screen. Each has its advantages, and all have the potential to become a positive feature in the garden, perhaps supporting a selection of climbers and wall shrubs to provide additional color and interest.

DEFINING YOUR BOUNDARY

The choice of a boundary style is determined partly by personal taste and partly by practical considerations of its function and position. A pretty picket fence will be almost useless if your primary purpose is to keep rabbits out of the garden, but a high wall would be equally unsuitable if that garden opened onto beautiful rolling countryside.

Nor should boundaries be thought of simply as territorial dividers. Well-planted fences and walls can both enhance the main planting design and, if you plan carefully, hedges can lure a range of wildlife into the garden as well.

Clearly, cost may be another major factor, but it is important to make this calculation carefully. A flimsy trellis may be cheaper than a more sturdy alternative, but if it lasts for half as long it could prove expensive in the long run. It is also important to consider local planning regulations – especially if you live in an ecologically sensitive area, or hope to erect a particularly tall structure – and, to avoid legal disputes with neighbors, check that the boundary is in the correct place.

HEDGES

A hedge can be anything from a formal feature clipped with mathematical precision to a relaxed collection of shrubs twined with wild roses and other climbers.

Although usually found in larger gardens, formal yew, beech, or privet hedges can be kept to a manageable size with regular attention, and so are perfectly well suited to even quite small plots. In contrast, the lovely but somewhat sprawling *Berberis julianae* and plants of similarly arching habit form informal but rather rambling hedges that need the space provided by a large garden.

In some cases, the hedging plants themselves can be prohibitively expensive. Two of my favorites for formal hedging, yew and beech, are fairly slow growing and, unless you have a lot of money to spend, are usually supplied as small plants that have little if any screening effect for quite some time. In cases like this, erect cheap fencing at the same time as you plant your hedge, and remove the fence when the hedge has grown to an acceptable height and density. For details about the different types of hedges and how to plant and maintain them, *see* "Hedges," pp.84–5.

FENCES AND TRELLISES

If you want a quick and relatively cost-effective screen, then fencing or a trellis makes a good choice. Both are now widely available in prefabricated sections in a huge range of decorative styles and

A trellis fence
Even prefabricated fencing can be given a stamp of individuality, as illustrated by this informal boundary draped with a golden hop.

finishes. A new or existing fence or trellis can be easily customized to fit in with surrounding plantings and adjacent buildings by painting it to the color of your choice using wood stain.

You can make up a combination of fence panels, trellises, and screening plants to suit not only your pocket but also the style of your garden. For information on materials for fences and trellises, *see* pp.70–71; for how to erect them, *see* pp.72–3.

A NEW PLANTING SPACE

Often an undervalued space in the garden, any structurally sound fence or wall will provide a good surface against which to grow a range of plants. In addition, the shelter provided by a solid barrier such as a wall may well allow you to grow more tender plants than would otherwise be possible. You can choose from a gorgeous selection of climbers and wall shrubs to create a display of flowers and foliage for every season and in virtually any color range. Always select plants carefully according to site and exposure.

Fruit, especially apples, cherries, peaches, and many of the cane fruits, will thrive if planted close to the protection and support of a sunny wall or fence. Both fruit trees and cane fruits can be trained in a variety of shapes, or simply tied in as they grow, to make an attractive and productive barrier where displays of beautiful blossoms are followed by a harvest of delicious fruits. For more planting ideas, *see* "Clothing with Climbers," pp.76–7.

Informal hedge
Challenging normal concepts of what constitutes a hedge, silver lace vine and rambler roses have been twined together in a mass of color. Since it takes up a great deal of space, this style of hedge is suitable only for larger gardens. However, the same plants could be trained up a fence or wall to create a similar effect in a more contained area.

SCREENS, ARCHES, AND PERGOLAS

Vertical features are a tremendous asset and provide a great planting opportunity in almost every garden. Laden with yellow-flowering laburnum, a simple arch becomes a breathtaking feature. A pergola planted with honeysuckle, roses, and other scented climbers creates a fragrant and beautiful walkway or a magical arbor in which to escape the heat, and stresses, of the day, while a well-planted screen will in time develop into a living tapestry of color that is as functional as it is lovely.

Always remember that a boundary structure or divider within your garden need not be solid. Adequate privacy can usually be provided by a screen that allows you to enjoy more distant views. Not only can arches, pergolas, and screens be used to divide neatly one area from another, but they will also add a whole new dimension to your garden designs.

MAKING USE OF SCREENS

A screen is one of the simplest garden structures – at its most basic being a single panel of a trellis or a wire frame – but can still be highly effective. Ornamental screens can be used to hide eyesores from view, to break up a long, thin garden into a series of garden "rooms," or simply to increase the available planting area.

Plant screens on one or both sides with a combination of climbing foliage and flowering plants. Alternatively, use fan-trained fruit trees and espaliers, or cane fruit trained against the screen, to create a feature that is both attractive and functional. For more planting ideas, *see* "Ornamental Dividers," pp.82–3.

POSITIONING ARCHES AND PERGOLAS

Arches and pergolas make even a new garden look as if it is developing well, and after a year or two will provide established,

A country retreat
Leading from a raised patio to the garden beyond, this delightful feature creates an easy transition between the two. Pergolas on either side of the steps are linked by a central arch laden with fragrant roses. A sophisticated combination of hydrangeas, echeverias, roses, foxgloves, and pansies grow in clusters around the base, softening the gray expanse of paving slabs.

Harvest bounty
Train apples and other fruiting trees along a system of straining wires to make an informal screen that is as productive as it is attractive.

eye-catching features. Both should be positioned carefully for maximum impact – used either to link one part of the garden to another or as a decorative means of separating areas.

A pergola running over the path between the front gate and house door can transform the front garden area, welcoming visitors as soon as they open the gate. Elsewhere, a pergola could be used to house a garden bench, making a peaceful spot in which to sit on a hot summer's day.

Alternatively, construct the pergola to adjoin the house or straddle a patio, and create a Mediterranean-style area of shaded seclusion, perfect for *al fresco* eating. In warmer areas you may even be able to train a fruiting vine over the structure to complete the effect.

As your imagination takes flight, be aware of the need to keep the design in proportion to its surroundings. A smaller garden may be dwarfed by a pergola, whereas a well-placed, sizeable arch would be perfectly suited to the dimensions.

Either structure can be carefully positioned to help draw the eye away from ugly nearby features or obscure an

unattractive view. Like screens, they can also be used as an inexpensive way to alter the proportions of awkwardly shaped edges or corners, or to break up a large, open garden into individual sections.

CONSTRUCTING ORNAMENTAL FEATURES

A screen or divider can be constructed cheaply and easily from trellises, posts, and sturdy wires. At first this structure will look rather bare, but a good selection of plants will soon transform it. What you choose to plant is determined partly by site and partly by personal preference, and it offers you the opportunity to create something unique – and is certainly more individual and exciting than bare walls and fences.

An arch or pergola can be anything from an ornate wrought iron structure to a simple wooden design. Arches are available in kit form in a wide range of styles and are designed to slot together easily and quickly with only a few basic tools needed to complete the job.

A homemade wooden arch, constructed from pressure-treated lumber or rustic-style unpeeled poles, will usually work out cheaper than a kit but will also take longer

to assemble. Given a little time and skill, however, making your own arch offers the real advantage of allowing you to create a structure to exactly the size and design you want. Remember that even the simplest arch made from rough lengths of lumber and a trellis will soon look impressive when covered with plants.

If you do decide to build your own feature, bear in mind that the larger the structure is, the sturdier your building materials and construction techniques must be. In addition, larger structures – especially in exposed sites – may need properly laid foundations to be completely stable. For practical instructions, *see* "Building Arches and Pergolas," pp.74–5.

SELECTING AND SUPPORTING A COLLECTION OF CLIMBERS

Many climbers are suitable for growing up an ornamental screen. Which plants you choose will depend largely on your personal priorities – do you need fast-growing cover to hide an eyesore, is fragrance important, or would you prefer a year-round season of interest? It is perfectly possible to meet any or all of these goals with the right planting.

When choosing a selection of climbers, do consider their compatibility – if one needs pruning just as another comes into flower, or grows at such a rate that it stifles all competition, then you are likely to have problems. Try to plan combinations that will give a long season of interest. For example, *Clematis tangutica* flowers in summer and early autumn, then produces fluffy seedheads that last into winter, so it could be combined with a spring-flowering climber for a nearly year-round display.

If you intend to grow some of the heavier or larger climbers, such as wisteria and

Rustic style
An open trellis of peeled, unshaped wood creates an informal feature with a decidedly rural character – enhanced in this example by a planting of vivid pink climbing roses and honeysuckle, which combine to form a fragrant display. The trellis alone would provide little privacy, but with its mantle of climbers creates an effective screen, particularly during the summer when the garden is most in use.

grapes, which both develop sizeable woody stems, it is essential that the arch or pergola is sturdily constructed from strong materials. Lighter-weight climbers, such as some clematis, honeysuckles, and roses, still require a well-built structure if they are to make a lasting feature, but will be adequately supported by a simple arch.

Choose a sunny part of the garden for your structure if at all possible. This will

make it much easier to plant the feature attractively, since there is a greater range of colorful climbers available for sunny situations than for shade. Away from full sun, consider angling your screen to make the most of all available light.

For details of plant supports and plant selection, *see* "Clothing with Climbers," pp.76–7, and for ongoing care, *see* "Pruning and Training Climbers," pp.78–81.

Pergola planting
A traditional wooden pergola provides ample planting opportunities. In this combination the Chilean glory flower (Eccremocarpus scaber) together with Clematis tangutica covers the structure in a mass of sunny color, while tubs of cool blue and white agapanthus are sited beneath.

Color impact
Laburnum – here trained over a prefabricated metal arch – produces cascades of yellow flowers from spring to summer and grows on almost any soil, although it needs full sun to give its best.

STYLES OF FENCES AND TRELLISES

The style of fencing or trellis you choose can have a great impact on the garden, potentially altering its appearance completely. The height and shape plus the materials the fences and trellis are made from can create anything from an angular, modern look to a rustic, rural character. Consider how the materials will blend with the house and any other existing features. All these structures are long-lasting elements in the garden and should not need to be replaced for years, so it is important that you select carefully at the beginning, choosing structures sturdy enough to bear the weight of any plants that may be grown over them. Take into account your future plans: for example, when putting up a wooden fence, think whether you may want to add a trellis on top of this – it is easier and cheaper in the long run to buy taller fence posts at the start than to add extension posts for the trellis later.

FENCING

Choose fencing to suit your needs – do you want a solid barrier for privacy, a secure and sturdy animal-proof structure, an effective windbreak, a means of attaching trellis and growing climbers to make a decorative feature, or just a functional way of marking out the boundary of your garden? Fences vary widely in cost and style, and you should be able to find one to suit both your budget and taste. Bear in mind when buying wooden fencing that it is worth spending a little more on materials that have been pressure-treated with wood preservative, since the fencing will then last much longer.

You can easily change the look of a wooden fence to suit the surrounding buildings and your own preferences by applying a differently colored wood preservative or stain. Even concrete pillars and posts can be painted to coordinate with paintwork on adjacent buildings.

Other sorts of fencing, especially wire fencing and post-and-chain fencing, are more basic, functional, and often cheap. They are most suitable for use in places where a completely solid or aesthetically pleasing barrier is not of the greatest importance – to keep a dog from escaping through a hedge, for example.

Woven fencing
Woven fencing panels – made from woody stems – are one of the most decorative and informal fencing or screening materials available, and they are an effective and instant way of providing a rural feel in the garden. Their strong brown color and hand-woven texture allows them to blend in easily with any natural background and also makes them an excellent surface for climbing plants, which can cling to the irregular surface.

Chain-link fencing
This is an inexpensive fencing material, held in place by wooden or concrete posts. The wire mesh is unattractive, but it may be concealed by the planting of lightweight climbers. It provides a good barrier to keep larger animals out, or in, as required.

Vertical closeboard panels
Fence panels made from vertical boards form a sturdy and attractive boundary. They are slightly more expensive than other types, but suit mature gardens and look good with a trellis added above.

Picket fencing
This type of fencing may mark your boundary but will not provide much privacy or screening. It is ideal for a small front garden and is neither expensive nor difficult to erect. It is not strong enough to support plants.

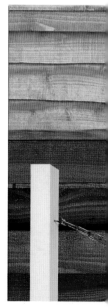

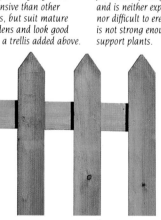

TRELLISES

Trellises are available in several different heights and shapes; they are usually made from treated wood, though plastic or coated wire trellises are available, too. Most trellises are designed to be mounted against walls or fences, or to form screens. Some types can be expanded or elongated to fit different areas. Others are suitable for adding to the top of a fence to alter its shape and extend the growing area. Be careful to choose a trellis strong enough to support the plants you will be growing.

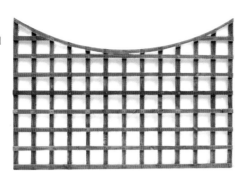

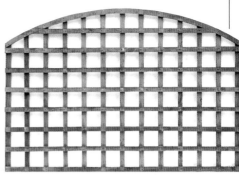

Shaped trellis

A convex or concave top to this trellis makes the design more interesting and brings an informal appearance to an otherwise regimented garden boundary. The trellis may be attached to the top of wooden fence panels.

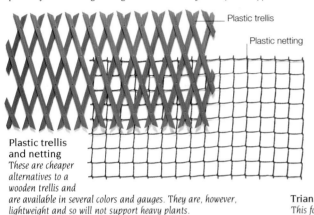

Plastic trellis

Plastic netting

Plastic trellis and netting

These are cheaper alternatives to a wooden trellis and are available in several colors and gauges. They are, however, lightweight and so will not support heavy plants.

Wavy-edged panels

These are readily available and commonly used fence panels. Reasonably priced, they provide a solid boundary, and a trellis can easily be added to the top of the panels.

Triangular trellis

This form of trellis is suitable for supporting a single climber and for mounting where space is limited. It can also be used for a climber in a container.

Interference fence panels

The horizontal boards mounted to either side of vertical posts create a windbreak that can be installed quickly and easily. Interference fencing is attractive and provides privacy.

Post-and-chain fencing

This is suitable only if more substantial fencing is impractical. Posts can be concrete or plastic but are usually made from wood, and can be painted in any color. The chain may be metal or plastic. Post-and-chain fencing is not sturdy enough to support plants.

Diamond-shaped trellis

The trellis may be edged with wood for easy mounting on walls, arches, and pergolas. Expanding types are available.

ERECTING FENCES AND TRELLISES

Putting up a fence is one of the easiest, cheapest, and most effective ways of giving your garden some privacy. A fence defines your boundary, provides a windbreak, and offers great potential for extra planting space. Adding a trellis to the top of a fence or against a wall gives you even more scope for planting. The most widely available and easily erected type of fence is panel fencing, which comes in several styles (see pp.70–71). To hold the panels firmly in position you will need either wooden or concrete fence posts. Concrete posts are sturdy and very long-lasting but are not particularly attractive. Wooden posts are readily available and lighter to install but need post supports to prevent them from rotting. Paint wooden posts and fences with wood preservative every few years to keep them in good condition – differently colored preservatives allow you to change the fence color, too.

ERECTING A FENCE

To save yourself time and money, check that the site of the fence you intend to erect is clearly on your side of the boundary, not on your neighbor's land.

BASIC TECHNIQUES

The picture sequence (right) shows how to erect a fence with concrete posts, set in concrete-filled holes and with the panels slotted directly into grooves along each post. First measure the line of the fence and calculate the number of panels and posts you will need, and then select posts long enough to support the height of fence you choose. For typical 6ft (2m) fence panels, the posts need to be 8½ft (2.75m) long, so that they can be sunk 30in (75cm) below soil level. If you intend to add a trellis to your fence, buy posts long enough to allow for the additional height.

If you are using wooden posts, follow a similar method, but secure the posts in the ground with concrete spurs or metal post supports to prevent the posts from rotting (see "Methods of Supporting Posts," opposite). To attach the panels to the wooden posts use 3in (7cm) galvanized nails, or screws and metal brackets. Saw the tops off the posts to the required height and treat with a wood preservative before attaching wooden caps.

YOU WILL NEED

- Measuring tape • String line
- Spade • Crushed stone
- Fence posts • Concrete
- Level • Gravel board
- Fence panels
- Wooden coping
- Hammer
- Galvanized nails
- Wood preservative
- Paintbrush

(SPR, SUM, AUT, WIN seasonal wheel)

Before buying, check that wooden posts have been pressure-treated with wood preservative since this prolongs their life. Attach wooden coping (if not already in place) to the top edge of each panel with galvanized nails.

FENCING ON A SLOPE

If the ground in your garden is simply uneven, you may be able to level it off and then put up a fence in the normal way. But if the slope is steep, you will need to put up the panels in a steplike arrangement, with each panel supported by a low wall. Unless your bricklaying skills are excellent, this is probably best left to professionals.

1 Prepare a hole about 30in (75cm) deep for a 6ft (2m) tall fence. Put a 6in (15cm) layer of crushed stone in the base. Firm the post, nestling it into the stone, and fill the hole with concrete. Check the post is at the correct depth, centered in the hole and vertical. Add more concrete if necessary.

ATTACHING A TRELLIS TO THE TOP OF A FENCE

The use of longer fence posts from the start allows the trellis to be nailed directly onto the post and is by far the best option. There are, however, two methods of extending fence posts to attach a trellis to an existing fence. Either join an extra length of post to each existing post with wooden battens, then mount the trellis to the extended post; or use metal post extensions – metal fixtures that slot over the top of the existing post – into which you slide the additional post. For both methods, remove the wooden caps on existing posts. A vigorous climber should cover ugly joins after a season or two.

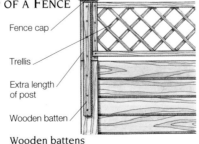

Fence cap
Trellis
Extra length of post
Wooden batten

Wooden battens

Secure sturdy battens to join the extra length of post to the existing one, overlapping each. Then attach the trellis to the extra post using galvanized nails.

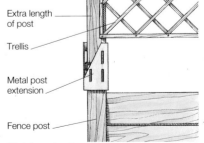

Extra length of post
Trellis
Metal post extension
Fence post

Metal post extensions

Remove the post cap and fit the post extension. Insert the extra length of wooden fence post and replace the post cap. Nail on the trellis.

METHODS OF SUPPORTING POSTS

Concrete posts can be set directly into concrete, but wooden posts need some form of protection to prevent them from rotting at the base. Either bolt them into concrete spurs bedded in a concrete foundation, to hold them just above ground level (right), or fit them with pointed metal post supports (far right).

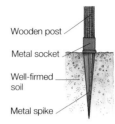

Wooden post
Bolts
Gravel board
Concrete spur
Foundation

Concrete spur
The concrete spur is embedded firmly into concrete. When the concrete is set, the wooden post is bolted onto the spur.

Wooden post
Metal socket
Well-firmed soil
Metal spike

Metal post support
The metal post support is driven into the soil (follow instructions). The wooden post is then slotted into it.

SPACING THE POSTS
Lay a panel on the ground and measure the correct distance to the next post using a peg and tightly stretched string.

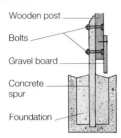

2 *To protect the base of each panel from moisture, fit a wooden or concrete gravel board between the posts. Carefully level the ground so that the board is horizontal, then check with a level. Alternatively, raise the level of the fence by 2in (5cm) so that the panel is clear of the ground.*

3 *Slot the fence panel into the groove in the first post, and measure the position of the next post. Put the next post in its hole, wedging it into the crushed stone. Add concrete. Repeat the process until all your posts are in position. Fit the panels when the concrete has set.*

BASIC REPAIRS

The better constructed the fence, the less likely it is to need mending, but after a number of years or following strong winds, repairs are often needed. Attend to repairs promptly: the longer a problem is neglected, the worse it is likely to get.

• Keep fences in good condition by painting regularly with creosote or other wood preservative (see below), and keeping soil and debris clear of the base.

• If one panel or board becomes wobbly, others may soon follow suit, so check the whole fence before starting the repair. Loose panels or boards are often easily fixed by using a few galvanized nails.

• If a panel does need to be replaced, try to obtain one from the original supplier to gain the best possible match; after a couple of years, the new panel should have weathered enough to blend in with the others reasonably well.

• Before attaching the new panel, always check whether the posts are in sound condition.

MOUNTING A TRELLIS ONTO A WALL

House, garage, or garden walls can all support plants if they have a trellis mounted on them. If you are in doubt as to whether a wall is suitable or sound, seek professional advice before mounting the trellis – mistakes could prove costly! To lessen any risk of causing damage to the wall, attach vertical wooden battens to the wall first, then mount the trellis to the battens securely using galvanized nails.

Attaching a trellis
Hammer ¾–1 x 1–2in (2–2.5 x 2.5–5cm) battens of wood to the wall and attach the trellis to the battens.

WOOD PRESERVATIVES

Treat fences with creosote or a water-based preservative every 3–4 years. Creosote is cheaper, but you will need to wear protective clothing, and it is unsuitable for fences supporting plants. Water-based treatments are less likely to harm plants or people but should also be used with care. Follow the manufacturer's instructions carefully and apply evenly to dry wood.

Sample colors

BUILDING ARCHES AND PERGOLAS

An arch or pergola literally adds a whole new dimension to a garden. It can help to make a new garden seem more established and, provided it is well built using sturdy materials, can be used to support a range of climbers. For practical reasons, the structure should be about 8ft (2.5m) high, or taller than the tallest person who is likely to walk beneath it when the top is covered in dense foliage or trailing flowers. The width will depend on how much space you have, but an arch or pergola makes a more striking and integrated feature if it is wide enough for two people to walk comfortably through it side by side. Both arches and pergolas need not be difficult to construct, and choosing your own materials and design gives you the chance to make one that best suits your garden. If time is limited, they are available in kit form, too, with ready-cut, treated, and shaped lumber that you slot together.

ARCHES

Simple rustic arch
A rustic arch is easy to construct and ideal for a rural or cottage-style garden. If the bark has been removed, ensure that the wood beneath has been pressure treated. The wood is simply nailed together; the diagonal struts give extra strength and support.
To ensure that the main posts are firm in the ground, use round metal post supports, or set the posts in concrete. This type of arch will support light- to medium-weight climbers.

DIAGONALS
The diagonal pieces are decorative and strengthen the arch.

Pointed rustic arch
This arch is also easy to construct yourself. Use galvanized nails or screws to attach the timbers to each other, and secure the posts into the ground in the same way as for the simple rustic arch. The pointed top provides extra height. Light- or medium-weight climbers are suitable for growing on this type of arch.

HORIZONTALS
The horizontal half-beams provide support for both the structure and for training plants.

Simple wooden arch
Sawed lumber, secured with simple joints nailed together, makes an attractive arch. The strong joints mean that it is safe to plant even heavyweight climbers to grow up this arch. Shaping the ends of the crossbeams creates a more professional result, but the cut ends will need to be treated with preservative.

BEAM ENDS
The ends of the beams are shaped to create a decorative effect – mark the shape you want on each beam before cutting it.

PERGOLAS

Wooden pergola
Using pressure-treated lumber ensures a long life for the pergola. Reapply wood preservative every few years. Sturdy uprights and cross-beams with housing joints for extra strength (see *opposite page* for how to make housing joints) enable the pergola to support a good selection of climbers.

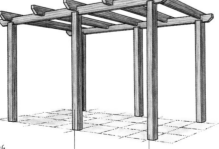

CLIMBERS
Plant a climber just outside each post and train it around the post and up over the crossbeams.

POST SUPPORTS
Secure the posts into the ground with metal post supports or embed them into concrete.

Rustic pergola
The informal style and material of this pergola blend in well with a cottage garden. Although sturdy, and reinforced with diagonal struts and simple joints, this pergola is strong enough to support only medium- or lightweight climbers. Many cottage-garden climbers are ideal, such as clematis, jasmine, and climbing and rambler roses – the roses will need to be kept in check so that their weight does not overburden the pergola.

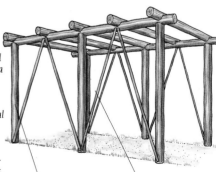

LUMBER
Use posts covered with bark, or ensure they have been pressure-treated.

PLANT SUPPORTS
Diagonal struts provide extra strength and support for lightweight climbers.

BUILDING AN ARCH

An arch can be as simple or as ornate as you like. In its simplest form it can be built using sturdy upright posts with beams or a trellis secured across the top. The lumber used can either be treated to retain a natural wood color, or stained to the color of your choice.

To secure the beams, always use galvanized nails or brass screws since neither of these will rust. The structure will be stronger if you use housing joints to interlock the beams. This sort of joint (described below) can be made with a chisel and saw, but more complex carpentry joints call for a template and a jig saw. Shaping the ends of the cross-beams before putting them in place will make the arch more decorative. This can be done simply by marking the shape you would like in pencil on the beam, and then using the marked line as a guide along which to saw.

YOU WILL NEED

- Metal post supports •Lumber
- Level •String and pegs
- Tape measure •Saw
- Wood preservative
- Hammer •Chisel •Mallet
- Galvanized nails •Brass screws •Screwdriver •Trellis

Chiseling out a joint
Carefully mark out the width of the joint so the beams will fit exactly. Saw 2 vertical cuts in the crossbeam, then chisel out the wood in between.

Installing the vertical posts
Use metal post supports to secure 4 x 4in (10 x 10cm) wooden posts into the ground; check that they are correctly spaced, upright, and level.

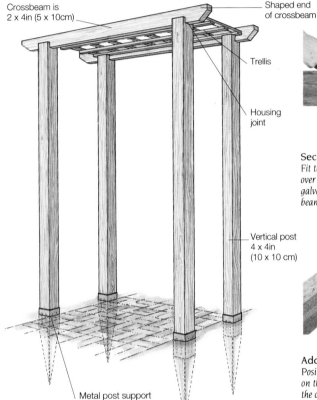

Crossbeam is 2 x 4in (5 x 10cm)

Shaped end of crossbeam

Trellis

Housing joint

Vertical post 4 x 4in (10 x 10 cm)

Metal post support

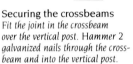

Securing the crossbeams
Fit the joint in the crossbeam over the vertical post. Hammer 2 galvanized nails through the crossbeam and into the vertical post.

Adding the trellis
Position the trellis so that it rests on the vertical posts and against the crossbeams. Attach the trellis to the vertical posts with brass screws.

MAKING A PERGOLA

A pergola can be built in the same way as an arch – the structure is similar but longer. Follow the instructions above but instead of using just four posts, add more posts, cross-beams, and trellises until the pergola is the length you want. The trellis on the top will support only lightweight climbers that are regularly thinned out. For more effective support and to enable plants to cover the structure evenly, attach wires between and vertically up the posts.

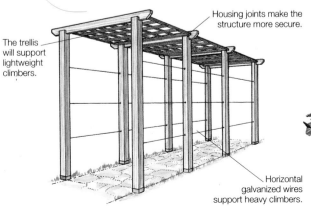

The trellis will support lightweight climbers.

Housing joints make the structure more secure.

Horizontal galvanized wires support heavy climbers.

Extra straining wires
Attach galvanized straining wires vertically up the posts using vine eyes at intervals of about 12in (30cm).

CLOTHING WITH CLIMBERS

In many gardens, a large growing area is often ignored – all the vertical surfaces. It is easy to clothe these unused areas of your garden with climbers and some shrubs, as long as there is enough soil in which to plant. You may decide to choose a colorful flowering or fruiting shrub, or perhaps a more vigorous climber to screen an unattractive wall or view.

Erect the support system before planting, since trying to make one around a growing plant is never successful. The support must be strong and large enough for the climber when fully grown with an extensive spread of stems and branches – otherwise it may collapse and damage the plant. Whatever you choose to grow, provided it is properly secured to the support, it will bring the walls and fences in your garden gloriously to life.

Star jasmine (*Trachelospermum jasminoides*)

MOUNTING SUPPORTS

Your wall or fence must be in good enough condition to carry the weight of the climber you choose and be sound enough for you to drive vine eyes or other hardware into it safely. Lightweight support can be provided by attaching netting to the wall with staples, or by a system of vertical or horizontal wires held in place with vine eyes. If the support system is likely to be used for heavier climbers in the future, choose something more substantial from the outset. Sturdy support is best provided by a system of galvanized wires held in place with vine eyes secured with wall anchors. The vine eyes hold the wires away from the wall or fence to allow air to circulate. The wires can be arranged horizontally, vertically, or in a fan shape according to whatever best suits the plant and the space. A heavy-duty trellis mounted on a sturdy wall also gives strong support; for how to attach a trellis, *see* pp.72–3. Use galvanized hardware for attaching plant supports; these do not rust so last longer than the ordinary ones.

Vine eyes and wires
Screw in a vine eye, wind one end of the wire around its head, pull taut, and secure to another vine eye.

Netting
Use galvanized U-staples to hold the netting away from the fence or wall surface.

see pp.72–3.

WHICH SUPPORT TO CHOOSE?

A few climbers, including English ivy and Virginia creeper, are self-clinging – they have aerial roots that cling to the surface of the wall or fence and therefore do not need any additional support.

LIGHT SUPPORTS
For annual climbers, such as sweet peas and morning glory (*Ipomoea purpurea*), use wire or plastic netting, or lightweight wires as supports. These plants often have twining stems or tendrils that do not need to be tied in.

STURDY SUPPORTS
Grow woody climbers, for example wisteria, and vigorous scrambling and twining climbers, such as honeysuckles and some clematis, on heavy-duty straining wires held in place with vine eyes. Alternatively, use a sturdy trellis, or strong wire netting, such as stock fencing.
  Many large, woody climbers need to be trained onto their supports with bamboo stakes while young but, once established, support themselves; scrambling climbers should be tied into their supports regularly to maintain a balanced shape.

DEALING WITH LOOSE FIXTURES

If vine eyes, nails, or U-staples become loose, try to remount them with the plant still in place rather than taking the risk of damaging or disturbing it. In a nearby, firm area of wall, drill a fresh hole, add a new wall anchor if needed, and remount the fixture. If wires break, even when the vine eyes or other hardware is still sound, it is usually worth replacing all of them since others may break soon after the first one.

PLANTING A CLIMBER

If your climber is container-grown, it can be planted at almost any time of year but will establish better if planted in spring or autumn. Bare-root and containerized climbers, such as roses, should always be planted in spring. Prepare the soil well before planting by adding organic matter and a slow-release fertilizer – this combination should be enough to get even the fussiest of climbers off to a good start.

Dig the planting hole about 12–18in (30–45cm) from the support so that the roots are not in the "rainshadow" – the area of ground that is sheltered from rain by the wall or fence. The hole should be at least twice the diameter and a few inches deeper than the container.

Climbers may be sold clinging to a support or mesh bag. Remove this gently, cleanly trimming away any damaged stems before planting. Plant climbers so that the top of the root ball is level with the soil, and in a slight dip so that the water runs toward the stems of the plant, which will help to conserve water. A layer of mulch applied after planting and watering will also prevent water from evaporating too quickly and effectively deters weeds.

1 *Prepare a large hole, mixing a little organic matter and fertilizer into the soil removed. Insert the climber, leaning it toward the support. Check that the root ball is level with the soil surface using a stake, adding or removing soil as necessary.*

2 *After carefully spreading out the roots, backfill the hole and gently firm down the soil. Prune away any dead or damaged stems, then space out and tie in the others, using bamboo stakes to guide them so that they will grow toward the wall.*

3 *Water the plant and surrounding soil thoroughly. Apply a 2–3in (5–8cm) mulch of bulky organic matter over the root feeding area, keeping clear of the stems. This will retain moisture in the soil, helping the plant to establish quickly.*

PLANTING CLEMATIS

Plant clematis slightly deeper than other climbers to enable the plant to form basal buds below ground from which it can renew if it is damaged by clematis wilt or slugs. Avoid heavy or wet soil, especially for evergreen or species clematis. Site the plant with its base in the shade to keep its roots cool; flat stones around the base shade its roots further.

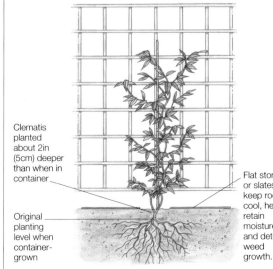

Clematis planted about 2in (5cm) deeper than when in container

Original planting level when container-grown

Flat stones or slates keep roots cool, help retain moisture, and deter weed growth.

SEASONS OF INTEREST

SPRING
Akebias ❧ ☀ ✚
Clematis [some] ❧❧ ☀ ✚ [some △]
Hops (*Humulus lupulus* and cvs, incl. 'Aureus') ❧ ☀ ✚ △

SUMMER
Actinidia kolomikta ❧ ☀ ✚
Coral plant (*Berberidopsis corallina*) ❧ ☀ ✚
Bittersweets (*Celastrus*) ❧ ☀ ✚ △
Clematis [some] ❧ ☀ ≡ [some △]
Climbing hydrangea (*Hydrangea anomala* subsp. *petiolaris*) ❧ ☀ ✚ ◉
Everlasting pea (*Lathyrus latifolius*) ❧ ☀ ≡ ◉ △
Sweet peas (*Lathyrus odoratus* cvs) ❧ ⊛ ☀ ☀ ≡
Honeysuckles (incl. *Lonicera* x *americana*, *L.* x *brownii* *L. tellmanniana*) ❧❧ ☀ [some ☀ △] ✚
Virginia creeper (*Parthenocissus quinquefolia*) ❧ ☀ ✚ ◉ △
Blue passion flower (*Passiflora caerulea*) ❧ ☀ ✚

Flame creeper (*Tropaeolum speciosum*) ❧ ☀ ≡
Wisterias (incl. *W. sinensis*, *W. floribunda*) ❧ ☀ ✚

AUTUMN
Chinese trumpet creeper (*Campsis grandiflora*) ❧ ✽ ☀ ≡ ◉
Trumpet creeper (*Campsis radicans*) ❧ ☀ ✚ ◉
Clematis [some] ❧ ☀ ✚ [some △]
Silver lace vine (*Polygonum aubertii*) ❧ ☀ ✚ △
Crimson glory vine (*Vitis coignetiae*) ❧ ☀ ✚
Grapevine (*Vitis vinifera*) ❧ ☀ ✚ △

WINTER/ALL YEAR
Winter jasmine (*Jasminum nudiflorum*) ❧ ☀ ✚
Ivies (*Hedera helix* cvs) ❧ ☀ ✚ ◉

KEY:
☀ Prefers sun
☀ Tolerates or prefers shade
≡ Lightweight
✚ Heavyweight
◉ Self-clinging
△ Fast-growing

PRUNING AND TRAINING CLIMBERS

All newly planted climbers need some pruning and tying in for the first few years to ensure that they produce a sturdy, vigorous, and well-shaped framework of stems. Mature climbers are not difficult to maintain – usually they can be allowed to grow as they please – but some routine pruning may be needed so that they continue to grow and flower well, without becoming too heavy for their support or swamping nearby plants. In some cases the plant may need to be kept in check so that it does not damage gutters, roof tiles, or masonry. Whatever type of climber you are pruning, a good, sharp pair of pruners is essential. On climbers with alternate buds, make a clean, sloping cut just above a healthy, plump bud that is pointing toward the direction in which you want the new shoot to grow. On climbers with opposite-facing buds, make a straight cut above a pair of buds.

MATERIALS FOR TYING IN

Coated twine is ideal, since it is flexible and weather-resistant, unlike ordinary twine, which breaks and rots more easily. Synthetic twine is also strong. Galvanized wire is useful for vigorous, strong-growing climbers. Other alternatives include plastic-coated wire, plastic rose ties, and ready-made fence clips. Tie in flexible new shoots regularly, spacing them out well. Tie stems loosely to allow some movement and prevent the tie from strangling the stem.

Twine
Use a loose figure-eight knot for tying in to prevent the plant stem from chafing against the support.

Plastic rose tie
This tie has ratchets and so can be gradually loosened in stages as the plant grows in size.

Fence clips
Specially made for attaching the stems of climbing plants to wavy-edged fences, the clips shown here are fastened directly to the tops of the horizontal panels. Each is used by first pushing one end onto the board, looping it across a stem, and then attaching the other end to the board to enclose the stem securely.

PRUNING AND TRAINING CLIMBING AND RAMBLER ROSES

In their first two years, most climbers and ramblers need no pruning except for the removal of any weak, straggly, or diseased wood. Train new shoots along horizontal supports where possible – the more horizontal the shoot, the more flowers it will produce. In subsequent years, train in all new growth while it is still pliable.

PRUNING CLIMBING ROSES
Climbing roses should be pruned in summer after flowering: shorten sideshoots and any main shoots that have outgrown the space. On old climbers with bare lengths of stem near ground level, renewal pruning may be needed to encourage new shoots to grow from the base – cut one or two older shoots back to within about 12in (30cm) of the ground, using loppers for thicker stems.

PRUNING RAMBLER ROSES
Ramblers should be pruned in summer. Prune established plants by carefully removing older stems from their support and cutting 25–30 percent of the oldest

ones back to ground level. Any remaining stems can then be tied back onto the support and trained horizontally. Cut back sideshoots above a healthy shoot to within two to four buds of the main stem.

Cutting to ground level
Prune a proportion of old, bare stems almost back to ground level to encourage plenty of new replacement shoots to develop on ramber roses.

Removing poor growth
Remove any weak, straggly, diseased, or dead stems, cutting back to healthy growth or flush to the main stem.

Pruning sideshoots
On rambler roses, prune sideshoots to within 2–4 buds of the main stem (as shown here). On climbing roses, trim the sideshoots by about 6in (15cm). For both types of rose, make a clean, sloping cut to just above a healthy, outward-facing bud. This will help encourage plenty of spreading new growth.

BASIC PRUNING OF CLIMBERS

Climbers perform better if you prune them regularly rather than letting them grow too large or congested. The season of flowering and the age of wood on which the flowers are produced determine when you need to prune a climber.

Climbers that flower on the previous year's growth (and sometimes on even older wood) need to be pruned soon after flowering is over. Remove weak or damaged growth, cutting out any branches that are crossing or congested, and prune flowered wood to a vigorous shoot or bud. This encourages new shoots to develop and ripen before winter so that they are ready to flower the following year.

Climbers that flower on the current season's growth need to be pruned at the end of winter or in early spring so that they have plenty of time to develop new flowering shoots. Prune out dead, damaged, or congested wood, and cut back sideshoots to five or six buds. This encourages strong, new shoots and keeps the plant in shape.

If you are worried about inadvertently pruning out the wrong type of stem, remember that shoots that are in their first year will still be green and pliable, while those in their second year are more rigid and usually gray or brown in color. For details of how to prune a clematis, *see* p.80.

CROSSING BRANCHES
Prune crossing branches, cutting flush with a main stem or just above a bud.

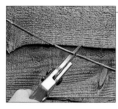

TYING IN
Tie in shoots to establish a well-spaced framework of stems.

PRUNING SIDESHOOTS
Prune back sideshoots to encourage strong, outward growth and an open habit.

REMOVING CROWDED BRANCHES
Prune out congested stems in the center to open out the plant and reduce risk of disease.

Prune shoots that have flowered to a healthy bud, then tie in.

see p.80.

WHEN TO PRUNE CLIMBERS

PRUNE AFTER FLOWERING
Actinidias ❧ [some ✽]
Golden trumpet (*Allemanda cathartica*) ❧✽
Birthworts (*Aristolochia*) ❧ [most ✽]
Beaumontias ❧✽
Bougainvilleas ❧✽
Gelsemiums ❧
Hoyas ❧✽
Climbing hydrangea (*H. anomala* subsp. *petiolaris*) ❧
Jasmines (*Jasminum*) ❧❧ [some ✽]
Passionflowers (*Passiflora*) ❧ [most ✽]
Schizophragmas ❧
Capa de oro (*Solandra maxima*) ❧✽
Streptosolen jamesonii ❧✽
Wisterias ❧

PRUNE IN WINTER OR EARLY SPRING
Akebias ❧
Coral vine (*Antigonon leptopus*) ❧✽
Bignonias ❧
Campsis ❧
Clerodendrums ❧❧ [some ✽]
Clianthus ❧✽
Hops (*Humulus lupulus* and cvs, incl. 'Aureus') ❧
Lapagerias ❧✽
Honeysuckles (*Lonicera*) ❧❧
Mandevillas ❧❧✽
Pileostegia viburnoides ❧
Plumbagos ❧ [some ✽]
Polygonums ❧
Pyrostegias ❧✽
Solanums (*S. crispum*, *S. jasminoides*) ❧✽
Stephanotis ❧✽
Thunbergias ❧ ✽
Snail flower (*Vigna caracalla*) ❧✽
Vitis ❧ [some ✽]

RENOVATING A NEGLECTED CLIMBER

If a climber is allowed to grow untamed, it can become congested, tangled, and very heavy. It may also outgrow its position, becoming so dense that it bulges into nearby paths or overhangs borders, shading plants underneath. A climber in this condition can almost always be saved by careful pruning. A few climbers will grow back if cut almost to the base but, unless you are sure your plant will recover from this, follow the less drastic method on the right, tackling the plant in stages over a period of at least two years.

Removing old wood
Prune away all large, woody stems almost down to the base, to leave only vigorous new growth.

Pruning an overgrown honeysuckle
When a honeysuckle has developed into a mass of tangled, dead growth, with only the ends of the shoots bearing leaves and flowers, trim away dead and damaged stems from underneath the new growth. Although you may lose some of the flowering stems for a season, they should rejuvenate and flower the following year.

PRUNING CLEMATIS

Clematis are often divided into three groups depending on when they flower, and consequently how they need to be pruned.

MINIMAL PRUNING

Vigorous species clematis that produce their flowers early in the season on stems that have ripened during the previous season should be cut back hard when planted, but then need no routine pruning. However, if they become too vigorous or grow into a congested, tangled mass, they can be pruned shortly after flowering to keep them in check. Clematis that can be treated in this way include *Clematis alpina*, *C. armandii*, *C. cirrhosa*, *C. macropetala*, and *C. montana*.

LIGHT PRUNING

Clematis cultivars that produce large flowers early in the season on the previous season's growth should be lightly pruned in very early spring before the plant starts to grow. Remove straggly, diseased, or dying stems and then cut back the remaining stems by about one-third, to just above a healthy pair of green buds; the stems that grow from these buds will produce the first flush of blooms in the season. Clematis in this group include 'Lasurstern', 'Marie Boisselot', 'Mrs. N. Thompson', 'Nelly Moser', 'Niobe', 'The President', and 'Vyvyan Pennell'.

Light pruning
Remove dead and weak growth, then prune back the remaining growth by one-third to a pair of strong buds.

HARD PRUNING

Hard pruning is used on the clematis species and cultivars that produce their flowers late in the season on the current year's stems. In early spring, before the plant starts to produce new shoots, all the previous season's growth should be pruned back to just above the lowest pair of strong, healthy buds (about 6–12in (15–30cm) above ground level).

Hard pruning
Cut out any diseased, dead, or dying stems. Prune the remainder back to a healthy pair of buds 6–12in (15–30cm) above ground level. Always cut back to a pair of strong buds with a clean, straight cut. In late spring and summer, tie in the new stems, spacing them out evenly; take care not to break any.

As new growth develops it can be tied into the support at regular intervals to train it into the shape you want. Do this carefully since the new stems can be very brittle. Clematis that should be pruned in this way include 'Comtesse de Bouchaud', 'Ernest Markham', *C. florida*, 'Hagley Hybrid', 'Jackmanii', *C. paniculata*, 'Perle d'Azur', *C. tangutica*, 'Ville de Lyon', and *C. viticella*.

PRUNING AND TRAINING ON A PERGOLA OR ARCH

Train climbers over a pergola, pillar, or arch so that they grow evenly over their support. Tie in new stems loosely as they appear—most climbers flower best if trained horizontally. In spring or late summer, depending on when the climber flowers, remove dead, diseased, or damaged wood, pruning the main stems to encourage new sideshoots to form. When the main shoots reach the top, prune them so that they do not outgrow their position. For climbing and rambler roses, encourage flowering shoots to form near the base by spiraling the main shoots around the uprights when the growth is pliable.

> **TYING IN SHOOTS AND STEMS**
> Always tie in shoots and stems gently and lightly, being careful to leave enough room for growth and movement. If the tie or string is too tight it can damage or even kill the stem as it cuts into the growing plant.

> **YOU WILL NEED**
> • Pruners
> • Twine or plastic rose ties
>
> SPR / SUM / AUT / WIN

Wisteria on a pergola
Tie in shoots regularly to form an even covering over the support. Prune back or tie in stems that are hanging down. Prune in late summer to encourage more shoots and flowers.

TYING IN
Shoots tied in horizontally flower more profusely than if tied vertically.

SPACING THE SHOOTS
Tie in young, pliable shoots as they develop so that you can train them in the direction you want and cover the support evenly.

PRUNING
In late summer, prune back any nonessential stems by one-third. In late winter shorten these shoots again to about 3–4in (8–10cm).

MAINTAINING CLIMBERS

Climbers are similar to shrubs and trees in the general maintenance they require. Regular watering, feeding, and the occasional application of a mulch should keep them in good condition. From time to time supports and hardware may need to be repaired and made more secure, or even replaced with something new. Climbers are often badly blown about by wind, so ties should also be checked frequently, and renewed when necessary,

especially following periods of severe weather. The regular removal of overvigorous stems encourages healthy new growth, and it prevents the climber from becoming misshapen or outgrowing the available space in your garden. Many climbers can easily be propagated by layering – they root naturally along their shoots, so you can take advantage of this and encourage the plant to produce more layers, giving you a new supply of climbers to plant elsewhere.

FEEDING, WATERING, AND MULCHING

In the spring of the first and second years after planting, climbers benefit from an application of about 50–85g (2–3oz) of a balanced fertilizer around their base. This will keep them growing and flowering well for the first few years. Once established, feed climbers annually in spring using a slow-release fertilizer to ensure the plant has a well-balanced and continuous

supply of nutrients throughout the growing season.

Climbers need plenty of moisture for the first few years; after that, keep the soil moist according to the plant's needs. For climbers, soil conditions will usually be drier as a result of the combination of the rainshadow created by the support and, next to walls, the drying effect of the bricks. Also the luxuriant growth of

many climbers means that they often lose a lot of moisture through their foliage. Where climbers are underplanted with other plants, ensure that you apply enough water (and fertilizer) for both the climber and everything else. To retain soil moisture and deter weeds, apply a spring mulch around the base of the climber. For details of different mulches, *see* "Which Mulch?" p.46.

MULCHING CLIMBERS ON A PERGOLA
Avoid mulching right up to the base of a wooden pergola or arch – the damp mulch will promote rot. Keep it clear of plant stems, too.

INCREASING YOUR STOCK OF CLIMBERS

Many climbers produce trailing shoots that naturally start to develop roots when they come into contact with the soil. This is known as self-layering, and taking advantage of this natural process is the simplest means of propagating some climbers. Along a stem, there may well be several rooted or self-layered sections. Separate those that have a well-developed root system – this will be obvious since they will have healthy new growth above ground – lifting them carefully without damaging the root systems. Most layers

should be potted into a container of soil mix, but if a new layer has already developed a strong root system, transplant it right into its permanent home, watering it in well. If your climber has not yet layered, you can encourage it to do so by carefully bending down a young stem and weighing it down with stones.

Many climbers are easily propagated by semiripe cuttings, too. For details of how to take these cuttings, *see* p.53.

YOU WILL NEED
- Hand fork • Pruners
- Multipurpose soil mix • Small pot
- Watering can

HOW TO PROPAGATE CLIMBERS

SELF-LAYERING
Bittersweets (*Celastrus*) ⚘
Creeping fig (*Ficus pumila*) ⚘
Ivies (*Hedera*) ⚘
Parthenocissus ⚘ [some ❄]
Trachelospermums ⚘

SEMIRIPE CUTTINGS
Euonymus ◆⚘
Hoyas ⚘❄
Jasmines (*Jasminum*) ⚘⚘ [some ❄]
Honeysuckles (*Lonicera*) ⚘⚘
Polygonums ⚘
Schisandras ⚘
Schizophragmas ⚘
Stephanotis ⚘❄

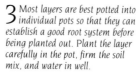

1 Carefully lift shoots that have grown toward the ground and started to root. Ease each layer out with a hand fork and use a sharp pair of pruners to cut off the rooted area with the new shoots.

2 Cut the stem into sections, each with a good root system, healthy-looking new growth, and some buds. Carefully strip off any leaves growing close to the rooted area, without damaging the stem.

3 Most layers are best potted into individual pots so that they can establish a good root system before being planted out. Plant the layer carefully in the pot, firm the soil mix, and water in well.

ORNAMENTAL DIVIDERS

An ornamental divider is a living screen of climbers or other plants which have been trained to grow up and cover a wall, trellis, or fence, dividing one area of your garden from another. Choose plants to achieve different effects, from a range of delicate flowers to a spectacular crop of fruits or berries. Ornamental dividers are particularly useful for screening off eyesores – perhaps a compost pile or garage – and are ideal for

providing privacy from neighbors. You could also use a divider to create separate areas within the garden – for vegetables, for children to play in, for ornamental beds, and so on. There are several types of support from which to create the divider – sturdy posts with horizontal straining wires, trellises, fence panels, or a wall (see "Erecting Fences and Trellises," pp.72–3, and "Mounting Supports," p.76). If you use fast-growing plants, the structure itself can be basic.

PLANTING BOTH SIDES OF A TRELLIS

If your divider is free standing, you can plant on both sides, creating a dense mass of color and foliage. Your screen will look good for several months if you select plants that flower in succession. Position the plants so that they are not quite opposite each other, to cut down on the competition between the two root systems. If your planting area is restricted, pay particular attention to regular watering and feeding both after planting and once the plants are established. For details about how to plant, see "Planting a Climber," p.77. Allow the climbers to intertwine as they grow, but check that one does not swamp the other, trimming it back if necessary.

Complementary planting
For a shaded site, combine a climbing hydrangea (Hydrangea anomala *subsp.* petiolaris) *with a sweet autumn clematis* (Clematis paniculata), *both of which have creamy white flowers. The late-blooming clematis extends the flowering season into autumn.*

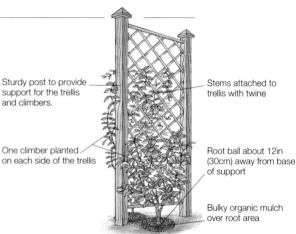

Sturdy post to provide support for the trellis and climbers.

One climber planted on each side of the trellis

Stems attached to trellis with twine

Root ball about 12in (30cm) away from base of support

Bulky organic mulch over root area

TRAINING FRUIT ON A DIVIDER

For beautiful blossoms, followed by a tasty crop, train a fruit tree or even some cane fruits (see p.147) on your divider.

TRAINING INTO SHAPES
Fruit trees can be trained into a range of forms, including the fan (see below and the illustrations, right), cordon, and espalier. A cordon, usually planted at 45°, is a tree trained as a single stem with the sideshoots cut back to form fruiting spurs. An espalier has one vertical stem and pairs of horizontal arms at 15in (38cm) intervals. These forms each need specific, sometimes detailed, pruning to keep them in shape and fruiting well – seek advice before starting to train.

TRAINING A FAN
Many fruit trees can be grown as fans, and in colder climates, peaches, apricots, and nectarines crop more heavily when protected by a

YOU WILL NEED

- Pruners
- Bamboo stakes
- Twine

sheltered wall or fence. In warmer climates they can be grown on free-standing posts and wires.

It is best to start training with a feathered maiden – a one-year-old tree with several well-placed sideshoots (equivalent to "Year of planting," right). These are inexpensive and should establish well. Alternatively, buying a partially trained fan (equivalent to "Following year", middle right) will save you work, but costs more; before buying, check that the central, vertical stem has been removed to leave two main arms and that each is developing evenly and strongly. Once you have formed the basic fan shape by the third year, routine pruning consists of cutting out the fruited shoots and tying in new shoots. Some shrubs, such as pyracantha, can also be fan-trained using these methods.

Training a fan, year of planting

EARLY SPRING
Cut the leader above a pair of laterals about 12in (30cm) from ground level. These will form the main arms.

PRUNING THE ARMS
At the same time, cut each of the arms back to about 15in (38cm). Tie in each of the 2 arms to a bamboo stake at an angle of about 40°.

EARLY SPRING
Prune back remaining lower laterals to one bud.

SUMMER
As new, flexible shoots develop, tie 2 on the top of each arm, and 1 beneath, to stakes. These shoots will form the basic fan shape.

COMBINATIONS WITH CLIMBERS AND WALL PLANTS

• For a display of trailing elegance with hanging clusters of blooms, combine a wisteria (in mauve, white, or pink) with the bright yellow Voss's laburnum (*Laburnum* x *watereri* 'Vossii').

• *Clematis montana* 'Tetrarose' grown with *Actinidia kolomikta* makes an attractive display since the pink clematis flowers pick up the color in the white- and pink-splashed actinidia leaves.

• The range of clematis from which to choose is vast. Combine two with different flowering times (but similar rate of growth and pruning needs, *see* p.80) for year-round interest. For a succession of beautiful flowers, select *C. alpina* for the spring, with a large-flowered, midseason clematis, such as 'The President'.

Clematis montana 'Tetrarose'   *Actinidia kolomikta*

• To give a pergola, arch, or wall a dense and luxuriant appearance using a rich combination of pinks and mauves, try growing rose acacia (*Robinia hispida*) as a wall shrub with a mauve Japanese wisteria (*Wisteria floribunda*).

English ivy 'Goldheart'   *Tropaeolum speciosum*

• To create a simple, pretty effect combine the English ivy 'Goldheart', which has yellow variegated leaves and clings to its support, with the vivid red flowers of the flame creeper (*Tropaeolum speciosum*) clambering through it. When the flame creeper dies down you will still have the attractive ivy foliage.

• Newly planted climbers may take a while to look established. For the first year or two plant annual climbers such as morning glory (*Ipomoea purpurea*), sweet pea, and flame creeper (*Tropaeolum speciosum*).

These will brighten up an otherwise sparse arch, fence, trellis, or pergola while a perennial climber or wall shrub matures.

• Honeysuckles often produce heavily scented flowers and then, later on in the year, attractive berries. Combine green-leaved forms with *Lonicera japonica* 'Aureo-reticulata', which has bright yellow veins on its leaves.

• In a large area, plant three pyracanthas of your choice – one each of red-, orange-, and yellow-berried forms adds a fiery autumn and winter effect. The profuse white flowers are a bonus.

• Pink and purple splendor comes from growing pink-flowered *Rosa* 'Mme. Grégoire Staechelin' together with Clematis 'Vyvyan Pennell'.

Rosa 'Mme. Grégoire Staechelin'   *Clematis* 'Vyvyan Pennell'

Following year

EARLY SUMMER
Train in the new sideshoots to bamboo stakes.

EARLY SUMMER
Prune out all shoots appearing below the two main arms.

EARLY SPRING
Prune back the 2 main arms by about one-third, cutting just above a strong, outward-facing bud.

EARLY SUMMER
Cut out any shoots that are pointing downward or away from the fence.

Routine pruning

SUMMER
Tie in developing sideshoots.

EARLY SUMMER
Thin excess side-shoots and those growing inward, leaving the remaining ones 4–6in (10–15cm) apart.

AFTER FRUITING
Prune each fruiting shoot to a replacement near its base. Tie in the replacements to maintain the fan shape.

SUMMER
Pinch back to 4–6 leaves any sideshoots that start to overlap the main framework.

HEDGES

With the exception of a brick or stone wall, a dense hedge is the best way to make an attractive and almost impenetrable boundary around a garden. Hedges have a few advantages over walls, too. They can be neatly clipped into decorative shapes, or allowed to grow informally, and, of course, unlike a wall or fence, they will change with the seasons. Apart from marking the boundary of your property, a hedge can also screen passing traffic, pedestrians, or neighbors, giving your garden some privacy. It can also provide secluded areas as well as shelter from wind or sun. Many plants make effective hedging, from a formal yew as a green backdrop, to a colorful barberry as a feature in its own right. The most time-consuming task is trimming your hedge. This is usually an annual job, though it might need to be done more often to keep formal or fast-growing hedges in shape.

CHOOSING A HEDGE FOR YOUR GARDEN

The first things to decide are whether you want a formal or informal hedge and whether you would prefer it to form an evergreen or deciduous barrier.

Yew is the ultimate in elegant, formal hedging but is relatively expensive and slow growing. At the other extreme, Leyland cypress is fast growing and cheap; if kept trim it quickly makes a dense,
regular hedge. A slower-growing, and more attractive, evergreen hedge can be made with arborvitae, Lawson cypress, or well-clipped green or variegated hollies. For low, formal hedging, boxwood makes a dense edging. Beech is an excellent deciduous hedge – both its purple- and green-leaved forms retain their leaves during the winter to provide a good degree of screening.
Many barberries make good informal hedges, especially Japanese barberry, with its many cultivars, and pyracantha, which has white flowers and colorful berries. Deciduous forsythia and flowering quince lose their leaves in autumn, but the interest they provide at other times makes them a good choice where an all-year-round barrier is not essential.

Leyland cypress (x *Cupressocyparis leylandii*)
This one of the cheapest and fastest-growing hedging plants, but it must be kept firmly in check to prevent it from getting out of control.

Darwin's barberry (*Berberis darwinii*)
This spring-flowering barberry makes an informal ornamental hedge, easily cared for since it needs pruning only after flowering.

Beech (*Fagus sylvatica*)
Although deciduous, the glory of beech is that it holds its tan-brown leaves in winter, providing an attractive screen all year.

FORMATIVE PRUNING

Pruning in the first few years after planting is vital if the hedge is to look good in the long term. The sides of the hedge should be tapered slightly toward the top to ensure that it grows into a strong, weatherproof barrier. Mature hedges that are uneven or sparse at the base have usually become so as a result of incorrect formative pruning.

EVERGREEN HEDGES
All evergreens, including conifers, are neatened up at the sides for the first few years. Keep the main vertical shoot trimmed back once it reaches
the height you want the hedge to be when it is fully grown.

DECIDUOUS HEDGES
Most deciduous hedging plants develop best if cut back by about one-third all over at planting, and again the following spring. Strong-growing hedges that have vigorous, upright growth, such as hawthorn and privet, should be cut back to about 6–12in (15–30cm) in the spring after planting and their sideshoots pruned again in summer.

Before pruning
Lonicera nitida *tends to become straggly and uneven, so it needs correct formative pruning at planting if it is to grow into an effective barrier.*

After pruning
Keep the main shoots trimmed evenly to the height you would like the hedge to be. Prune back the sideshoots by half to encourage dense, bushy growth.

TRIMMING A HEDGE

The time of year to trim depends on the type of hedge and how neat you want it to look. Formal hedges generally need pruning more frequently than informal ones to keep them in shape.

Hand shears are ideal for most hedge-trimming jobs, especially if you want a good, even finish. Remember to keep the blades parallel to the hedge to maintain a straight line. For larger areas, it may be easier to use a power hedge trimmer, although these are unsuitable for use on large-leaved hedges, such as laurel, since they tend to rip the leaves rather than cut them. Always wear protective goggles when using a power hedge trimmer.

When clipping, slope the sides of the hedge inward slightly, so that the base is wider than the top. This will ensure that all parts of the hedge receive enough light. For conifers, keep the sideshoots trimmed regularly to avoid the brown interior stems being exposed by a sudden drastic cut – they generally will not resprout.

PLANTING A CLIMBER THROUGH A HEDGE

Brighten up a plain hedge by planting climbers to grow through it. Clematis and rambler roses look attractive, as do some annuals, such as nasturtiums and morning glory (*Ipomoea purpurea*). Regular watering is essential, especially while the plants are establishing.

Pointed top
This hornbeam hedge has been clipped so that it has a pointed top. In areas that are prone to heavy snowfall, this will prevent snow from settling on the hedge and distorting its shape.

Flat top
This yew hedge is narrower at the top than the base, and so will be less easily damaged by snow or wind.

RENOVATING A HEDGE

Neglected hedges can often be renovated – though most conifers will not produce new growth if cut back into old, bare wood. Avoid cutting back all the shoots severely at once, or you will place too much stress on the plant. In the first year, trim one side back to encourage healthy new shoots from the center. The next year, trim these shoots lightly and cut the other side back hard. The following year there should be new, healthy growth over the whole hedge.

Cut back growth on one side almost to the main stem in the first year.

Trim the growth on the other side lightly into shape.

HEDGES FOR PLANTING AND PRUNING

HEDGING PLANT	PLANTING DISTANCE	WHEN TO PRUNE	HOW TO PRUNE
Japanese barberry (*Berberis thunbergii*) ⬠□□△	12–15in (30–38cm)	After flowering	Clip to shape
Boxwood (*Buxus sempervirens*) ⬤□□	12in (30cm)	2–3 times in the growing season	Clip to shape
Flowering quince (*Chaenomeles speciosa*) ⬠△	24in (60cm)	Immediately after flowering	Clip to shape
Lawson cypress (*Chamaecyparis lawsoniana*) ♥⬤□	24in (60cm)	Spring and autumn	Remove new growth, clip to shape
Hawthorn (*Crataegus monogyna*) ♀□△	12–24in (30–60cm)	□ summer and autumn; △ summer	Clip to shape
Leyland cypress (x *Cupressocyparis leylandii*) ♥□△△	30in (75cm)	2–3 times in the growing season	Clip to shape
Beech (*Fagus sylvatica*) ♀□	12–24in (30–60cm)	Late summer	Clip to shape
Forsythia x *intermedia* and cvs ⬠△△	18in (45cm)	Spring, after flowering	Remove old wood, clip to shape
Garrya elliptica ⬤△	18in (45cm)	Spring, after flowering	Neaten vigorous or damaged stems
Hollies (*Ilex* species and cvs) ♥⬤□□	18–24in (45–60cm)	Late summer	Clip to shape
Lavenders (*Lavandula*) ⬤□△	12in (30cm)	□ spring; □ and △ after flowering	Remove flowerheads, clip to shape
Privets (*Ligustrum*) ⬤⬠□□△	12in (30cm)	2–3 times in the growing season	Clip to shape
Lonicera nitida ⬤□	12in (30cm)	2–3 times in the growing season	Clip to shape
Pyracanthas ⬤△	24in (60cm)	Midsummer	Remove spindly and vigorous shoots
Shrub roses (incl. 'Roseraie de l'Haÿ') ⬠△	18in (45cm)	Spring	Remove weak growth
Arborvitae (*Thuja*) ♥□△△	24in (60cm)	Spring and early autumn	Clip to shape

KEY □ formal △ informal △ fast-growing

·6·
PATHS AND STEPS

Paths and steps may be functional, or even essential, but they can also be an attraction in their own right – provided paving materials are selected with as much care as plants, and routes are planned to draw the eye as well as the feet. In this chapter you will find both inspiration and practical advice.

GARDEN WALKWAYS

Paths and steps play an important role in the garden. On the one hand, they are highly practical features, facilitating access to the house and different garden areas, while protecting grass from heavy wear and providing a firm surface for moving equipment. On the other hand, they can be a valuable part of the overall design – adding an architectural element to modern plantings, or emphasizing the informality of a cottage-style design.

FORM AND FUNCTION

Since they are permanent features, any new walkways should be planned carefully to take full advantage of the site, complement garden designs, and fulfill the function required of them. Both the design and the materials you choose for these elements will have a strong impact on the garden, for better or for worse. Certainly, if paths and steps are to fit in well, they should harmonize with the architectural style and building materials of the house and any surrounding structures.

A path can be anything from a formal, straightforward access route to a wide and sprawling trail. But beyond its practical purpose and immediate impact, a path can also be used to alter perceptions of garden proportions. For example, a straight, narrow path can make a short garden look longer – especially if the end point is obscured by foliage to give the impression that it goes on even farther. Conversely, a path laid on the diagonal or planted in clumps along its length will draw the eye from side to side and counteract an excessively elongated appearance.

In square or oblong gardens that are largely devoted to lawn, a meandering trail of stepping-stones will help break up the expanse of green, and also make a useful, dry path in bad weather. In icy conditions such paths really come into their own, since stepping on frost-covered grass can seriously damage it.

Steps can form a practical link between different levels or make a visual bridge between areas of contrasting design in the garden. They can be built out of traditional stone slabs, rustic poles and gravel, modern paving materials, or even painted wood for a hint of oriental style.

Before you go to the expense of lifting existing features to lay new steps and paths, look carefully to assess the potential of what you already have. It may be possible to make significant improvements simply by mending or cleaning dirty or damaged areas – and established features will already have that wonderful weathered appearance which helps them blend with their surroundings.

SELECTING SUITABLE MATERIALS

When choosing new materials, consider practicality, suitability, and expense. The amount and type of use paths or steps will get, the width necessary to make them useful rather than just decorative, and the look and texture of the surface will all affect your choice. Remember that better-quality materials may cost more initially but, since they invariably last longer, could actually save you money in the long run.

ADDING PLANT LIFE TO PATHS AND STEPS

Steps and paths can both be enhanced by careful planting into cracks and crevices. Small rock plants are ideally suited to this purpose since their native habitats offer similarly spartan growing conditions, and they will thrive in even the smallest pocket of soil without spreading too much. Herbs are another attractive and interesting choice for pathside planting. If steps are wide enough you could also use pots and planters to introduce color, break up an uninteresting area, and maybe even hide damaged or discolored slabs.

However, it is important to mention one word of warning. Don't allow yourself to get carried away with path and step planting – too much overhanging vegetation obscures step edges and can make paved surfaces dangerously slippery.

Rock planting
Bellflowers (Campanula) *sprawling down from the joints in the wall and* Welsh poppies (Meconopsis cambrica) *spreading upward to meet them from crevices in the steps bring a cheerful splash of color to the weathered, mellow tones of this old stone wall and steps.*

Material benefits
Wood-edged stairs, backfilled with gravel, lead down in a gentle sweep to an informal path almost completely obscured by the adjacent planting. The bold, contrasting, architectural foliage of the plants beside the steps forms a series of focal points and softens the look of the wooden edging.

MATERIALS FOR PATHS AND STEPS

Paths and steps form a permanent part of the garden, linking its various areas and the house, so it is worth investing in something that lasts well and looks good. Having decided where to site them, what materials should you use? There is a wide range available, and although each will provide you with the same feature, they are all very different in character and appearance. Factors to consider include, of course, the cost and availability, but more importantly, which materials will blend best with the rest of the garden (and the house) and suit your own personal taste. If the garden and house are informal in style, natural materials, such as rustic wood or stone (or good imitations), invariably look best. A more formal garden and house would be better complemented by a design incorporating straight edges and more regular paving, such as pavers or bricks.

MATERIALS FOR PATHS

A path can be made using just one or several different materials – a combination often gives a softer appearance and allows you to mix cheap and expensive materials or contrasting textures. Brick paths are long-lasting, versatile, and attractive (see p.90). Stone setts and clay or concrete pavers can be used in many situations and are available in a variety of shapes and sizes. Paving slabs come in a wide range of sizes, colors, and textures, and are one of the cheapest materials for paths. Natural stone slabs (such as field stone) are also suitable but are very expensive (see p.96). Gravel paths are cheap and easy to lay (see p.91).

Engineering brick

Red brick with "frog"

Terracotta brick with "frog"

Bricks
Choose bricks that are weatherproof so they will not crumble in frosty conditions. Engineering bricks are suitable as are bricks with "frogs," or indentations, which must always be used with the flat side upward. Different colors are available, and these can be used singly or in combination. Multicolored and mottled bricks give a more informal look to a path. Bricks can be laid in a range of patterns, including herringbone and basketweave, or end to end; they are easy to lay around awkward corners.

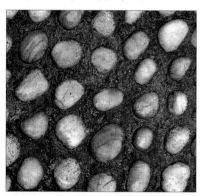

Cobblestones
These large, naturally rounded stones have been set in mortar for a firm, regular finish. The end result is an informal blend of subtle colors and varying shapes. Since they are uncomfortable to walk on, they should be used only for small paths or those that are used infrequently.

Imitation stone setts

Setts
These small paving blocks are usually made of stone, such as granite, or imitation stone, and look less regular than bricks when laid. Extremely hard-wearing, they are also easy to lay in straight lines or curves. The slightly uneven surface created by setts has an attractive, informal look, but it may not always be suitable for wheelbarrows or bicycles.

Small setts
These are expensive to use over a large area but make a richly textured and natural-looking path when softened over a period of time by moss forming in the joints. The colors of these imitation stone setts change to become deeper and stronger in appearance when wet.

Granite setts

Concrete blocks

Concrete paving blocks
Cheaper than stone blocks, these form a regular, hardwearing surface. They come in a range of shapes and sizes and can be used for curves or interlocking patterns, or combined with other materials.

MATERIALS FOR EDGING PATHS

Path edging can make or break the appearance and practicality of a path, so it is essential to choose carefully. Like paving materials, edgings vary in style and price. You can choose an edging either to match your path or to contrast with it. The more decorative the edging, the more informal the look; plain, straight lines are more suited to a formal garden. Raised edgings form a transition between a path and a border, but they are not suitable next to a lawn since they interfere with mowing (for edging a path next to a lawn, *see* p.57). Wood with or without the bark still in place gives a rustic or rural character to a path and is relatively inexpensive. To be long lasting, however, the wood must be pressure treated.

Raised edgings

Glazed or unglazed rope edging is fairly expensive but long lasting. Ceramic edging is often more decorative than other edgings and is attractively old-fashioned. Precast materials range from concrete strips to shaped edgings. Bricks placed on the diagonal look striking and can be laid individually or bought premolded and laid in sections.

Terracotta post

Precast diagonal bricks

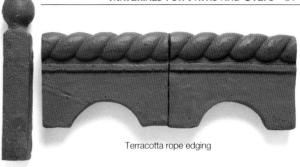

Terracotta rope edging

Decorative ceramic edging

MATERIALS FOR STEPS

So long as they are carefully constructed, the longest-lasting, sturdiest, and safest flights of steps are usually made from a combination of brick or molded concrete risers, with slabs for the horizontal treads (*see* p.96 for a choice of slabs). Informal steps can be made with pressure-treated wooden risers and gravel treads. For the construction of steps, *see* pp.92–3.

Gravel and wooden steps

The materials for these steps, apart from gravel and lengths of wood, include long pegs to hold the wood in place and boards to form the edging and contain the gravel.

Gravel

Red gravel

Gray gravel

Gravel

Choose from different grades and colors of gravel to match other materials and suit your garden. Gravel made from local stone harmonizes well with local buildings. Although cheap and easy to use for steps, it does not make very solid or stable treads.

Slate chips

Board   Peg

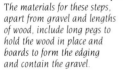

Molded brick risers

Molded concrete risers

Risers

Molded risers provide an easier-to-use alternative to laying your own risers with individual bricks. They are available in several colors and brick combinations to suit most budgets. Make sure they are set firmly in place with concrete so that they support the slab treads.

Lengths of pressure-treated wood are used as risers for gravel and wooden steps.

MAKING PATHS

A well-constructed path, however simple, is an asset to any garden. It provides a way of linking various areas, allowing easy access without damaging grass or flowering plants. When deciding where to site and how to construct a path, remember that it should be at least wide enough for one person and a wheelbarrow, if not for two to walk comfortably side by side. For stepping-stones, space them to fit your stride easily. Choose

materials that harmonize with existing or planned garden features, and at the same time suit your budget. Whether you choose brick, gravel, paving slabs, setts, or stepping-stones, make sure your path looks good on its own and with the surrounding plants. Edgings, both manmade and planted, can be used in practical ways – to make mowing easier or to contain a gravel path – or simply to soften the hard edges of a newly laid path.

LAYING A BRICK PATH

Brick paths may be more expensive and time-consuming to lay than gravel ones, but if the job is done well, they are almost indestructible, look tremendous, and provide a good surface for feet, wheelbarrows, wheeled toys, and strollers. A brick path can be laid at any time of year unless temperatures are freezing, or if soil is waterlogged, both of which can cause problems with mortar cracking or failing to set properly.

   Measure out and mark the area of the path with pegs and string; allow space for including edging bricks when you are calculating the width of the path. Construct a good, firm foundation in the same way as for a patio (*see p.98*).

   Once the foundation is complete, lay the edging bricks (or edging strips) first, using string lines and pegs to ensure they are set straight and at the correct height. They will need to be bedded on a concrete footing and then the joints filled with mortar.

   The bricks for the main area of the path can be laid in a variety of decorative patterns. Although the bricks can be laid on sand, bedding them on mortar provides the most stable path in the long term. Mortaring between them will deter weeds from growing in the joints and ensure that bricks do not become loose.

YOU WILL NEED

- Pegs •String •Level
- Crushed stone •Concrete
- Bricks •Mortar
- Length of wood
- Club hammer
- Broom •Watering can

LAYING BRICKS EVENLY

To create an even effect when laying bricks, insert strips of lumber between each joint as you lay the bricks. Remove the strips before adding the mortar.

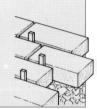

1 Mark out the path using pegs and string, and excavate the area to the depth of the bricks plus the foundation. Lay and compact the crushed stone, leaving room for a footing for the edging.

2 Make a concrete footing at the edges of the path and lay the edging bricks. Apply mortar between the joints, tamp down the bricks, and check the level.

3 Lay 1in (2.5cm) of mortar on the crushed stone, and bed the bricks onto it leaving spaces for joints. Tamp down the bricks until level using a length of wood and the handle of a club hammer.

4 Sprinkle dry mortar over the completed path and brush it into the joints. Using a thin piece of wood, press the mortar between the joints to eliminate air pockets. Clean up any excess mortar.

5 If the weather is dry, use a watering can to sprinkle water over the pointing to set it. In wet weather, moisture from the soil and air will do this. Clean up the surface of the bricks if necessary.

MAKING A GRAVEL PATH

Gravel paths are easy to make and relatively cheap to lay. It is essential that a gravel path is well edged so that the gravel does not spread onto adjacent lawns or beds. Choose from concrete, bricks, or pressure-treated lumber; lumber edging strips need to be held firmly in place with pegs. If you are laying your path next to a lawn, sink it deeper than you would if making it next to a border or patio to allow you to mow right up to the edge of the lawn. A sound base will ensure that your path performs well and looks good; for instructions on laying a foundation, *see* p.98.

Alternatively, if you want a path with a firmer surface, embed the gravel into a thin layer of soil spread over the foundation. This method is particularly suitable if you need an access route for wheelbarrows, bicycles, or strollers.

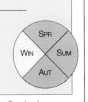

YOU WILL NEED

- String •Shovel •Level
- Boards •Wooden pegs
- Roller •Crushed stone
- Gravel •Sand
- Pea gravel
- Rake

1 *Dig down to a depth of 7in (18cm), or 8in (20cm) if the path is next to a lawn. Set the edges using boards secured with wooden pegs at 3ft (1m) intervals. Compact the base using a roller.*

2 *For the base use 4in (10cm) of compacted crushed stone. Add 2in (5cm) of coarse gravel and sand, and top with a 1in (2.5cm) layer of pea gravel. Rake to produce a slope for drainage.*

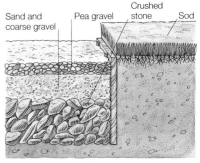

Sand and coarse gravel | Pea gravel | Crushed stone | Sod

Edging a path next to a lawn
Edging boards should be slightly greater in depth than the path and set just below the level of the lawn for easy mowing.

STEPPING-STONE PATHS

Not all paths need to be built for regular or heavy use: sometimes a lightweight, easy-to-lay path is all that is needed. Paving slabs, arranged as a formal path or, less formally, as stepping-stones, look most attractive. If the soil beneath is compacted firmly, the slabs can be bedded on sand rather than crushed stone.

1 *Mark out the position of the slabs and remove sufficient depth of sod to sink the slabs just beneath the level of the grass, allowing for at least ½in (1cm) of sand. Note the depth, and repeat for each slab along the whole path.*

2 *Compact the ground firmly, and then add the sand as a base for each slab. Nestle the slabs securely into the sand and check the level, adjusting the slabs where necessary.*

PLANTS AS PATH EDGING

Plants make an attractive edging to any border-side path. It is important to check when choosing plants that they naturally form a compact shape or respond well to being cut back. Use upright or dense plants, such as boxwood, to create a formal edging that emphasizes the line of the path, or choose irregular, sprawling plants, such as aubrieta, alchemilla, or *Geranium dalmaticum*, to soften the edges or hide brand-new or unattractive path edging.

Choose plants that will not spread over the path too rapidly, and avoid planting very close to the path or the plants will soon encroach. Check the suggested planting distances, using these as a guide to the distance needed between path and plants.

Rock plants including hens and chicks and dwarf thymes give a more informal effect, but they will need to be thinned or trimmed once they are well established since they tend to spill out all over the path.

Planting a lavender hedge
Compact plants, such as 'Hidcote' lavender used here, can be planted en masse along the edge of a path: they will quickly grow together to form a beautiful, scented hedge. Space the plants at intervals of 12–16in (30–40cm), and 8in (20cm) from the edge of the border to prevent them from encroaching too far over the path.

BUILDING STEPS

A bove all, steps need to be both safe and practical to use. The more care you take building them, the longer they will last. Shallow steps are often the safest for gardens, especially if you have children or will need to use the steps with a wheelbarrow or lawnmower. If you have space, steps wide enough for two people to walk side by side look far more inviting than a narrow flight. Choose materials that blend in with the style of the garden and any

surrounding buildings, and that are appropriate to the amount of wear the steps will receive (*see* "Materials for Steps," p.89).

To soften the hard edges of newly built or existing steps, add a few small, low-growing plants in crevices. You could even leave spaces for plants during the building process, but be careful to use enough mortar between bricks and slabs so that the main structure of the steps is secure.

MAKING BRICK AND SLAB STEPS

Steps made with brick risers and slab treads mortared into position are long-lasting and sturdy. For safety reasons and to keep the steps in proportion, the risers should be about 6in (15cm) high and the treads (from the front of the slab to the next riser) at least 15in (38cm) deep. If you want the tread to overhang at the front, allow an extra 1–2in (2.5–5cm).

Once you have decided on the proportions, calculate how many steps you will need to build by dividing the vertical height of the slope where the steps are to be by the height of a single riser (including the depth of the paving slab, mortar, and bricks). You may need to adjust the height of the risers slightly to fit the height of your slope. Having calculated the number of steps, work out the quantities of bricks and slabs you will need to make them.

BUILDING THE FOUNDATIONS

Once you have dug out the steps from the slope, the lowest riser will need a concrete footing. Make this a few days before the rest of the steps to allow time for it to set. Dig out a level trench about 6in (15cm) deep and twice the width of the bricks you are using to make the riser.

Pour water into the trench to soak the surrounding soil, allow it to drain, then add a 3in (7cm) layer of crushed stone and tamp this down. Pour in concrete, mixing it slightly with the crushed stone using a spade. Firm down the concrete to make a level surface and to ensure that it fills the trench to the edges. Once the footing has set, the steps can be built as shown below.

1 Use pegs and string to mark out the sides of each step and the front of each tread. Using the string as a guide, dig out the steps, compacting the soil on each tread.

2 Make a concrete footing for the first riser and when this has set, build the riser. Use taut string to ensure that you lay the bricks level and straight; check them with a level.

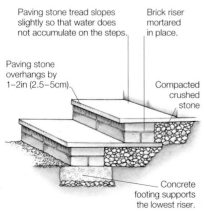

Paving stone tread slopes slightly so that water does not accumulate on the steps.

Brick riser mortared in place.

Paving stone overhangs by 1–2in (2.5–5cm).

Compacted crushed stone

Concrete footing supports the lowest riser.

3 Backfill the area behind the riser with crushed stone until level with the top of the bricks. Lay mortar ½in (1cm) deep and set the slabs on it, sloping forward slightly, with an overhang if desired. Tamp down, leaving a small gap between the slabs.

4 Mark out the position of the second riser on the slabs and lay the bricks in place using mortar. Backfill and lay the second tread. Continue until all the steps are completed. Finally, mortar the spaces between the slabs.

MAKING WOODEN STEPS WITH GRAVEL TREADS

A simple way to make steps is to use gravel for the treads, held in place at the sides with wooden boards, and lengths of wood for the risers. The risers are usually made with railroad ties or pressure-treated lumber. For a more rustic effect, use lengths of tree trunk, but even if these are hardwood, their life expectancy is not as great as that of treated lumber and they may start to rot after a few years. Calculate how many steps you need as for the brick and slab steps (opposite) – the depths of crushed stone and gravel will depend on the depth of the material used for the risers – then dig out the steps. Compact the soil and then fit the risers and edges, holding them firmly in place with pressure-treated wooden pegs.

YOU WILL NEED

•Treated lumber or railroad ties •Saw
•Club hammer •Pegs
•Crushed stone •Pea gravel •Spade •Rake

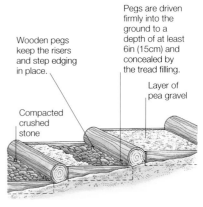

Pegs are driven firmly into the ground to a depth of at least 6in (15cm) and concealed by the tread filling.

Wooden pegs keep the risers and step edging in place.

Layer of pea gravel

Compacted crushed stone

1 Cut the lumber risers to the exact width of your steps, and mount them in place using wooden pegs. Check that the risers are straight and level as you position them, working up the slope.

2 Firm down the soil for each tread, and add a layer of crushed stone. Compact this well, then spread pea gravel to just below the top of the riser. Rake the gravel level, and firm down.

PLANTING IN CREVICES

Steps can easily be brought to life with a little strategic planting. Mortar or concrete that has crumbled can be carefully scraped away to reveal the soil beneath or behind it – but do not remove any that could endanger the structure of the steps. Add soil mix or fresh topsoil to make a suitable planting hole. Plant on either side of the steps so that the plants soften the edges rather than obstruct the pathway. Choose compact plants, checking their potential height and spread and avoiding ones that will sprawl over the treads, making them dangerous to use. Also avoid plants with soft, succulent leaves since they become slippery if stepped on.

YOU WILL NEED

•Widger or knife
•Hand fork •Soil mix
•Compact plants

1 Scrape crumbling mortar from the edge of the steps. Use a widger or knife to press soil mix or moist soil into the crevice.

2 Ease the plant into the hole to the correct depth, and cover the roots with soil mix. Firm the mix to settle the plant into its niche.

3 Water the soil mix or soil carefully without washing it away. Since the roots are in only a small amount of soil, plants in crevices need to be watered more than those in open ground, particularly during the first year or two.

PLANTS FOR STEPS

Androsaces 🌿
Antennarias 🌿
Snapdragons (*Antirrhinum*) [some] 🌸
Sandworts (*Arenaria*) [some] 🌿
Thrift (*Armeria maritima*) 🌿
Aubrietas 🌿🌿
Aurinias 🌿
Campanula poscharskyana 🌿
Maiden pinks
   (*Dianthus deltoides* and cvs) 🌿
Drabas 🌿 🌿
Dryas octopetala 🌿
Fairy foxglove (*Erinus alpinus*) 🌿
Rock roses (*Helianthemum*) ▲
Candytuft (*Iberis sempervirens*) 🌿
Lobelia erinus 🌸
Sweet alyssum (*Lobularia maritima*) ⊛
Phloxes 🌿 🌿⊛
Moss rose (*Portulaca grandiflora*) ⊛
Saxifrages 🌿
Thymes 🌿
Thymophylla tenuiloba ⊛
Violets (*Viola*) 🌿

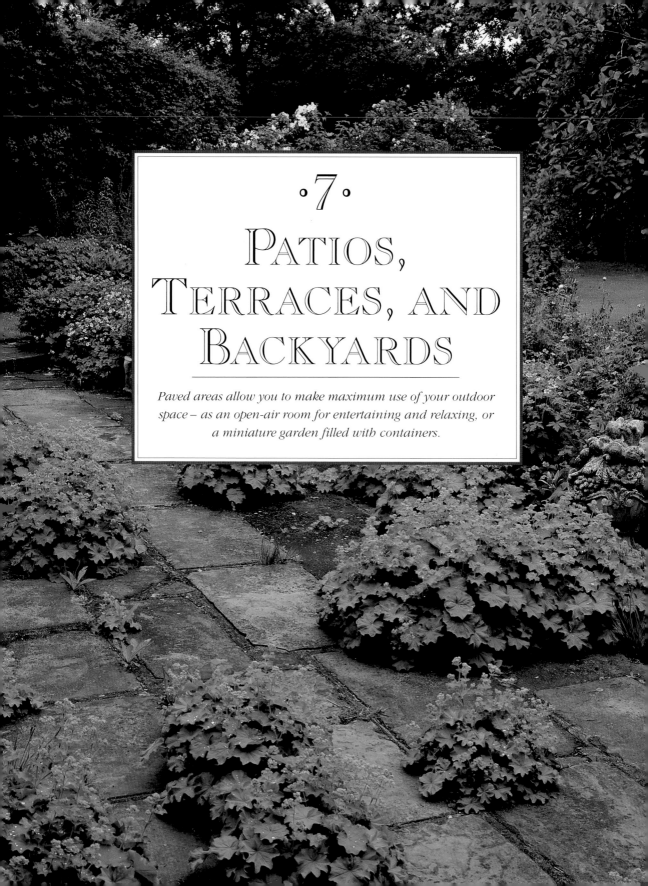

·7·
PATIOS,
TERRACES, AND
BACKYARDS

*Paved areas allow you to make maximum use of your outdoor
space – as an open-air room for entertaining and relaxing, or
a miniature garden filled with containers.*

CREATING A PLACE TO RELAX

For many people, the garden is an open-air extension of their indoor living space. A paved and planted outdoor "room" will soon become a hub for household activities, whether you decide to construct a terrace adjacent to the house or a patio elsewhere in the garden.

DESIGNING A PATIO OR TERRACE

A paved area can, of course, be absolutely any shape you like, but to be a real success the design must take into account certain practical considerations. Think carefully about both the type and amount of use the area will receive, and how the design will look in relation to the rest of the garden. If you intend to do much al fresco entertaining or eating you will probably need a fair amount of space, but a smaller area would suffice if you just want a quiet corner in which to sit and enjoy the sun (or shade).

The most common patio plan seems to be a simple square or rectangle, but don't let this put you off from trying something a little more adventurous. Experiment with steps and different levels, or irregular or curved edges. In general, a curved perimeter complements a traditional-style garden, while geometric shapes look good with modern surroundings. However, there is only one real rule of patio planning, and that is to choose the shape and size of the feature to blend with the rest of your garden rather than intrude on it.

Color and pattern

Wonderfully mellow, old bricks are used to full effect in this decorative paving plan. Circles of decreasing size artfully play with perspective to make the small courtyard look much larger than it actually is. A limited color scheme, ranging from purple through to white, echoes the pinkish hue of the bricks to create an impression of harmonious tranquility. The plantings, spilling onto the paving, add to the relaxed feeling.

Height and texture

Here, a combination of raised beds (edged with railroad ties) and gravel walkways creates an attractive backdrop for a selection of sun-loving plants. Both the planting and the hard landscaping make full use of contrasts in texture and height to get maximum impact from minimum space.

CHOOSING MATERIALS

Your choice of materials may be dictated primarily by budget, but you should also bear existing structures in mind. You can create a pleasingly established effect by matching the existing stone or brick of your house. Alternatively, a sharp contrast in style can create an interesting change of mood. Select materials suited to the patio shape you want: it is simple to make curves with bricks, setts, and preformed slabs, while square or rectangular slabs usually limit you to a geometric shape (*see* "Materials for Paths and Steps," pp.88–9, and "Materials for Paving," pp.96–7).

CHOOSING A SITE

When positioning a paved area, you will find that some sites are immediately ruled out because of problems with terrain or the existing planting. Within these constraints, your final choice of site will be determined by whether you prefer a sun trap or a shady retreat. Whatever your other priorities, remember that easy access is essential, especially if the area is to be used for entertaining and eating.

REVAMPING AN EXISTING FEATURE

An inherited patio or terrace, however uninspiring, can usually be adapted to suit your needs. Even subtle alterations can have a surprising impact and, provided an area is structurally sound, you can do a lot without resorting to radical reconstruction.

Disguise a dull or badly proportioned shape by planting trailing and cushion-forming plants around the edges. Build raised beds onto the patio, or simply amass a collection of well-planted tubs and other containers. You may also be able to break up a large paved area by lifting the occasional slab to provide more space for planting.

A BACKYARD GARDEN

Even a tiny paved or concreted backyard can look marvelous – although the smaller the area, the more important it is to plan your designs carefully. Regardless of exposure, plants can be selected to give year-round color and interest, making full use of every planting space – including fences, walls, and trellises – with a combination of tubs, troughs, baskets, and windowboxes (*see* "Gardening Within Limits," p.105). The lack of a conventional garden needn't prevent you from creating a few surprises, either – perhaps making a small pond in a half barrel (*see* p.124). An area may be small, but its potential is very often enormous.

MATERIALS FOR PAVING

A hard surface such as a terrace, patio, or deck needs to complement the rest of the garden in style, rather than stand apart from it. Paved areas are prominent, long-term features that have a major impact on their surroundings, so they are worth planning and constructing with great care. The type of materials used, how they are laid, and the colors and textures chosen should always be sympathetic to the existing or planned elements of both the garden and the house. On a patio you can combine several different paving materials to give a variety of textures, colors, and patterns; this also enables you to mix expensive materials with those that are slightly cheaper. If you intend to include other hard landscape features in the garden, such as steps or paths, the overall effect will be enhanced if each of these elements has at least one material in common.

PAVING SLABS AND FLAGS

These are available in a range of sizes, shapes, colors, and textures; they are made from natural stone or cement and are smooth or textured. Natural colors, such as grays and buffs, are easier to incorporate into a design than some of the more artificial yellows and pinks, since they harmonize well with the garden. For a more unusual surface, try combining different materials within the same area, such as bricks or setts between slabs (*see* p.88 for a choice of bricks and setts). Most slabs are square or rectangular; the standard sizes are 24 x 24in (60 x 60cm) and 24 x 36in (60 x 90cm). Hexagonal, octagonal, circular, and interlocking shapes are also available. For details on how to lay a patio, *see* pp.98–9.

Hexagonal slabs
These can be used to create an unusual pattern within the patio design. The slightly mottled finish turns a deeper color when wet.

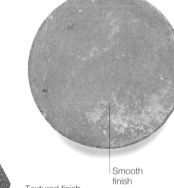

Textured finish

Circular slabs
Circular slabs make an ideal stepping-stone path, but on a patio are only really practical for a tiny area, where they can be combined with cobblestones, pebbles, or gravel.

Shaped slabs interlock with others to make a pattern.

Smooth finish

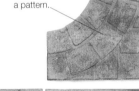

Cement molded into patterns
Some paving materials are molded to look like several slabs joined together. These are easy to lay, and can be used to create quite complex paving patterns.

Mottled colors produce a naturally weathered appearance.

Textured cement
Textured cement slabs (above and right) are sometimes available readyweathered to resemble natural stone; once laid they continue to weather, harmonizing with their surroundings. Their colors are usually muted and may be mottled. They are a reasonably priced alternative to natural stone slabs for both formal and cottage gardens.

Combining sizes creates an informal effect.

Natural stone
Although expensive, natural stone, such as sandstone (shown here) or field stone, is the classic, traditional material to use. It blends well with most garden styles.

MAKING PATTERNS WITH PAVING

Smaller slabs, tiles, and molded pavers can be laid to form a variety of interlocking patterns, from a simple, regular design, to a more complex arrangement of different shapes. Provided they are laid at the correct height, several different materials can be used; a combination of two, or at most three, types of material looks best.

Hexagonal tiles
Hexagonal terracotta tiles make a subtly colored but quite formal surface. Because many are not frost-proof, they should be used only in warm or sheltered places.

Interlocking pavers
Interlocking pavers are made in a limited range of shapes that are designed to fit together in whatever combination you choose. Although time-consuming to lay at the start, they make a very hardwearing surface, suitable even for bicycles and wheelbarrows.

Red brick pavers
These rectangular pavers make a complex but regular basketweave pattern. Their warm colors look good in cottage gardens and blend well with other brickwork.

WOODEN DECKING

Wooden decking imparts a modern, informal character to a garden. It is best suited to relatively dry, warm climates since wet weather may cause it to rot and can make the surface rather slippery. Decking is a useful means of making a flat surface on uneven ground. The lumber used, whether specifically made decking panels or individual boards, must be pressure-treated with preservative, even in the driest of climates. The easiest way to buy and lay decking is by using ready-made panels; these are available in a wide range of patterns.

Always lay panels so that the struts forming them are not all facing the same way. This gives an interesting surface and makes the decking less slippery in wet weather.

Single-colored decking over a large area may look rather monotonous; to avoid this, the panels can be painted or stained in two or more different colors.

Decking for damp climates
Chicken wire tacked firmly to the decking in autumn and winter gives extra grip to the surface.

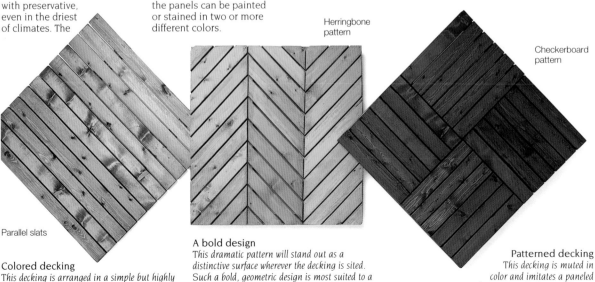

Herringbone pattern

Checkerboard pattern

Parallel slats

Colored decking
This decking is arranged in a simple but highly effective pattern. The choice of green-stained wood ensures that it blends in well with the garden.

A bold design
This dramatic pattern will stand out as a distinctive surface wherever the decking is sited. Such a bold, geometric design is most suited to a large, modern-style garden; in a smaller one it might be too overpowering.

Patterned decking
This decking is muted in color and imitates a paneled design; it is ideal in small areas since it will not dominate the garden.

BUILDING A PATIO

When you are planning where to site your patio, think first about what functions you want it to provide. Do you need to allow room to set up a barbecue or table and chairs? Is it to be a spot for sunbathing, or a shady oasis on a hot day? Watch how much shade is cast by nearby trees and buildings at different times of day before finally deciding on your site. Think also about whether you might need an electricity supply – for lighting

perhaps – and, if so, consider how easily and safely you can lay cables to the patio site. Plan the size and shape of the patio carefully before you start work – if it is too small there may not be room for garden furniture and pots or containers, and if too large it may look out of place or dominate the garden. For the best results, choose paving materials that suit the style of your house and the surrounding garden.

LAYING A PATIO WITH SLABS

Before starting to lay the slabs, clear the area of all debris and weeds, and roughly firm the site. Also, make sure to locate (and protect, if necessary) any utility meters and underground utilities in the general area to avoid damaging them. The site must slope slightly so that rainwater and groundwater can drain away (*see* opposite). Calculate how many slabs you need – if you are using mortar in the joints, allow for ¼–½in (0.5–1cm) between each slab.

Mark out the site of your patio with pegs and string, using a builder's square to keep the corners at right angles. Use a roller or a plate compactor to firm the base. For the foundation, use layers of crushed stone and sand deep enough to withstand your local winter conditions. Consult local contractors for specific depths.

To lay the slabs, work from an existing straight edge, such as the wall of the house. If you want to plant alongside a wall or next to the house, leave an area unpaved.

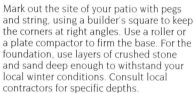

YOU WILL NEED

- Pegs •String •Builder's square •Roller or plate compactor •Level
- Spade •Crushed stone
- Sand •Paving slabs
- Trowel •Mortar
- Wooden spacers
- Stiff broom

1 After marking the area out with pegs and string and removing the topsoil, compact the subsoil with a roller or plate compactor. Allow for the depth of the foundation, plus the thickness of the slabs you are going to lay.

2 Use marked pegs every 6ft (2m) and a level to ensure that there is a slight drainage slope (*see opposite*). Shovel a layer of crushed stone over the area, then compact and level it again. Add a layer of sand if necessary.

3 After preparing the foundation, you can start to lay the paving slabs. Use a builder's trowel to lay mortar in a square to lie just within the edges of each slab. For large slabs, make a cross of mortar through the center, too.

4 Put the slab in position, and then tamp it down onto its mortar bed using the wooden handle of a tool. Use equal-sized wooden spacers between the slabs. Check with a level that each slab is laid level, both side to side, and with its neighbors.

5 Remove the spacers as soon as possible. After at least two days, fill the joints with a stiff mortar mixture, firming it and smoothing it so the mortar is just below the surface of the slabs. Use a stiff broom to clear away all debris and loose mortar.

CREATING A SLOPE FOR DRAINAGE

To drain properly, the patio needs to slope away about 1in every 6ft (2.5cm every 2m). Add the depth of the surface material to the depth of the foundation and mark a line at this distance from the top of pegs. Insert a row of pegs at the top of the slope, add another row 6ft (2m) farther down, and place a 1in (2.5cm) wood scrap on each peg. Lay a board and level between pegs in both rows, adjusting the lower pegs until level. Rake the soil to the lines on the pegs.

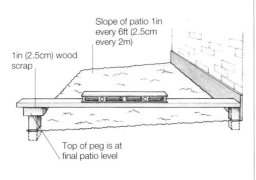

Slope of patio 1in every 6ft (2.5cm every 2m)

1in (2.5cm) wood scrap

Top of peg is at final patio level

CUTTING PAVING SLABS

Wear safety goggles to do this job. With the slab on a firm surface, use the corner of a chisel against a straight edge to score a ¼in (6mm) deep groove. Raise one section of the slab off the ground using a length of wood, aligning the groove with the straight edge. Use a wooden handle to tap the slab – it will split neatly along the marked line.

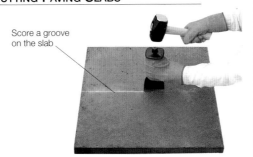

Score a groove on the slab

RANDOM PAVING

Random paving is good for an informal patio but has a slightly uneven surface. The paving can either be bedded into sand, to allow space for planting in the crevices, or into mortar. Start from one corner and use pieces of varying sizes. Lay a block of wood over a few pieces of random paving at a time and tap with a mallet to firm them into position. Check that the area is as level as possible with a level. Fill the joints with sand or dry mortar. If using mortar, bevel it slightly along each joint to assist drainage.

Laying random paving
Start in a corner and lay the edging pieces first, with the straight edges outward. Fill in the rest of the area with different-sized pieces of paving, choosing them so that the gaps between are as small as possible.

BUILDING A DECK

In most landscapes, a deck in the garden connects with the house. In fact, that is a deck's usual role: to supply a useful, flat, outdoor surface that can be walked directly onto from the house. Because a deck actually attaches to the house – and becomes part of its structure – deck construction must follow more codes and calls for considerably more planning and advance work than most other garden construction. (You can design and build a raised bed, a fence, a trellis, or an arbor with just a few instructions, a load of lumber, some concrete, and the needed tools, but not so a deck). Most amateurs should seek qualified help from a designer and a contractor or carpenter.

A deck attached to the house requires: a ledger board (the substantial lumber that supports the deck structure on the house side); a number of concrete footings, one for each supporting pier; the properly dimensioned lumber to serve as posts, beams, joists, joist headers, decking, and perhaps bench posts, railing posts, benches, and railings; and special hardware including bolts, lag screws, nails, joist hangers, and post caps.

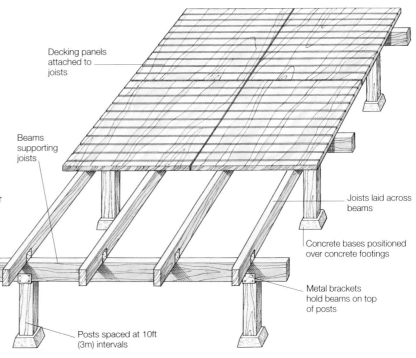

Decking panels attached to joists

Beams supporting joists

Joists laid across beams

Concrete bases positioned over concrete footings

Metal brackets hold beams on top of posts

Posts spaced at 10ft (3m) intervals

ADDING PLANTS TO THE PATIO

Adding plants to a patio can soften hard edges and introduce new colors and shapes to liven up the area. Simply arranging planted containers on the patio works wonders (*see* "Creating a Place to Relax," p.95), but there is also plenty of scope for planting in holes made in the structure of the patio itself. Seeds and small plants can be sown or planted in crevices or gaps between paving, and, with a little preparation, small shrubs and climbers can easily be added. These will not just make the area prettier but can bring life and interest to what may have started out as a boring paved square. Patio plants growing between the paving slabs need a little extra care and attention, especially soon after planting, since all the surrounding stone, brick, or concrete has a drying effect on the soil. Once established, however, they require only a little more watering than those grown in other areas of the garden.

SOWING SEEDS BETWEEN PAVING STONES

The easiest, cheapest, and quickest way to brighten up a patio is to sow seeds in the crevices between paving stones; once filled with flowers, the area is less likely to become colonized by weeds. Bear in mind, however, that plants may be slippery when wet, so leave some areas clear for garden furniture or for a walkway from the house to the rest of the garden.

Clean up the whole area before planting. Using a hand fork or a strong stick, clear out any loose mortar, debris, stones, and weeds from between the slabs that you are about to plant. Before planting, drizzle a small amount of sieved garden soil or soil mix down the gaps and firm it down.

YOU WILL NEED

- Hand fork or stick
- Soil or soil mix
- Horticultural sand
- Seeds • Watering can

(seasonal dial: SPR, SUM, AUT, WIN — SPR and SUM shaded)

Water gently to avoid washing the soil away. Sow the seeds, covering them with a small amount of soil if necessary (check the packets for details). Fine seeds are much easier to sow thinly if they are first mixed with a small amount of horticultural sand in a salt shaker.

CLEANING ALGAE OFF PAVING
Algae and moss form a dangerously slippery layer on paving. Clear them using a broom and soapy water or a chemical treatment – follow the manufacturer's instructions and test on a small area first.

Sowing seeds in crevices
Clear out the crevices, and add sieved garden soil or compost to within ¼in (0.5cm) of the surface of the paving. Water the area, then sow seeds finely. Keep the soil moist as the seedlings grow.

PLANTS FOR SOWING IN CREVICES

Candytufts (*Iberis*) 🌱 ✤ ❧
Violet cress (*Ionopsidium acaule*) ✤
Poached-egg plant (*Limnanthes douglasii*) ✤ ❧
Lobelia erinus 🌱
Sweet alyssum (*Lobularia maritima*) ✤ ❧
Virginia stock (*Malcolmia maritima*) ✤ ❧
Swan River daisy (*Brachycome iberidifolia*) ✤

KEY
❧ self-seeding

Planting between paving stones

PLANTING AT THE EDGE OF A PATIO

When designing a paved area from scratch, you may decide to incorporate planting areas around the edge or leave a strip of ground that you can use as a flower bed. If your existing patio or terrace adjoins a wall or fence, the problem of bare walls can be resolved by lifting a slab or two and planting climbers. Other plants are worth considering, too, including some low-growing perennials, bulbs, and annual bedding. The bricks and mortar in walls have a drying effect on soil, so it is especially important here to incorporate plenty of new topsoil and organic matter before planting, or to lift two or more adjacent slabs to create a larger area where the soil is easier to improve and less likely to dry out. After planting, feed and water regularly, and apply a mulch to keep the moisture in.

(seasonal dial: SPR, SUM, AUT, WIN — SPR and AUT shaded)

Planting a climber against a wall
Mount a support to the wall about 12in (30cm) above soil level. Plant the climber about 18in (45cm) from the wall with its stems angled toward the support. Train in and tie the stems loosely.

PLANTING IN THE MIDDLE OF PAVING

To break up an area of solid paving, it is usually quite simple to lift some of the slabs so that you can then plant in the soil beneath. If the patio is in poor condition and has loose slabs, so much the better.

CHOOSING PLANTS

A quick improvement can be made with a selection of annuals. For longer-term planting, choose slow-growing plants or ones that will tolerate regular clipping so you can keep them from spreading too far. Near an area of seating, choose plants with fragrant flowers and foliage. Since patios are usually within easy reach of the house, you can even make a miniature herb garden – many herbs also like the dry soil conditions in the middle of paving.

REMOVING SLABS

Before removing slabs, take some time to consider which areas need to be left clear for an adequate-sized seating area, or an easy passage from the house to the terrace or patio. It is easy to get carried away and plant in places that may look pretty but will not necessarily be practical, especially as the plants start to spread a little. Lifting loose slabs is usually easy – just use a spade to lever up the edge. If the slabs are held firmly in place, scrape out any remaining mortar or debris from between the slabs using an old chisel or screwdriver, then lift in the usual way.

PREPARING FOR PLANTING

Once the slab has been removed, the soil beneath will probably be of very poor quality, heavily compacted, and mixed with stones and mortar. Remove this, clearing back to less compacted soil, and loosen up the soil slightly beneath adjacent slabs with a fork. Provided you add a layer of good-quality topsoil mixed with extra bulky organic matter, and water regularly, your plants should grow well.

YOU WILL NEED

- Spade •Fork or trowel
- Topsoil •Bulky organic matter •Plants and bulbs
- Watering can

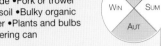

SEASONAL BEDDING

To add interest while the main shrubs or perennials are still relatively small and to brighten up the area throughout the year, try planting seasonal bedding and a selection of small bulbs. You can also change the design from season to season by replanting with new bedding. Keep the plants well watered.

1 Clear out any debris or old mortar around the slab, then insert the blade of a spade in the gap. Maneuver the spade so that it digs in lower than the base of the slab, then ease it underneath and lever out the slab.

2 Remove the compacted soil and any sand or stones from beneath the slab using a spade, then loosen the soil around the edges of the hole you have made with a fork. Dispose of this soil since plants are unlikely to grow well in it.

3 Fill the planting hole with a mixture of topsoil and bulky organic matter (such as well-rotted manure, compost, or planting mixture) to improve its texture, fertility, and ability to retain moisture. Incorporate some beneath adjacent slabs, too.

5 As the plants grow, they will become established and look more attractive. Water and feed regularly throughout the growing season, and trim back the plants if they start to encroach too much on the surrounding paving.

4 Plant your chosen plants in the normal way, teasing roots out first and making sure the root balls are at the correct depth. Add a few bulbs if you wish, and water well.

MAINTENANCE AND AFTERCARE

Plants in paving need regular watering and feeding since paving and mortar quickly deplete the area of moisture and nutrients. Adding mulch helps to retain moisture around the plant's roots. Use a watering can with a fine rose to avoid dislodging new seeds or washing away the soil. Deadhead annuals and shrubs regularly to keep them flowering for as long as possible, cutting back any that are spreading too far.

PERMANENT PLANTING ON THE PATIO

The dullest of patios, terraces, or decks can be brought to life instantly with a few large containers brimming over with plants. They can be displayed individually or grouped together to make a miniature garden. Large containers, such as old stone troughs or sinks, whiskey barrels, and hollowed-out tree trunks, can be bought or made quite cheaply. More unusual containers, especially made for fitting into awkward sites or for covering eyesores such as utility covers, are also available. Raised beds provide a permanent feature on a patio or elsewhere in the garden, and they can support a wide range of plants – in some cases, even small to medium-sized trees and fairly large shrubs. Both large containers and raised beds allow you to add color in what might otherwise be a dull area. Filled with a specialized soil mix, they also enable you to grow plants not suited to your natural garden soil.

RAISED BEDS ON THE PATIO

Choose materials to suit your site and budget. Railroad ties make a good option, but if you prefer a more rustic look, use sawed logs treated with a water-based wood preservative (see p.73). Concrete blocks are suitable for making a large and deep bed; however, if you intend to grow acid-loving (lime-hating) plants, the sides of the bed must be lined, either with several layers of sealant or a rubber liner. Bricks are ideal for a circular or curved bed, but again the bed should be lined if you intend to grow lime-hating plants. Stone beds, although expensive, look best on stone patios.

To prepare your raised bed, fill the bottom third with a layer of rubble or broken bricks. Top this with peat or coarse compost, and then add topsoil up to the brim. Water thoroughly before planting. After planting, add a layer of stone or bark chips or coarse grit to conserve moisture and deter weeds.

Using railroad ties

Railroad ties are extremely sturdy, blending in well with both plants and soil. They can be bought quite cheaply and can be used to make a very attractive, low raised bed.

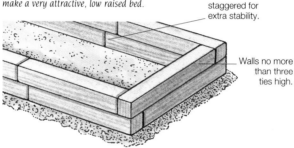

Joints are staggered for extra stability.

Walls no more than three ties high.

Using bricks

Bricks can be used to create a raised bed of any size or shape, with changes in levels. To build the bed use frostproof bricks, not ordinary house bricks.

First layer of bricks is below soil level.

A brick raised bed needs a crushed stone base and 1in (2.5cm) concrete footings.

PLANTS FOR RAISED BEDS

Maples (*Acer*) ♀ [some ᵖᴴ]
Aubrietas 🦋 🐝
Camellias ● [some ❋] ᵖᴴ
Campanulas [some] 🦋 🐝
Ceanothus thyrsiflorus var. *repens* ●
Clematis 🌿🌿🐝
Cotoneaster dammeri ●
Broom (*Cytisus demissus*) ◯
Chilean glory flower (*Eccremocarpus scaber*) 🌿 ❋
Fothergillas ◯ ᵖᴴ
Fuchsias ◯ [many ❋]
Hardy geraniums 🦋
Rock roses (*Helianthemum*) ● [some ❋]
Heucheras 🦋
Hostas 🦋
Jasmines (*Jasminum*) [some] 🌿🌿[some ❋]
Deadnettle (*Lamium maculatum*) 🦋 🐝
Sweet peas (*Lathyrus odoratus* and cvs) 🌿 ❋ ❋
Lavenders (*Lavandula*) ●
Sweet alyssum (*Lobularia maritima*) ❋🐝
Honeysuckles (*Lonicera*) ●🌿🌿
Small crabapples (*Malus*) ♀
Evening primrose (*Oenothera missouriensis*) 🦋
Passionflowers (*Passiflora*) 🌿🌿 [most ❋]
Pieris ● ᵖᴴ
Shrubby cherries (*Prunus*, some cvs) ◯
Lungworts (*Pulmonaria*) 🦋
Rhododendrons and azaleas ●◯ᵖᴴ
Sedum 'Ruby Glow' 🦋
Spiraeas ◯
Nasturtiums (*Tropaeolum*) 🌸 ❋🐝

KEY
🐝 Trailing

SUNKEN PATIOS

To create planting areas around a sunken patio, retaining walls can be added. The beds behind can either be planted in the same way as a raised bed, including trailing plants to camouflage the edges, or they can be grassed over.

If made from bricks, the lowest row needs to have "weep holes," or unmortared joints, incorporated to allow any excess water from the soil to drain away easily.

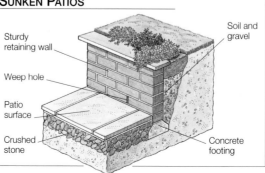

Sturdy retaining wall

Weep hole

Patio surface

Crushed stone

Soil and gravel

Concrete footing

LARGE AND PERMANENT CONTAINERS

Containers, particularly larger ones, make it possible to plant trees, shrubs, climbers, and perennials, as well as smaller plants, on the bleakest patio. Imaginatively positioned and planted, they can be used to screen walls, fences, and trellises, as well as eyesores such as drainpipes.

Most container-grown plants do best if placed in an open position, with a fair amount of sun, but you can brighten up a very shady corner using a selection of shade-loving plants. Avoid windy sites if possible since the wind may cause leaf scorch and, even on tougher plants, it has a drying effect. All containers need regular watering, so try to position them

within easy reach of the tap or hose – you will be glad of this in hot summers or if you have many containers!

TROUGHS AND SINKS

If you are lucky, you may be able to buy an old stone trough or sink, although these are increasingly rare and expensive. It may be easier to find an old-fashioned glazed sink and use hypertufa – a substance resembling stone – to coat the outside. The hypertufa mix is made using 1 part cement, 1 part coarse sand, and 1–2 parts peat or similar material. Mix these to a thick consistency with water. Paint the sink with a PVA adhesive and allow it to dry –

this ensures the hypertufa will stick. Press a ½–¾in (1–2cm) thick layer of hypertufa all over the outer surface of the sink, over the rim, and part of the way down the inside to below the intended level of the soil mix.

1 Stand the trough in position, using bricks to keep it clear of the ground. Check it is level and stable. Place fine galvanized mesh over the drainage hole, then cover the base with large pieces of broken pots, keeping the drainage hole clear. Cover the base with 3–4in (7–10cm) of coarse grit.

2 Fill with gritty soil mix to within about 3in (8cm) of the rim, firming gently as you fill. If you wish, partly bury some rocks or pieces of tufa in the soil mix. Then top up with soil mix to within about 2in (5cm) of the rim, and check that the rocks or tufa are stable.

3 Arrange your selection of rock plants, allowing each enough room to mature; spreading plants often look good near the rim of the trough where they can sprawl over the edge. Plant to the correct depth and then water in well, allowing time for the excess to drain.

4 Add extra soil mix and firm it down if the level has fallen too low. Top-dress the surface of the soil mix up to the neck of each plant with a 1in (2.5cm) layer of gravel or stone chips. This will improve drainage and discourage wet soil conditions around the plants.

5 The completed trough should last for years and, provided the plants have been selected carefully, there should be interest from both flowers and foliage throughout the seasons. Extra plants can be added later, if the trough has not been planted too densely, either to fill spaces or extend your collection. Deadhead regularly to prolong flowering, and trim back any plants that have become leggy or outgrown their space.

Campanula raineri

Daphne jasminea

Dianthus myrtinervius

Thrift (Armeria maritima 'Dusseldorf Pride')

Phlox amoena 'Variegata'

Oxalis lobata

Sempervivum 'Schleehanii'

Campanula garganica 'Dickson's Gold'

·8·

CONTAINER GARDENING

Grow plants in pots, and suddenly it becomes possible to create
a garden almost anywhere. This chapter shows how
a courtyard, balcony, flat roof, or even the narrowest of
window ledges can be transformed into a wonderfully leafy,
colorful – and maybe even fragrant – oasis.

GARDENING WITHIN LIMITS

Well-planted containers can be put to quite a number of different uses. They may simply provide your only opportunity to garden – on a balcony, roof garden, backyard, or patio – where they will introduce much-appreciated color, foliage interest, and possibly even scent into an otherwise sterile environment.

Growing plants within the confines of a container opens up a whole new set of inspiring gardening opportunities. The beauty of container gardening is that you can create, and then control, your planting environment to an extent that land-bound gardeners can only dream about.

The first advantage you will enjoy is that plants in containers can be moved from place to place. This gives you a marvelous opportunity to try out several different arrangements until you discover the optimum position for each plant. It also allows you to adapt the design through the season, bringing plants to center stage when they are at their best, then shunting them to a less prominent position when their moment of glory has passed.

Another advantage is that tender plants will thrive in cooler climates if container-grown. Unlike in the border, where a plant becomes a permanent feature the minute it is planted, a container specimen can be displayed during warm weather, then moved into a protected spot when the temperature drops.

Since containers enable you to select the precise growing medium you need, they are particularly useful if your soil type restricts the range of plants you can grow. If, for example, you have a passion for acid-loving plants but your garden soil is alkaline, a container full of acidic soil mix gives you the growing opportunity you have been looking for.

Patio planting
A collection of well-planted containers can bring a vibrant splash of color to the garden in spring. Here, an attractive selection of terracotta pots has been filled with tulips, prolific-flowering purple pansies, and fragrant wallflowers. Care should be taken when placing pots along the top of a wall in this way, to ensure that they are stable enough to withstand buffeting from strong winds or clumsy passersby.

CONTAINERS IN THE BORDER

Clearly, containers are invaluable in paved areas where there is no soil available. However, they can also add a whole new dimension to more conventional gardens. If a garden design turns out to be slow to establish, less interesting than you had expected, or a specimen plant dies and leaves a hole in the planting, ready-planted pots can be plunged into the border to add instant splashes of color or to fill a gap. These pots can be removed or replaced as soon as the best of their display is over. If you acquire a particularly beautiful

container, you might even consider incorporating it in a permanent border design. This could create an interesting focal point for your design which would look good when empty, and stunning when well planted.

WHAT CAN YOU GROW?

Most plants can be grown in containers, provided, of course, that the capacity of the pot is suitable for the ultimate size of the plant. Bulbs, annuals, perennials, shrubs, climbers, and even small trees will all grow well. Rock plants thrive in such free-draining conditions and are often grown in a stone trough or old glazed sink where their delicate beauty can be shown off to perfection. Many vegetables will also do well in containers, and it is even possible to plant a barrel pond complete with miniature waterlilies.

PLANTS FOR DIFFERENT SITUATIONS

Planted containers can also be extremely useful in places where you would like to screen off an unattractive feature – perhaps a shed or trash can area – but have no possibility of planting a hedge or erecting a fence. In these circumstances, carefully positioned container plants, especially climbers, shrubs, and small trees, can provide the ideal solution. Similarly, pots can be used to draw the eye away from a messy area of the garden; to help soften hard, angular edges on a square patio; or to brighten up a dull flight of external stairs.

Creative designs
Although often used simply to provide a colorful focal point, containerized plants can also be grouped into quite sophisticated arrangements. This lovely group uses geraniums, Helichrysum petiolare, *white* brachycome, *and various succulents within a limited color range to exploit differences in plant texture and form, turning a plain terrace into a stunning feature.*

BALCONIES

The scope for creating beautiful displays on a balcony is huge. However, if your designs are to prove successful, it is important to take a number of practical considerations into account when planning the planting.

Most balconies are subjected to extreme weather conditions, and in particular to strong gusts of wind and heavy shading from above. The precise conditions on your balcony will have a profound effect on your planting plans.

In addition, the weight of the plants, together with their containers and soil mix, is an important factor to consider. Before you get started, find out how much weight the balcony can safely support, and don't allow your imagination to exceed this limit. If you are at all unsure about its strength or safety, have the balcony examined by a qualified contractor to satisfy yourself that you are creating a lasting, legal, and safe garden.

If you need to put down new flooring, choose materials that are weather-resistant and as light as possible. Good-quality pressure-treated lumber decking is one popular option, since it is attractive, affordable, and makes a very pleasant surface to sit on.

MAKING THE MOST OF YOUR SPACE
Space on most balconies is at a premium, so it is sensible to try to make the best possible use of every available surface.

If your balcony is very windswept, the first thing to do is erect a good-quality screen or trellis to act as a windbreak. The more sheltered conditions this will create allow you to grow a wider range of plants and makes the balcony a more enjoyable place in which to sit. In addition, the windbreak, as well as the walls and railings around a balcony, can be fitted with a trellis or training wires to create a new growing

Outdoor living
Here, mature shrubs and climbers, including bougainvillea, abutilon, clematis, and bamboo, combine to turn an essentially featureless balcony into a charming, secluded bower. A sturdy trellis increases the available growing surface and creates a useful windbreak.

surface – invaluable in a confined area. Cover vertical surfaces with wall shrubs and vigorous climbers, such as the cup-and-saucer vine (*Cobaea scandens*), morning glory (*Ipomoea purpurea*), and *Convolvulus tricolor*. Remember to check that the exposure will suit your plants, and on windy surfaces grow only climbers, such as the golden hop, that are resistant to wind scorch. Pots and hanging baskets can also be used to increase the vertical planting area.

Make the most of horizontal surfaces with an array of containers planted with perennials, or maybe small trees, such as

Japanese maples, chosen for year-round interest. Supplement the skeleton planting with a selection of annuals and bulbs.

CONTAINERS FOR BALCONIES
Choose your containers with care, wherever possible selecting lightweight examples made from plastic or fiberglass to keep the weight on the balcony to a minimum – after all, the less your containers weigh, the more plants (and soil mix) you can use. There are many attractive containers available that are made from these materials, including some excellent imitations of terracotta.

If you have a limited budget, even cheap plastic pots or similar containers can still look quite good, especially if they are camouflaged by clever planting with a selection of trailing plants. Choose containers to suit individual plants, and bear in mind that some taller plants may need a reasonably heavy base to provide a counterbalance in windy conditions.

ARRANGING CONTAINERS FOR EFFECT
Even a single container can be displayed to great effect, but arranging several assorted containers in a group opens up many new possibilities. Maximize the options open to you with a selection of plants of differing heights growing in containers of varying shape and size.

Group containers of taller plants at the back, with the smaller ones close to the

Limited space
A well-planted windowbox can transform the exterior of a house, as this beautiful example clearly shows. An artful combination of soft gray and variegated foliage with bronze-black begonia and heuchera leaves makes the perfect foil for pale pink osteospermum and mauve brachycome, in a design which is unashamedly romantic.

Wall planting
A simple terracotta wall pot (right) is easy to attach to the side of a house and can bring a bold splash of color to an otherwise featureless surface. With regular watering and deadheading, this simple planting of single-colored pansies would produce masses of flowers right through spring and on into early summer.

Balcony collection
A balcony planting does not need to be on a grand scale to be effective. Here (left) an eclectic mixture of plastic and terracotta pots, planted with inexpensive miniature roses, pink and white hydrangeas, and a birch tree – secured to the railing – creates a cherished haven from the stresses of city life.

front, to create a solid bank of color. Arrange tall or bushy plants to provide shade for smaller ones that would scorch in full sun, use topiary shapes to add a touch of formality, or place large specimen plants on either side of the balcony doors to create an impressive entrance. With a little trial and error, you will find that a garden in miniature is both easy to establish and satisfying to arrange.

SELECTING PLANTS
One fast way to make a new balcony garden look more established is to invest in several large shrubs. These can be rather pricey, but they are worth the expense if you can afford them. Where a limited budget or awkward access rules out grand plants, consider growing a hibiscus (*Hibiscus rosa-sinensis*). They are reasonably priced, and a small plant will grow rapidly and produce large, showy blooms every year. Although some shrubs have the potential to grow very large, and are therefore considered less suitable than medium to small varieties, most can in fact be kept relatively compact by regular and careful pruning. Even if a plant proves unsuitable and is impossible to keep in

check after a few years, it will still have given you a fair period of enjoyment, so do not allow lack of space to restrict your choice too much.

THE SCENTED BALCONY
Plants bearing sweet-smelling flowers are ideally suited to pots and tubs in balcony gardens, since their scent will be enjoyed from inside the house as well as outside. Quick-growing scented annuals, such as sweet peas and night-scented stocks, or bulbous plants, such as freesias, paperwhite daffodils, and hyacinths, are excellent choices.

For the longer term, consider growing fragrant climbing jasmine (either *Jasminum officinale* or *J. polyanthum*). Wisteria is another option, but will need hard pruning if it is to be kept under control.

A SELECTION OF TRAILING PLANTS
Almost any container planting is enhanced by the addition of trailing plants, which allow you to experiment more with color and texture. In their season, trailing plants such as lobelias and petunias will bring almost instant bright color to a dull spot. For a more subtle effect, choose ivy

geraniums and *Verbena* x *hybrida*. Trailing and some climbing plants can also be encouraged to sprawl over and through railings if containers of a suitable height are arranged close to the edge. Many plants, including trailing plain and variegated English ivies, aubrieta, periwinkle (*Vinca minor* or, in larger containers, its big brother V. *major*), and ivy geraniums are suitable.

Enhance the display of trailing perennials with a selection of annual trailers such as Swan River daisies (*Brachycome iberidifolia*) and nasturtiums – which are extremely easy to raise from seed and are edible as well. Also explore the potential of plants such as helichrysums, which are not strictly trailers but sprawl so expansively that they perform much the same function.

THE PRODUCTIVE BALCONY
Many vegetables and some fruits can be grown in containers on the balcony and, except in extreme conditions, should produce a good harvest. Apples grafted onto dwarfing rootstocks, and most strawberry varieties, will grow well in pots. Also try tomatoes, potatoes, zucchini, sweet peppers, and salad vegetables, among other crops, which will enlarge the scope of your aerial gardening further. Consider using stacking pots with planting holes on their sides, hanging baskets, and strawberry jars with tiered planting holes that make maximum use of precious floor space to produce a cascade of fruit. Climbing vegetables, such as lima beans, pole beans, hyacinth beans (*Lablab purpureus*), and peas, look good grown up wires, on a wigwam, or on the balcony railing. Combine your favorite crops with a selection of culinary herbs grown in pots or troughs to create a miniature kitchen garden right where people would least expect to find one.

ROOM AT THE TOP

If you ever have the chance to turn a roof into a roof garden, jump at it! Whether it is your only available growing space, or it provides an alternative to a conventional ground-level site, a roof garden offers such scope for development into something very special that you really shouldn't pass up the opportunity.

Unlike balconies, which tend to be small and rather hemmed in by house walls and railings, a roof garden usually offers enough space for your imagination to run riot without the interruption of too many logistical considerations. There certainly will be some restrictions – the strength of a roof and its ability to hold extra weight are the most common problems – but a qualified contractor will be able to advise you on their extent.

Classical look
Restrained planting, a limited color scheme, and an emphasis on quality combine here to create an impressively formal garden. Raised wooden beds and large terracotta pots are filled with dwarf evergreens, variegated ivies, and bronze-leaved begonias.

GARDENING CONDITIONS ON THE ROOF

Conditions at roof level do present a number of challenges to the would-be gardener. The temperature range is often extreme and, if the area is not adequately protected by a windbreak or sheltered by surrounding buildings, wind may be a problem. In areas where plants are likely to suffer from wind scorch, it is important to construct a windbreak, using either large, hardy plants or a commercial screen.

Provided the site is protected from wind, the warmth given off by the building will increase local temperatures, enabling you to raise tender plants with far better results than would be possible at ground level. The added warmth also tends to extend the season, so it is well worth growing some vegetables, too.

However, during sunny weather, a lack of shade may lead to extremely high temperatures, and roof surfaces – especially if they are dark in color or constructed from asphalt – can get uncomfortably hot. Wooden decking, or even good-quality woven matting, will make the roof far more pleasant to walk on – and improve its appearance as well.

DESIGNING THE GARDEN

A roof garden can be ordered to give a regimented or formal style, or arranged in a more haphazard and natural fashion, as if the containers had grown there of their own accord. Whichever style you prefer, arrange the containers in such a way as to create areas of shade, allowing you to add some shade-loving plants to your list. If the roof is strong enough, you could also include a small pond, perhaps in a half barrel (*see* "Making a Pond in a Half Barrel," p.124), in a slightly shaded spot.

When planning which plants you want to include and where to position them, do leave room for some sort of seating, because after all that hard work you will

Relative heights
Using containers in a range of sizes, and exploiting a full range of supports – ornamental trellises, bamboo frames, and even an old stool – this corner arrangement makes an attractive feature. The sweet peas and English ivy should screen out enough sun to keep the shade-loving fern happy.

Rustic style
Here, masses of fragrant sweet peas, lavender, pelargoniums, nasturtiums, and petunias recall the rambling informality of a traditional cottage garden. A container-grown tree provides an element of shade and lends extra height to the tiered arrangement of smaller plant pots.

want somewhere to sit and admire the results. And last of all, do not forget your surroundings. Rooftops generally offer some of the best views around, so modify your planting to take advantage of them.

SELECTING CONTAINERS

As for balconies, you will probably need to restrict the weight of containers and soil mix that you use so that you don't overburden the roof. Since there are many good-quality, attractive, yet lightweight containers now available, this concern with weight need not be much of a restriction. For further details, *see* "Containers for Balconies," p.106.

CHOOSING PLANTS

Faced with a completely empty roof area, it can be daunting to try to plan – and pay for – the creation of an entire garden all at once. Fortunately, containers can be planted during much of the year, so you can ease yourself into the task over several months, or even years. You may find it easier to concentrate on a single corner to start with, and work out from there, learning from your successes – and failures.

In the first year, annuals and bedding plants will quickly brighten up pots, boxes, and planters. In the long term, however, the optimum planting is probably a combination of temporary or seasonal varieties, together with shrubs and other more permanent plants. For example, a dwarf conifer will look good all year and act as a foil and support for the yellow-flowering canary vine (*Tropaeolum peregrinum*). Underplant these two with 'Tête-à-Tête' daffodils, and you will introduce a splash of gold in winter and late spring to create a combination with all-season interest.

There are lots of suitable shrubs to choose from, including *Lonicera fragrantissima*, *Weigela* 'Bristol Ruby',

dwarf azaleas, and *Pieris* 'Forest Flame', all of which provide a good long season of interest. These more permanent plants make maintenance easier, too.

With a little trial and error, you will discover that a massive number of different plants can be successfully grown in containers. If in doubt as to the suitability of a particular plant, it is always worth experimenting, but remember that

regular watering, feeding, deadheading – and, in some cases, pruning – are essential if you want to achieve the best results.

FOLIAGE EFFECTS

Foliage is an important element in a roof garden. Although plants with a good show of flowers certainly deserve a place, any plant that offers attractive or interesting foliage or stems should be high on your list. The advantage of these multitalented varieties is that they look good for much of the year, not just when they are in flower. Choose plants for their range of leaf size, shape, and texture.

Many deciduous trees and shrubs, such as cotinus, many Japanese maples (including *Acer palmatum* 'Dissectum Atropurpureum'), and fothergilla, have autumn color or attractive berries to provide interest in more than one season. Evergreens are essential too, unless your roof garden is to be used solely in spring and summer. This needn't mean cultivating a dark green wall of bland conifer foliage. Choose carefully and you can enjoy a range of texture and color – many evergreens, including *Aucuba japonica* cultivars, *Hedera helix* cultivars, and *Elaeagnus pungens* 'Maculata', have variegated foliage. This will supply you with a reliable backdrop of color, and some wind protection, all year.

Relaxing retreat
Were it not for a glimpse of the chimney pots beyond, it would be impossible to guess that this well-established garden was in fact created on a roof. Masses of mature climbers scramble over the trellis and walls, with roses framing the ironwork bench to create a fragrant and tranquil place to sit.

CHOOSING CONTAINERS

Gardening in containers is becoming ever more popular, and with the new surge of interest there has been a tremendous increase in the range of styles and sizes of containers available. The colors, shapes, and materials are so diverse that, regardless of your taste or budget, there is bound to be something that is right for you and the plants you plan to grow. Even the cheapest options, such as large plastic flower pots and troughs, make serviceable containers – they are frostproof and have drainage holes, and, if trailing plants are used, it is easy to conceal the sides of the pot. There are, of course, many more attractive and even unusual objects that can be used, some of which are illustrated on these pages – ultimately, the only limitation is that your container is of the right size and has adequate drainage.

WHICH CONTAINER?

There are several practical points you should consider when choosing a container. Very small pots tend to dry out quickly, and in pots that are too large, soggy soil mix may become stagnant around the plants' roots, even if the drainage is adequate. The weight of the container can be especially important if it is to be used on a balcony, because when filled up with plants and moist soil mix, it will be extremely heavy. If the container is to be kept outside throughout the year, choose one that is labeled as frostproof and insulate it if necessary (*see* "Protection Against Frost and Cold," p.159).

Anisodontea capensis

Daffodil
(*Narcissus* 'Jetfire')

Daffodil
(*Narcissus* 'Midget')

Grape hyacinth
(*Muscari*)

Dusty Miller
(*Senecio* x *hybridus*)

Terracotta pots
The warm orange-brown of terracotta suits most situations and weathers attractively. It is fairly heavy but is useful where a degree of stability is needed. Terracotta pots usually come with a central drainage hole; add broken crocks or a piece of screening to cover the hole.

Classic urns
Urns are attractive and suit a wide range of plants, but avoid planting them with particularly large or rapid-growing plants.

Glazed pots
These are available in a range of colors and designs and are often Oriental in style. Some are brightly colored, while others have natural tones that blend in more easily with their surroundings. Most are quite heavy and not frostproof, so they will need extra winter protection. They often have a single drainage hole.

Hanging baskets

The best hanging baskets are made from strong plastic-coated wire, usually in black, white, or green. Once the plants are growing strongly, the wire should be well concealed. They are practical for year-round use. See "Planting Pots and Containers," pp.112–13, for how to plant them.

Helichrysum petiolare 'Aureum'

Half baskets

Half baskets or troughs for use on walls are usually made from plastic-coated wire or wrought iron, and vary greatly in size. For the planting, a combination of upright and trailing plants looks especially attractive.

Snapdragon (Antirrhinum 'Sweetheart')

Pansy (Viola x wittrockiana Crystal Bowl Series)

Winter-flowering pansy (Viola x wittrockiana 'Imperial Light Blue')

Variegated English ivy (Hedera helix 'Harald')

Pansy (Viola x wittrockiana 'Rhine Gold')

TRAINING A CONE
Boxwood (Buxus sempervirens) is trained by trimming side-shoots as the plant develops.

Variegated English ivy (Hedera helix 'Eva')

Winter-flowering pansy (Viola x wittrockiana 'Blue Blotch')

Wooden containers

Wooden tubs and half barrels are particularly useful for siting in windy areas, such as roof gardens, because they are relatively stable. They make ideal containers for larger plants, including shrubs and some trees. For drainage, drill several large holes through the base of the container.

Chimney pots

From tall and narrow to small and squat, from terracotta to black or gray earthenware, chimney pots can be simple or ornate. Drainage is good; keeping soil mix moist is more likely to be a problem. Trailing plants are ideal for planting in the top, with smaller plants tucked into side holes.

PLANTING POTS AND CONTAINERS

Small containers are ideal for special plants, experimenting with new specimens, and adding an instant splash of color. They are also easily moved into a sheltered spot in frosty weather if the plants are tender. A container of tall plants, such as lilies or agapanthus, can be used to brighten up a dull border – conceal the container in a gap among other plants and remove it once the plants have finished flowering.

Large containers are perfect for growing more permanent plants, such as shrubs, perennials, and even small trees. Provided that you feed and water the plants properly, and repot them if their roots become congested, they should last for years. If you add seasonal bedding plants (and perhaps a selection of spring-flowering bulbs) to the container, you can create a complete miniature garden that has something to offer throughout the year.

WHICH SOIL MIX?

Garden soil may be wonderful stuff in the border, but in a container it tends to lose its structure and harbor diseases. Specially formulated soil mixes provide a better growing medium. A soil-based one should normally be your first choice: it retains moisture well, and once dry is easier to wet again than peat-based products.

SOIL MIXES FOR LARGE POTS

For large containers or those on balconies, peat-based and peat-substitute soil mixes are better choices since they are light and the container will be easier to move when full. Plants in these soil mixes will need more frequent feeding.

LIME-FREE SOIL MIX

With containers you have a new freedom to grow plants that do not suit your soil: use lime-free soil mix to grow acid-loving plants, such as azaleas and camellias.

MAKING THE MOST OF YOUR CONTAINER

The larger your container, the more you can pack into it, especially if you plant at several depths. Plant large bulbs toward the base of the container and smaller bulbs or corms above; these can be left undisturbed to come up year after year. A shrub or perennial can be put in the center where it has most space to spread its roots, and then you can add annual bedding plants in the clear areas around the edge.

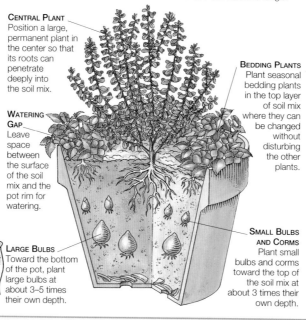

CENTRAL PLANT
Position a large, permanent plant in the center so that its roots can penetrate deeply into the soil mix.

WATERING GAP
Leave space between the surface of the soil mix and the pot rim for watering.

LARGE BULBS
Toward the bottom of the pot, plant large bulbs at about 3–5 times their own depth.

BEDDING PLANTS
Plant seasonal bedding plants in the top layer of soil mix where they can be changed without disturbing the other plants.

SMALL BULBS AND CORMS
Plant small bulbs and corms toward the top of the soil mix at about 3 times their own depth.

FEET OR SAUCERS?

Poor drainage can be the downfall of many plants: if the roots are always soggy they may rot. Check that your pot has enough drainage holes to let excess moisture drain away; if not, add new ones.

FEET
Terracotta or china feet are available to put under pots and raise them off the ground. This helps to keep the drainage holes clear. For a half barrel, tuck bricks under the base.

SAUCERS
Plastic or terracotta saucers are sometimes used under containers; these can be cleared of debris but hold water at the base of the pot, which causes waterlogging.

CONTAINER PLANTS FOR DIFFERENT SEASONS

SPRING
Camellias ● [some ✲] ᵖᴴ
Crocuses ☼
Hellebores (all incl. *H. foetidus, H. viridis*) ☽
Dwarf irises (incl. *Iris reticulata* and cvs) ☼
Star magnolia (*Magnolia stellata*) ♀ ○
Dwarf daffodils (*Narcissus*, some cvs) ☼
Azaleas (*Rhododendron*) ●○ᵖᴴ

SUMMER
Marguerites (*Argyranthemum frutescens* and cvs) ☽✲
Begonias ☽☼✲
Fuchsias ○ [many ✲, some ᵗ]
Helichrysum petiolare ☽✲ᵗ
Impatiens ☽☼✲
Lobelia erinus ☽ [some ᵗ]
Nasturtiums (*Tropaeolum*) ☽✲ᵗ
Geraniums (*Pelargonium*) ☽✲
Petunias ☼
Verbenas ☼

AUTUMN
Japanese maples (*Acer palmatum* and cvs, incl. 'Atropurpureum' and 'Dissectum') ♀
Ajuga reptans ☽
Cyclamens ☼
Chrysanthemums (*Dendranthema*) ☽ [some ✲]
English ivies (*Hedera*) ☽ᵗ
Deadnettles (*Lamium maculatum* and cvs, incl. 'White Nancy' and 'Beacon Silver') ☽☽ᵗ

WINTER
Daphnes ●○
Winter-flowering heathers (*Erica*) ●ᵖᴴ
Hollies (*Ilex*) ●
Junipers (*Juniperus*) ●
Pieris ●ᵖᴴ
Winter-flowering pansies (*Viola x wittrockiana* cvs) ☽

KEY
ᵗ Trailing

PLANTING A HALF BARREL FOR WINTER AND SPRING COLOR

A large, well-built container is excellent for winter plantings; the volume of soil mix it holds and its thick wooden sides help to protect the plants' roots from cold and frost. Before planting, make sure the barrel has clear drainage holes. Move it to its final position away from windswept areas or frost pockets and raise it off the ground on bricks – once planted it will be very heavy and hard to move. As you plant, add slow-release fertilizer and water-retaining granules to the soil mix to make maintenance easier. For more ideas on choosing containers, *see* pp.110–11; for suggestions of where to site them, *see* pp.105–109.

YOU WILL NEED

- Half barrel •Bricks
- Trowel •Soil mix
- Slow-release fertilizer
- Water-retaining granules

Coarse grit

Pieris 'Flaming Silver'

1 Place broken pots or coarse grit in the base of the barrel, then shovel in the soil mix without displacing the drainage material.

2 Place the pieris at the correct level and surround it with bulbs; here 'Tête-à-Tête' daffodils are being closely planted for a dense mass of spring color.

Top layer of bulbs

3 Add more soil mix, taking care not to disturb the bottom layer of bulbs. Towards the top, plant a layer of crocus corms around the pieris.

4 Add soil mix to within 1½in (3.5cm) of the rim. Firm the pieris, plant winter-flowering pansies, and water well.

SIMPLE MAINTENANCE Deadhead and neaten the pansies regularly to keep them looking good.

5 The completed barrel is a mass of color instantly. The pieris will provide year-round interest, while the pansies will flower in late winter and spring and can then be replaced with summer bedding. In spring, the crocuses and daffodils will grow and flower through the pansies.

SOIL MIX Lime-free soil mix suits the acid-loving pieris.

MAINTAINING CONTAINERS

Like a full-sized garden, a container needs attention to keep it looking good. In such a small space, the competition for food and water is intense, especially in spring and summer when the plants are growing rapidly.

Water as needed to keep the soil mix just moist – in summer this may need to be done every day. Start feeding from six to eight weeks after planting and continue into autumn while the plants are still growing. A liquid feed is easiest to use in containers. Choose a high-phosphorus one to encourage flowering, and follow the recommended rates. For a rapid effect use a foliar feed, but do not apply in bright light or the leaves may be scorched. Established containers need to have their soil replenished every spring: remove the top 1–2in (2.5–5cm) and replace it with a fresh layer.

CHECKING YOUR PLANTS

Deadhead regularly to keep plants flowering for as long as possible. While deadheading, take off any dead or dying leaves or stems, and check the plant for pests and diseases. Remove any infested or diseased leaves promptly before the problem spreads (*see* "Plant Doctor," pp.161–8). Replace plants that start to look shabby or leggy.

Deadheading

To keep plants flowering for as long as possible, pinch out dead or fading flowers individually. This prevents the plant from wasting energy in producing seeds. For tough-stemmed plants you may need to use scissors or pruners.

PLANTING BASKETS AND MANGERS

A hanging basket or manger can bring instant life and color to your house, garden, or balcony. You may choose to combine a mass of bright flowers, or to create a more subtle effect with pastel colors or foliage plants. Or you can select the plants from within a limited color range, or even an elegant, single color. With a huge range of plants to choose from, you can make the basket as simple or extravagant as you want! Don't abandon your basket at the end of the summer: with careful choice of plants and liners, and resiting of the container to a more sheltered spot, baskets may be used throughout the year. They need not be restricted to your house wall, but also look spectacular on garages and garden walls. Hanging baskets look particularly effective suspended from a pergola or arch – in fact they can be hung anywhere that is sturdy enough to take the weight.

PLANTING HANGING BASKETS

Hanging baskets are available in a range of sizes. Try to avoid very small sizes, however, since a tiny basket dries out easily and starts to look scruffy quite quickly as the plant becomes stressed. Hanging baskets with built-in saucers and hangers prevent dripping after watering, but should not be very densely planted since this makes them too heavy. Wire baskets coated in plastic or special paint look best and last longest. Baskets usually do best in fairly sheltered sites where they are protected from wind. Most summer bedding needs plenty of sun, although too much will shorten its flowering span. For a shady spot, select the plants carefully: some, such as impatiens and bellflowers (*Campanula*) thrive, but many others grow leggy and will not flower well if deprived of sun – check labels before buying.

1 Rest the basket on an empty flower pot to hold it steady. Use pliers to remove the basket chain. Lay the liner over the base and press into position.

2 Mix water-retaining granules with the soil mix, then add water. When the granules look like blobs of jelly, add a layer of soil mix to the basket.

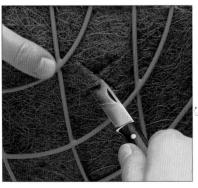

3 To plant trailing plants in the sides, make an X-shaped cut in the liner for each plant. Firm down the liner again if necessary. Plant through the holes, gently compressing the root ball of each plant to push it through the gap into the soil mix.

4 Build up another layer of soil mix around the sides, planting as you go. Plant trailing plants angled outward at the top, with an upright plant in the center. Add more soil mix and firm well, leaving space for watering. Reattach the chain.

WHICH BASKET LINER?

The traditional, and most attractive, basket lining is sphagnum moss, which retains moisture well; harvesting the moss for garden use does, however, damage its natural habitat. Alternatives include foam, which is easy to shape for a snug fit, and coconut fiber, which provides good insulation.

Foam liner

Sphagnum moss

Coconut fiber liner

A SCENTED BASKET

Once you have planted a summer basket, sprinkle a few seeds of quick-germinating scented annuals, such as night-scented stocks, on the surface of the soil mix, and later in the summer you will be able to enjoy enticing wafts of sweet scent.

PLANTING UP A MANGER FOR AUTUMN

As summer turns to autumn, add some fresh color to your garden with a manger or wall basket. These can be used in almost any season and in cold weather benefit from the protection of a wall, conservatory, or sunporch. They are available in various shapes, from half baskets to wrought-iron mangers up to 3ft (1m) long.

Larger half baskets or mangers can be planted to last for several seasons with a selection of plants, including some to give the container a more permanent feel, such as euonymus, dwarf junipers, heathers, or other compact evergreen shrubs.

If you are planting initially for autumn interest, you can always add seasonal bedding or bulbs to brighten up the basket or manger all year. Bulbs and corms of autumn-flowering crocuses and miniature cyclamens add an autumnal flavor as do the deeper colors of pot chrysanthemums and, for acidic soil mix, some compact heathers. Trailing or cascading plants

suitable for autumn displays include variegated ivies, deadnettles (*Lamium*), and periwinkles (*Vinca*) – these all tolerate some frost if given adequate protection.

1 *Line the base with a ½–¾in (1–2cm) deep layer of moss and firm down well. Add more moss to start covering the sides. Put in a shallow layer of multipurpose soil mix at the base of the manger.*

2 *Plant trailing plants through the sides, gently compressing each root ball before passing it between the uprights of the manger and firming the roots into contact with the soil mix.*

3 *Continue to build up the moss layer around the sides to the top of the manger. Add more soil mix. Plant the central area then fill with more plants around the rim, angling them outward to encourage them to trail over and cover the sides.*

EUONYMUS FORTUNEI 'EMERALD GAIETY'
Brightly colored, variegated foliage always looks good in containers.

CYCLAMEN CILICIUM
With its pretty, delicate flowers and beautifully marked leaves, this miniature cyclamen provides interest for months on end.

AJUGA REPTANS 'BRAUNHERZ'
Glossy, dark brown foliage sets off lighter colors well.

LAMIUM MACULATUM 'WHITE NANCY'
Trailing plants are useful for adding fullness to a mixed planting.

4 *Water carefully and top up the soil mix level if necessary. As the plants grow and establish themselves, the manger will become fuller and more colorful. Water and feed the plants regularly; this is particularly important when growth is at its* peak. *Deadhead plants as needed to prolong their period of flowering and neaten up leggy growth to encourage bushiness. Trim back plants that outgrow their place, removing any growth that has been damaged by weather.*

MAINTAINING HANGING BASKETS AND MANGERS

Hanging baskets and mangers can look beautiful for many months – indeed for much of the year – providing they are looked after with care and consistency.

WATERING AND FEEDING
The key to success is regular, thorough watering; this may need doing more than once a day in warm weather. If your hanging basket gets very dry, remove it from its bracket and carefully stand it in a tray of water for an hour or two until the soil mix is wet through. If you added water-retaining granules at planting, your basket will also benefit from a long soaking so that the granules can swell again properly. Baskets are surprisingly heavy when fully planted and watered, so check regularly that the brackets you have are sturdy enough to hold the weight.

Your basket will also need regular feeding since plants packed so tightly together soon use up the fertilizer in the soil mix. Start to feed them regularly five or six weeks after planting, depending on the type of soil mix and how quickly the plants are growing. Incorporate slow-release fertilizer granules at planting, or feed twice a week with a high-phosphorus fertilizer, to stimulate flower production. Water before feeding, or most of the fertilizer will run off the soil surface.

KEEPING PLANTS HEALTHY
Deadhead regularly and pinch back the plants when necessary to promote new growth. Look out for pests and diseases, and treat before they spread; lower the basket to a safe spraying height if using pesticides. In autumn, clear baskets of fallen leaves since these spoil the display and may cause the plants beneath to rot.

PLANTING A WINDOWBOX

A windowbox full of plants provides a mini garden right outside your window – and if you include some scented flowers, wafts of fragrance will fill the room as well. Foliage plants can add a mixture of shapes and colors to provide an attractive display throughout the year. Windowboxes need not be limited to your windowsill – they can be mounted on railings and balconies, positioned at the side of your patio, or perhaps raised on a wall in your garden. Choose your windowbox carefully and buy the best you can, since the more expensive terracotta and treated wooden ones last longer and look more attractive when planted. Plastic windowboxes provide an inexpensive alternative and come in a range of colors, but they have a tendency to bow outward in the center when full of soil. A planted windowbox complete with moist soil mix is very heavy, so make sure it is well secured.

SEASONAL WINDOWBOXES

Because windowboxes often benefit from the shelter of a wall, you can choose slightly more tender plants than you could for open ground. This gives you a wider range from which to select. Choose one or two evergreen foliage plants to provide a permanent framework, and then add flowering plants for different times of year, or plant bulbs to keep the windowbox looking interesting without too much work. Alternatively, start from scratch to create a different look each season.

Unless the box is in a sheltered place, avoid very tall plants since they may make it top-heavy and even blow over. Many plant species have compact forms that are ideal for the main body of the windowbox. These can be used on their own to create a dense, upright arrangement, or combined with trailing plants for a softer look.

Spring
This subtle arrangement of long-lasting hellebores and striped, low-growing tulips makes an attractive spring display, offset by the weathered terracotta windowbox. Both plants thrive in semishade and, since they are fairly compact, should not be wind damaged. In cold areas, replace this hellebore hybrid with a hardier one.

Helleborus x sternii

Waterlily tulip (*Tulipa* 'Ancilla')

Golden marjoram (*Origanum vulgare* 'Aureum')

Golden feverfew (*Chrysanthemum parthenium* 'Aureum')

Zinnia elegans

Gazania uniflora

Summer
Summer windowboxes are the easiest to fill since the choice of readily available plants at reasonable prices is unrivaled. Try restricting the color range to produce a subtle effect. Here gold, silver, and green make a bright, warm arrangement for a sunny spot.

Lawson cypress (*Chamaecyparis lawsoniana* 'Nana Glauca')

Late-flowering heather (*Calluna vulgaris*)

English Ivy (*Hedera helix* 'Elegance')

Winter
The warm colors of the skimmia and winter cherry fruits make a cheerful winter display for sun or semishade. Feed and water to prolong the display. The senecio will last well through mild winters but is damaged by severe frost. In mild areas, all the plants may last until early the following summer.

Skimmia japonica 'Rubella'

Senecio maritima

Winter cherry (*Solanum capsicastrum*)

Autumn
An effective way of achieving autumn color is with late-flowering heathers. A backdrop of Lawson cypress and some trailing, variegated English ivies make a cool arrangement in a pure white windowbox. Use a lime-free, or acidic, soil mix.

PLANTING A SUMMER WINDOWBOX

If possible, place your windowbox in position before you start planting. If the window will be opened, bear this in mind when choosing plants and positioning the box. Select plants that suit the situation – in summer you should be able to find something for conditions ranging from full sun to fairly deep shade. It does not matter if the plants are quite closely spaced, and this will certainly produce the most impressive display, provided they are kept well watered, fed, and maintained as they grow. To make aftercare easier, mix a few slow-release fertilizer granules and water-retaining granules into the soil mix before filling the windowbox. Leave room at the top of the box for watering – if the soil mix is too high, the water will run off.

SECURING WINDOWBOXES

Stabilize a windowbox by using brackets to attach it to the adjacent brickwork. Alternatively, attach the box beneath the sill by supporting the base with metal or wooden brackets mounted to both the wall and the base of the box. Secure to the wall with wall anchors.

Prepared windowbox

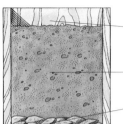

⅜in (1cm) space between top of soil mix and rim of box

Moistened multipurpose soil mix

Expanded clay granules or broken crocks

1 Plants in window-boxes need good drainage if they are to flourish; place a layer of broken pots in the base before filling with soil mix to prevent the soil from becoming waterlogged.

2 Half-fill the box with moistened soil mix and firm it down. Remove the plants from their containers.

Handle root balls with care

3 Loosen the root balls of the plants without damaging the roots. Plant them quite closely, but leave some space between each plant. Leave a ½in (1cm) gap between the neck of the plant and the top of the box.

4 Continue to plant, firming each root ball gently and adding soil mix between the plants. Leave a watering gap at the top of the box. Water thoroughly and allow excess to drain away. Add extra soil mix to fill any sunken areas.

Compact plants placed in the center

5 Water and feed the windowbox regularly, and deadhead promptly so that the plants keep flowering for as long as possible. Here, a couple of months after planting, the begonias, impatiens, and lobelias have grown bushier to fill out the available space and make a bright, exuberant windowbox.

Trailing plants arranged around the edges

RENOVATING WINDOWBOXES

Treat wooden window-boxes with a water-based preservative every few years; painted ones may need to be stripped and repainted if the surface starts to peel. Check metal screws, nails, and brackets annually and replace any that are deteriorating. Clear blocked drainage holes. When plants look straggly or stop flowering, replace them with fresh plants or with bulbs to keep the box looking good into the spring.

·9·
WATER
FEATURES

*The sight and sound of flowing water seems to captivate and
calm in almost equal measure. Introduce a water feature into
any garden design, and it will be completely transformed.
The wide range of options available means that there is
a style to suit even the smallest garden.*

POND STYLES

A garden with a pool or water feature will always have the edge over one without, and there are so many different types to choose from that you are certain to find one that suits your garden.

Creating a pond or boggy area not only improves the appearance of your garden, it also encourages wildlife. Birds will come to drink and bathe; dragonflies, mayflies, frogs, and newts will all pay a visit; and, as a bonus, some even help to keep garden pests at bay.

In and around the pond you will be able to grow a variety of water and moisture-loving plants (*see* "Plants for Ponds," pp.120–21). This increased planting diversity will be appreciated both by wildlife and those gardeners who have been bitten by the plant-collecting bug.

CHOOSING A POND STYLE

The design, size, and shape of a pond can be tailored to suit any garden. While a wildlife pond with a natural appearance would suit a cottage-style garden very well, it might look out of place in more formal grounds – where a pond with paved edges, fountains, and some statuary could look stunning. In a courtyard garden, a square pond with a neat brick edge would complement its surroundings.

The design you finally decide on will largely be determined by personal taste, but there are also a number of practical considerations that you will need to take into account. To grow the widest possible range of plants, you will need a pond with several different levels that can accommodate deep water varieties, marginals, and moisture-lovers at the edges. If your aim is to attract wildlife, you should make sure that the pond has at least one gently sloping side to make access easier.

As a way of introducing moving water to the garden, you could construct the pond on two levels, and install a pump to circulate the water from one level to the other. For more ideas, *see* "Spouts, Barrels, and Fountains," pp.122–3.

FINDING THE BEST SITE

Selecting a suitable site is very important if the pond is to be a success. Although water features look lovely in full sun, the combination of bright light and still water can cause unsightly algae to develop, blocking the light to submerged plants and water creatures. A slightly shady site is preferable – perhaps shielded by a wall or low-level poolside planting – but ponds should not be positioned near overhanging trees. All trees, and in particular deciduous ones, tend to cause problems since falling leaves clog the pond and may encourage disease. The pond surface can be netted (*see* p.131) but, if at all possible, it is better to select an alternative (tree-free) site.

Lush planting
Moisture-loving plants such as hostas and sedges combine with waterlilies to obscure almost completely this small but very pretty pond, where goldfish thrive in the cool, shady conditions.

Imitating nature
Despite its casual appearance, this pond has actually been very carefully planned, incorporating several different depths to accommodate a wide range of water plants. The pebble "beach" is both attractive and functional, providing ideal conditions for a selection of bog plants and a visual link between the pond and adjacent borders.

PLANTS FOR PONDS

All too often you see a pond which has been well built, but which lacks the last, and most fundamental, ingredient – a good selection of plants. Yet there are so many plants available for different parts of the pond and different depths of water that there really is no excuse for such an omission. If anything, the immense range available can be a handicap for beginners, and you may find it easier to start with a few favorites, then add to your collection gradually. With a combination of bold foliage and some well-chosen flowering water plants and marginals, a faceless pond will soon be transformed into a watery oasis you can be proud of.

PLANTS FOR DIFFERENT DEPTHS

Water and moisture-loving plants all have their own preferred planting depth and are broadly classified as bog plants, marginals, deep-water plants, surface floaters, and oxygenators. Deep-water plants need their roots to be in soil at a depth of up to 30in (90cm) underwater. Surface floaters are not rooted in soil at all, nor are most oxygenators – these help keep oxygen levels in the pond high and carbon dioxide levels low, boosting the health of other plants and water creatures. Marginals thrive at the edges of ponds

Planting depths
When constructing a new pond, try to include a range of different depths to accommodate water plants from every category. This medium-sized pond includes the full range, from moisture-loving bog irises, foxgloves, and golden meadowsweet to deep-water species such as the waterlily.

with their roots just covered with water, and bog plants like constantly moist soil. For more details about how to plant each type, *see* "Planting Water Plants," pp.128–9.

PLANNING WHAT TO PLANT

Using plants from each category enables you to make the most of all areas of your pond and create a feature which looks

Modern style
Although sparse planting is popular in and around contemporary water features, it is not essential to the effect. This pond is bordered by a lush selection of marsh and bog plants, including primroses and irises, but architectural brick edging and a formal waterfall combine to create a thoroughly modern effect.

good for most, or all, of the year. To make informed planting choices, it is well worth visiting an aquatic nursery or garden center several times over a number of months to see the greatest possible range of plants at different growth stages.

When planning what to plant, do bear in mind the ultimate size of the plants – you don't want to end up with a stately plant that looks tremendous but completely dwarfs the pond. Remember, too, that some pond and marginal plants grow rapidly and are potentially invasive, while others may be swamped by vigorous neighbors. Also check that the plants will survive local conditions – if you live in a cold region, you may well need a sheltered spot (such as a greenhouse) to keep tender plants during winter. As with all plant purchases, seek advice and read labels carefully before buying.

PLANT COMPOSITIONS

Unless you have a particular design style in mind, probably the most harmonious effect will be achieved by combining many different types of plants with a variety of contrasting leaf shapes – perhaps the pointed, straplike foliage of Siberian iris (*Iris sibirica*) with the rounded leaves of clumps of hostas. A range of foliage color and texture will also improve the display, particularly if combined with the occasional splash of color from flowering deep-water or marginal plants.

The plants you choose will be determined by the style of your pond. For a wildlife pond, native plants, such as marsh marigolds (*Caltha palustris*), are ideal, since they thrive with little attention and attract local wildlife. For a more formal or modern pond, plants such as cattails, bog irises, and others with angular leaves and compact shapes are more suitable.

DEEP-WATER PLANTS

The deepest areas of a pond, at 12–36in (30–90cm), can accommodate quite a number of water plants. Popular varieties include the yellow pond lily (Nuphar advena) and golden club (Orontium aquaticum), both of which add a cheerful touch of green and gold which enlivens pond planting. But, though these and many more are well worth growing, there is no doubt that the most spectacular deep-water plants are the waterlilies (Nymphaea). The precise planting depths for waterlilies vary from species to species, but there are a number suitable for deep ponds. Initially even deep-water varieties should be planted quite shallowly – stand the containers on blocks and gradually lower them to their preferred depth as they grow. Varying in color from deep red-pink to blue to pure white and shades of yellow, there is a waterlily to fit any color scheme – and I guarantee that their presence will add an instant touch of elegance.

OXYGENATORS AND SURFACE FLOATERS

Oxygenators perform a vital function in the pond, helping to supply oxygen for the healthy growth of water plants and animals, and prevent blooms of algae from forming. Although they are an essential, and practical, addition to pond planting, some oxygenators are also rather attractive. Water starwort (Callitriche), the lovely, lilac-flowered water violet (Hottonia palustris), and the water crowsfoot (Ranunculus aquatilis) – which produces tiny white flowers in late spring – are all as pretty as they are practical.

Surface floaters can also be very useful, helping to shade the water and thus restrict the growth of algae. Some however, including azolla and the duckweeds (Lemna minor and L. gibba), may form a carpet of growth that is too dense and clogs the surface. Consequently, these should be used only in very large ponds – or be controlled vigorously – but there are many less invasive varieties, such as frogbit (Hydrocharis morsus-ranae), which look good, grow at a more reasonable rate, and therefore require less maintenance in smaller ponds. Another surface floater, the water soldier (Stratiotes aloides), forms a rosette of erect leaves and, though submerged for most of the year, comes to the surface in mid- to late summer when it produces lovely white flowers.

MARGINALS

Marginal plants can help make a pond look natural, softening the otherwise sharp line between water and land. Marginals are grown in shallow water, usually at depths of about 6–12in (15–30cm), and can make attractive additions to a planting design. The choice includes such beautiful varieties as Iris laevigata, the blue flag (Iris versicolor), and many species of Mimulus.

However, like so many water plants, marginals are not just chosen for their looks – they also perform a practical function. A good dense planting of marginals provides a diversity of hiding and feeding places, which should lure the local wildlife, and will shade the edges of the pond at certain times of day.

BOG PLANTS

If you have, or can develop, an area for growing plants that need a boggy or constantly moist soil, then you will be able to treat yourself to some of the prettiest water plants of all.

Gunnera manicata puts on tremendous growth and develops gorgeous, umbrella-like foliage if you have space and sufficient moist soil to house it. But be warned that since it can grow up to 8 x 10ft (2.5 x 3m), it will completely hide an average garden pond. Other attractive bog foliage plants with more manageable growing habits include the variegated and golden forms of hostas. These do produce delicate flower stems in their season, but for real impact, try growing the stately cardinal flower (Lobelia cardinalis) alongside.

Alternatively – or elsewhere, if your pond is large enough – grow the globeflower (Trollius europaeus), with its golden spheres of color, and some primroses (Primula), for a very colorful scene.

Making use of color
Pondside plantings needn't be subdued, as this riotous combination clearly illustrates. Purple bog irises, with bold, variegated leaves, and candelabra primroses in clashing shades of pink and red, combine for a show-stopping effect.

Wildlife pond
Mimicking nature, this small but very pretty pond is densely planted with marginals which shade the water, provide a cool retreat for the goldfish, and shelter visiting wildlife. The planting, dominated by plants chosen for their foliage, such as alchemilla, creates a scene that will look good all year. The natural appearance of the pond is enhanced by the inclusion of cow parsley and buttercups.

Spouts, Barrels, and Fountains

A well-chosen water feature can bring the garden to life. The ever-changing sound of flowing water, and its dancing surface reflecting the surroundings, add a whole new dimension to garden design. Use of water in the garden need not be restricted to ponds or pools; it can be incorporated in many other, less static, ways.

Features such as spouts, fountains, bubble fountains, and freestanding ponds in barrels can even be used in relatively small gardens, where a traditional pond might prove too large. Although personal taste will play a large part in your choice, the feature you ultimately select should also suit the style of your house and garden, and be of a suitable size for its site – and remember that fountains appear much larger when they are working.

Formal fountains
Even a small and simple fountain will add a real touch of elegance to the garden. Here the fountain spurts from an ornamental urn, bringing the peaceful sound of flowing water to an already tranquil courtyard garden.

POSITIONING THE FEATURE

Since most water features are a permanent addition to the garden, it is important to put some careful thought into where best to position them. A single feature could create a whole range of different effects depending on its site. For example, a spout, barrel, or fountain can be used as the central feature in a garden, adding a new focal point as well as a touch of formality and order. Alternatively, it could be artfully concealed from casual glances so that the sound of moving water will entice visitors to explore the garden in search of the source of the noise.

Whatever effect you are trying to create, there are still a number of practical considerations to be taken into account. Like ponds and pools, other types of water feature are best kept out of the sunniest spots in the garden, since too much direct sunlight encourages the growth of algae – particularly if the water is not kept moving constantly. Instead, choose an area of the garden that catches sun for only part of the day and enjoy the magical effect of moving water as it is caught by a sudden beam of sunlight. Alternatively, imitate the cool seclusion of a grotto, and site your spout, barrel, or fountain in a shaded spot, reached only by an occasional shaft of light on a sunny day.

Also beware of sites close to deciduous trees, which can clog up the feature as they shed their leaves. It is easier to keep a small feature clear of debris than it is a larger pond, but all the same it is a job you might as well avoid if you can.

CHOOSING A SUITABLE STYLE

First and foremost, the style of water feature you choose should fit in with the type of garden you have or are trying to develop. A large and elaborate fountain may look stunning in a formal garden of fair size, but it could easily dwarf a smaller, more informal site – causing a garden that once looked cozily intimate to appear cramped and shabby in comparison. In this situation, a small barrel with a water spout creating a succession of gentle ripples might be preferable to restore the sense of casual harmony.

However, this is not to suggest that there is a straight choice between formal features for large gardens and rustic ones for small gardens. It is not the style, but the scale, of the feature that really counts.

Semisunken barrel
Making the best of both worlds, this half-barrel pond has been partially buried in a cool, shady corner where not only water plants but also a couple of goldfish thrive. The use of gravel and pebbles around the barrel helps to create an air of oriental simplicity.

Portable ponds
This novel water garden contains miniature water-lilies and several other small aquatics, including the water hyacinth (Eichhornia crassipes).

Bubble fountain
Ideal for a controlled water feature, especially if young children use the garden, a bubble fountain circulates water between a hidden underground reservoir and an ornamental arrangement of cobblestones and a millstone.

FOUNTAINS AS FEATURES
A fountain can be incorporated within a pond, or constructed as a feature in its own right, with water circulating around a bed of stones rather than a pool. An array of simple pumps, with varying strengths and adjustable sprays, is available. Pumps are generally quick and easy to install, although – as with any job involving electricity – if you have any doubts about your abilities, it is safer to call in a professional (for instructions, *see* p.124).

WATER SPOUT STYLES
Water spouts come in a variety of shapes and guises, offering something for any garden, however tiny, and any gardener, however restricted the budget. Whichever shape you choose, a spout will provide the soothing sound of running water without taking up a significant amount of space. Spouts are usually attached to a wall, and it is important to have access to both sides of the vertical surface to allow the mechanism of pump and reservoir to be hidden out of sight. It is also, of course, necessary to fit an ornamental receptacle to allow the water to be recirculated.

MINI-WATERCOURSES
My idea of the ultimate in water-feature luxury is a mini-watercourse, made from a series of clay or terracotta pots in a step-like arrangement, with a spout of water cascading down from top to bottom. These tend to look best in largish gardens where, though rather expensive to create, they make attractive long-term assets. In oriental-inspired gardens, use a series of bamboo spouts instead, to make a feature which is similar in style to a watercourse, but with a real flavor of the East.

While a single barrel pond might look lost in a large garden, a collection of several barrels or pots in a single arrangement, with larger quantities of water moving through and over the whole lot, could be used to make a grander feature with more impact. Similarly, a water spout can look splendid or strange depending on its surroundings. An ancient-looking gargoyle has great potential to impress, but not if attached to a brand-new, ultra-modern wall. Choose a spout of more contemporary design in this situation, and both wall and water feature will look all the better for it. Don't neglect the element of humor, either. Many gargoyle spouts have amusing – or downright wicked-looking – faces, and a little light relief can be a welcome find in even the prettiest garden.

WATER AND CHILDREN
All too often there is a worry that water and children do not mix. In fact, there is a range of features available that do not incorporate large or deep areas of water. Provided you do not rush into a decision, you should be able to find a feature which satisfies both your sense of garden style and your sense of parental obligation.

One useful childproofing technique is to create a feature in which water trickles over large pebbles or maybe a millstone, or through a series of pots or barrels. Since the water is not deep at any point, the element of danger is effectively removed. Even existing water features can be made child-safe with minimum

disruption if they are carefully filled with smooth pebbles (sharp edges may cut through a pond liner). Whatever its style, a water feature will invariably act like a magnet to small children since they, like many adults, are captivated by the sight, the sound, and the feel of running water.

FREESTANDING POND IN A BARREL
If you long for a pond but simply don't have enough space to create one, a half barrel could be the answer. It allows you to have a pond where it would not normally be possible. Half barrels are readily available at many garden centers and, if you buy one which is made from a real wine, whiskey, or beer barrel, it will be well adapted to hold pond water. If you have any doubts about its waterproofness, or want to make a decorative barrel completely watertight, it is advisable to treat it properly first (*see* p.124).

Small ponds in half barrels can be used above ground, maybe even on a sturdy balcony or roof garden, or partly plunged in the ground to imitate a traditional, larger pond. Unlike a conventional pond, a barrel pond can be moved around the garden as your designs develop, or even taken with you when you move!

Planting a barrel pond is relatively easy. There is a good range of smaller and less invasive aquatic plants that are suitable – although these may need regular care to keep them in check. If the barrel is simply placed on the ground, it will be necessary to insulate it during severe winters to protect the plants.

Simple spout
A water spout need not have ornate surroundings; it can act simply as a source of water, protruding from a wall and flowing onto the surface below.

CREATING WATER FEATURES

The allure of water is unmistakable, and for many people, a garden is not complete unless it has a pond. Certainly, adding a water feature allows you to try a whole new type of gardening and a new range of plants, and water is excellent for attracting wildlife. Even if space is at a premium, you will probably be able to make the room for a smaller feature, such as the pond in a half barrel described on this page, or a small fountain or bubble jet,

which will introduce a new dimension to the atmosphere of your garden. If you do have the space for a pond, you will need to decide whether to construct it using a preformed pond liner (shown on these two pages) or a butyl liner (shown on the following two pages). Preformed liners are not as long-lasting or as flexible as those made from butyl, but they do provide the quickest and simplest way to create an attractive pond in your garden.

MAKING A POND IN A HALF BARREL

A miniature pond in a half barrel is simple and quick to establish in a garden of any size. It has the additional advantage that it can be positioned as a focal point when it is looking its best, and then moved to a less prominent position as the leaves of the water plants die down in autumn.

Choose small aquatic plants for a pond in a barrel, and be prepared to trim them back as necessary. By selecting native plants, you will also be able to attract some local wildlife on a small scale. As in larger ponds, you will need to remove blanketweed and algae regularly (*see* "Keeping Plants Healthy," p.130).

YOU WILL NEED

- Half barrel • Scraper
- Wire brush • Sealant
- Paintbrush

Most barrels need to be treated to ensure they are watertight. Check that the sealant is not toxic to fish or plants before applying it to the clean, dry, inner surface of the barrel. Leave the barrel for a day or two, and once the sealant is dry, fill the barrel with water. Allow it to stand for a few hours, then discard the water and refill with a fresh supply before adding plants.

Preparing the barrel
Scrape off all loose, rotten wood and debris using a scraper and a wire brush. Let the wood dry out before applying the sealant liberally to the inside of the barrel with a paintbrush.

SEALING THE HALF BARREL
Coat the inside with sealant, being careful not to leave any gaps.

INSTALLING A FOUNTAIN

A gently trickling fountain brings a pond to life, and its sound is refreshing on a hot summer's day. It also helps to oxygenate the water and improves the environment for fish, although if the fountain is very vigorous, it may prove disturbing rather than beneficial. Installing a fountain, either in a new or existing garden pond, is not difficult. For all but the largest fountain, use a submersible pump; these

are easy to obtain from garden centers or water-garden suppliers. The pump or fountain you choose should be fitted with armored cable – if in doubt always check with the supplier before you buy. When you lay the cable, make the trench as deep as you can to prevent possible damage if the area is forked over for planting. It is essential to use a ground fault circuit interrupter as another safety precaution.

ELECTRICITY IN PONDS
Electricity and any kind of moisture is a lethal combination so, for safety's sake, it is essential that you buy a good quality pump or fountain with waterproof fixtures and armored cable. Follow instructions when installing a feature that uses electricity, or leave it to a professional.

Installing a fountain
Keep the apparatus raised, using bricks if necessary, so that it doesn't get clogged with debris. Hide the cable in a deep trench to the nearest electrical source, concealing it at the edge of the pond using carefully positioned stones or slabs.

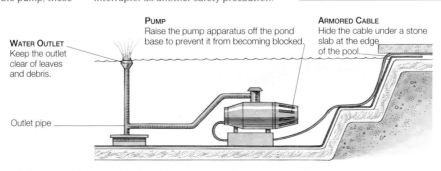

WATER OUTLET
Keep the outlet clear of leaves and debris.

Outlet pipe

PUMP
Raise the pump apparatus off the pond base to prevent it from becoming blocked.

ARMORED CABLE
Hide the cable under a stone slab at the edge of the pool.

INSTALLING A PREFORMED POND

Preformed liners are easy to install, sturdily built, and, if the preparation is done properly, they should last for at least ten years. A pond made in this way may not last as long as a pond made with a butyl liner (see p.126) however, and although preformed liners are available in a good selection of shapes and sizes, it may be hard to achieve the wide range of water depths possible using a flexible liner.

When marking out the site of the pond, use the liner as a template for the outline before excavating the different levels. The hardest and most essential job when installing a preformed pond liner is to make the liner level – if it is at a slant,

all the water will run to one end when you fill the pond. Avoid this by using a level and a board to check as you work that the base and planting shelves are level. You can adjust how the pond sits by adding or removing sand and soil as you bed the liner into the ground. Keep the rim at the same height as the surrounding soil level.

Once installed, your pond is ready for planting. It is a good idea to soften the edges of a new pond with marginal plants to make it look less stark (see pp.128–9 for details on planting water plants).

YOU WILL NEED

- Bricks •Bamboo stakes •String or rope
- Preformed pond
- Spade •Tape measure
- Board •Level
- Sand •Hose

CHOOSING A PREFORMED POND LINER

Preformed liners are commonly made from plastic or fiberglass; the latter is more expensive but should last longer. Choose one with an unobtrusive color and a natural curved outline that blends in with its surroundings. Plenty of planting shelves will allow you to plant marginals as well as deep-water plants.

Planting shelves are wide enough for planting baskets.

A simple shape is easier to install than one with lots of shelves.

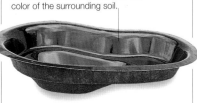

A black liner blends in well with the color of the surrounding soil.

1 Clear and level the site, then mark out the top edge of the liner on the ground. If it is symmetrical, invert the liner. For asymmetrical ponds, position the liner, stabilize it with bricks, then drive stakes into the ground around its edge and mark the outline with string.

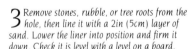

2 Dig out a hole to match the shape of the liner, but 2in (5cm) deeper. Excavate the planting shelves, matching the sides to the slope of the liner, and check the depth using a board and level.

3 Remove stones, rubble, or tree roots from the hole, then line it with a 2in (5cm) layer of sand. Lower the liner into position and firm it down. Check it is level with a level on a board.

4 Fill the pond with water to a depth of about 4in (10cm). Backfill the gap around the edges with soil or sifted sand to a similar depth. Firm the soil or sand. Continue in the same way, adding water to the pond, backfilling around the edges, and tamping down the soil. Check the pond is level as you go. Use sod, mortared stones, or paving to hide the exposed edges of the pond.

MAKING A POND WITH A BUTYL LINER

Using a flexible butyl liner allows you to make a pond of any size and shape. The liner can easily be molded to fit a natural shape, which incorporates a range of planting levels, that suits both your design and the size of your garden. It is particularly suitable for making an informal pond with shallow, sloping sides for attracting wildlife.

PLANNING THE POND

Plan the size and shape of your pond before buying the liner. If you want to include marginals, create shelves 10in (24cm) wide and deep around the edge. For deep-water plants, the central area should be about 20–24in (50–60cm) deep.

Once you know your pond's size and shape, calculate how much liner you will need. Add the maximum width of the pond to twice its depth to find out the width required, and its maximum length plus twice its depth for the length. To allow for the butyl to be buried or covered with paving around the edge, add at least 6–12in (15–30cm) to both the width and the length. For a long-lasting pond,

choose ¼in (7mm) thick butyl since it is hard to puncture and it has a life expectancy of about 40–50 years.

FITTING THE LINER

Mark out the shape of the pond on the ground with rope or string and score the outline on the soil just within the line. Start digging, ensuring that the sides of the pool slope inward at an angle of at least 20° from the vertical – this makes the sides less likely to crumble and easier to cover with a liner. As you dig, check that the edges of the pond are level with a board and level – water will flow out of any dips around the sides. If you want to add stones around the edge, dig out a 2in (5cm) hollow for each stone so that it will fit snugly once the pond is complete.

Before fitting the liner, carefully remove anything sharp, for example roots or stones, then fit a cushioned underliner (such as fiberglass insulation material) – this makes your liner less likely to be punctured. Once the liner is in position and as you fill the pond, add gravel and small stones around the edges to hide

MAKING YOUR LINER EASIER TO HANDLE
Build your pond on a warm day, or keep the liner indoors while you are digging out the shape of the pond. The extra warmth will make the fabric of the liner more flexible and much easier to fit to any planting shelves.

the liner and provide footholds for water creatures. Finally, check that the edges are level before tucking in and concealing the liner with pieces of rock or paving.

1 *Mark out the shape of the pond. Dig out the area, incorporating shelves at different depths for marginals and making the deepest areas 20–24in (50–60cm) deep. Ensure that the pool sides slope inward.*

2 *Check the edges of the hole are level, remove all sharp objects, and line with pool liner or fiberglass insulation. Place the butyl liner loosely over the dug area and press it into position, fitting it into the shelves and over the edges.*

3 *Check the liner is in the correct position, then weigh down the sides with bricks. Fill the pool slowly, gently pulling on the liner to minimize wrinkling. Trim the liner to leave an overlap at the edge of up to 12in (30cm).*

6 *Fill the pond to its final level. Arrange the stones to blend in naturally with the gravel. Once water plants have been added, the liner should no longer be visible.*

4 *Keep the liner anchored in position by covering the edges around the top with a thick layer of soil to within a distance of 6in (15cm) from the pond edge. Firm down the soil well.*

5 *Add stones or rocks to keep the liner securely in place and to disguise the edges. Use mortar if necessary to make the stones stable. Gravel laid from the edge into the water provides access for wildlife.*

MAKING A BOG GARDEN

A bog garden is an area of constantly moist soil in which you can grow bog plants. This can be created as a completely separate area or adjoining a pond. To make a separate bog garden, dig out an area deep and wide enough for several mature plants then line it with punctured butyl liner. Once filled with soil and watered, the area will stay moist and can be planted with bog plants. To make a boggy area around a new pond, dig out a site of varying depths around the edge and line with pond liner before replacing the soil. You can also convert an old pond into a bog garden: drain and fill the pond with soil, then moisten well before planting.

YOU WILL NEED

•Butyl liner •Scissors
•Fork •Spade •Bog
plants •Watering can

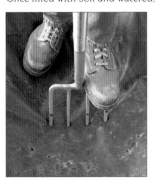

1 Measure a length of butyl liner large enough for your bog garden and cut it to the correct size. Puncture some drainage holes in the liner with a garden fork.

2 Dig out the site of your bog garden, lay the butyl liner in the excavated area, and fill it with soil. Firm down the soil and water thoroughly before planting.

PLANTS FOR A BOG GARDEN

Anemone rivularis ❧
Goat's beard (Aruncus dioicus) ❧
Astilbes (A. chinensis or A. simplicifolia) ❧
Marsh marigold (Caltha palustris) ❧
Joe Pye weed (Eupatorium spp) ❧
Gunnera manicata ❧
Hostas ❧
Japanese iris (Iris ensata) ❧
Siberian iris (Iris sibirica) ❧
Ligularias ❧
Cardinal flower (Lobelia cardinalis) ❧

Water forget-me-not (Myosotis scorpioides) ❧
Royal fern (Osmunda regalis) ❧
Umbrella plant (Peltiphyllum peltatum) ❧
Drumstick primulas (P. denticulata and cvs) ❧
Giant cowslip (Primula florindae) ❧
Candelabra primrose (P. japonica) ❧
Rodgersia aesculifolia ❧
Globeflower (Trollius europaeus) ❧
Cattail (Typha latifolia) ❧

FEATURES TO ATTRACT WILDLIFE

A wildlife pond should be made with plenty of variation in depth so that it can support a wide range of water plants and animals by containing several different habitats. Include as many native plants as you can in the planting design to help attract local wildlife and insects. Plant berrying shrubs around the pond: along with grasses and flowering perennials, these will attract birds, butterflies, and other insects and provide a good source of food for animals in winter.

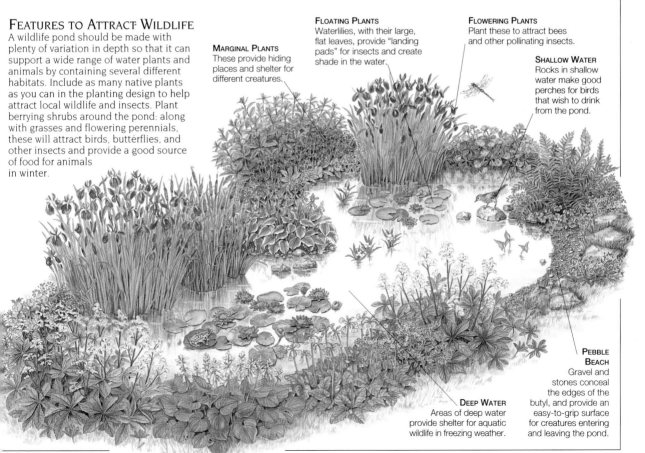

FLOATING PLANTS
Waterlilies, with their large, flat leaves, provide "landing pads" for insects and create shade in the water.

FLOWERING PLANTS
Plant these to attract bees and other pollinating insects.

MARGINAL PLANTS
These provide hiding places and shelter for different creatures.

SHALLOW WATER
Rocks in shallow water make good perches for birds that wish to drink from the pond.

PEBBLE BEACH
Gravel and stones conceal the edges of the butyl, and provide an easy-to-grip surface for creatures entering and leaving the pond.

DEEP WATER
Areas of deep water provide shelter for aquatic wildlife in freezing weather.

PLANTING WATER PLANTS

A pond is a self-contained water garden, and the plants you choose to grow in and around it give the pond its individual character. Water (or aquatic) plants are often classified by the depth of water they need to flourish. Deep-water plants are planted deeply with their leaves floating on the surface. Marginal plants need to be grown in shallow water, so they are often planted around the edges of ponds. Floating plants float on the surface of the water and do not need to be rooted in soil. To maintain oxygen levels and also help to keep algae at bay, oxygenators are essential; they also provide an instant source of shade in a new pond. Some oxygenators float; others are planted in containers. Bog and moisture-loving plants thrive in constantly wet soil, and a few prefer waterlogged conditions; these plants are ideal for planting in moist soil around the edge of a pond.

PLANNING YOUR PLANTING

To create an interesting, varied pond, choose plants for all areas including any shelves. This enables you to select a range of deep-water and marginal plants as well as oxygenators, surface floaters, and even some bog plants if you have a waterlogged area at the edge of your pond. If the pond does not have planting shelves, you can still include a range of plants suited to different depths and position them in containers standing on bricks; this enables you to raise the plants to the level of water they need. Include a good selection of plant shapes, sizes, and textures, and remember that striking or lush foliage often plays as important a role as flowers. If you want to create a wildlife pond, the more native water plants used, the better – but it is worth bearing in mind that many of these can soon become invasive.

SOIL FOR WATER PLANTS

Specially formulated aquatic soil mix should be used for planting aquatics and is available from water plant suppliers. It retains its texture and structure well under water and does not contain many nutrients, since these are easily leached out into the water.

Garden soil, particularly if it is heavy, may be suitable for some water plants but is generally best avoided; peat, sand, leaf mold, and compost should not be used. Some plants, notably waterlilies, need a fairly fertile soil; for these, a slow-release fertilizer, preferably with a high phosphate level, should be added to the soil before you start planting.

STORING WATER PLANTS

If you are unable to plant aquatics immediately, store them in the bottom of a refrigerator, or clean them under running water and submerge in buckets of water. Try to store them for only a few days or they will start to deteriorate.

CHOOSING CONTAINERS

Containers for pond planting come in a range of sizes, shapes, and depths. Several small plants can be planted together in one large container. Water-plant containers are usually made from strong plastic mesh; because the mesh is open, it prevents the soil in the containers from stagnating.

A curved shape is useful for planting near irregular edges.

A large, round pot will hold a vigorous plant.

A small container is ideal for young plants.

Planting depths

Nursery tags on all water plants should give the preferred planting depth – always follow these instructions. Remember that not all marginals need to be planted in the same depth of water, and often closely related plants have differing needs. Choose the recommended soil mix, too; the wrong growing medium can kill a water plant.

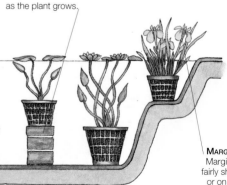

ADJUSTING THE DEPTH
Precise planting depths can be achieved by standing containers on bricks. Bricks can be removed to lower the container as the plant grows.

SURFACE FLOATERS
Floating plants help to keep down levels of algae by creating shade.

BOG PLANTS
Moisture-loving plants thrive in the constantly wet, but not submerged, soil around the extreme edges of a pond.

DEEP-WATER PLANTS
Plants requiring deep water can be placed on the floor of the pond.

MARGINAL PLANTS
Marginals grow in fairly shallow water or on a shelf near the surface.

PLANTING DEEP-WATER AND MARGINAL PLANTS

When planting a water plant, minimize the amount of stress to the plant by keeping it out of direct sunlight, especially when its roots are exposed – if possible, handle it in a shady spot. Remove dead or badly damaged foliage – if left in place these leaves may encourage rot and dieback. Invasive types of duckweed may be lurking among the roots or crown of a plant, so rinse your new plants carefully under a tap before starting to plant.

Most deep-water and marginal plants should be planted in soil-filled water-plant containers to prevent vigorous specimens from swamping neighboring plants. When deep-water plants are still quite small, place them on bricks that raise them so that their foliage floats on the surface; as they increase in size, they can be lowered to the correct depth. Marginals should be placed at the recommended depth, usually allowing 3–6in (8–15cm) of water above their crowns. Once filled, the

container often weighs too much to be safely lowered into the pond by just one person. Make sure you have someone else to help you, and if this means delay, cover the watered containers with wet burlap or wet newspaper until you are ready.

Plants grown in the wet or boggy areas around the pond are planted as described for perennials (*see* p.44).

1 *Choose a container large enough to retain the root system of a vigorous plant once it has grown to full size. Unless the mesh of the container is very small, line it with burlap.*

2 *Fill the container with moist aquatic or other suitable soil to a depth of 2in (5cm). Place the plant in the center. Add more soil, firming it to within 1in (2.5cm) of the rim.*

ANCHORING PLANTS

If young water plants are too light to stay where they are planted, put some large stones or a layer of grit on the surface of the soil mix to help weigh down individual containers.

3 *Top-dress with a layer of gravel to just beneath the rim. This weighs down the container and prevents soil from floating away into the water.*

4 *Trim off the excess burlap and attach string handles to opposite sides of the container's rim; use these to lower the container into position.*

WATER PLANTS

DEEP-WATER PLANTS
Cape pondweed (*Aponogeton distachyos*) ✿
Yellow pond lily (*Nuphar advena*) ✿
Brandy bottle (*Nuphar lutea*) ✿
Waterlilies (*Nymphaea*) ✿ [some ❋]
Floating heart (*Nymphoides indica*) ✿❋
Fringed waterlily (*Nymphoides peltata*) ✿ ❋

MARGINAL PLANTS
Sweet flag (*Acorus calamus*) ✿
Flowering rush (*Butomus umbellatus*) ✿
Bog arum (*Calla palustris*) ✿
Glyceria maxima 'Variegata' ✿
Irises (many, incl. *I. versicolor*) ✿
Juncus effusus ✿
Lysichitons (incl. *L. americanus* and *L. camtschatcensis*) ✿
Mimulus guttatus ✿
Pickerel weed (*Pontederia cordata*) ✿
Ranunculus lingua 'Grandiflora' ✿

OXYGENATORS
Water starworts (*Callitriche*) ✿
Ceratophyllums ✿
Canadian pondweed (*Elodea canadensis*) ✿
Water moss (*Fontinalis antipyretica*) ✿
Water violet (*Hottonia palustris*) ✿
Lagarosiphon major ✿ ❋
Pondweeds (*Potamogeton*) ✿
Water crowfoot (*Ranunculus aquatilis*) ✿

SURFACE FLOATERS
Water hyacinth (*Eichhornia crassipes*) ✿ ❋
Frogbit (*Hydrocharis morsus-ranae*) ✿
Duckweeds (*Lemna*) ✿
Water soldier (*Stratiotes aloides*) ✿

OXYGENATORS AND SURFACE FLOATERS

Most pond plants hold their foliage above water, so the oxygen they release is lost into the atmosphere. Oxygenators release their oxygen into the water. They are vital since, without them, a pond will soon turn into a green, opaque mass of algae, particularly during warm weather. Some oxygenators are planted as bunches of unrooted cuttings tied together: prepare a small container as for deep-water and marginal plants (*see* above), then insert several bunches of cuttings. Others are simply left to float on the surface.

Floaters are placed on the surface of the pond where they provide shade and discourage algal buildup. If they grow too rapidly, the excess shading may put oxygenators under stress, so thin them out when necessary.

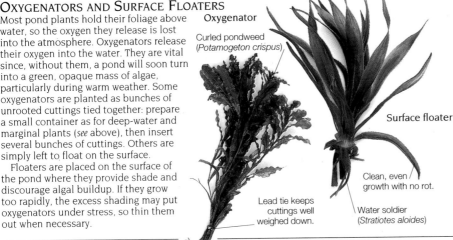

Oxygenator

Curled pondweed (*Potamogeton crispus*)

Surface floater

Clean, even growth with no rot.

Lead tie keeps cuttings well weighed down.

Water soldier (*Stratiotes aloides*)

LOOKING AFTER YOUR POND

A well-sited and well-planned pond stocked with a carefully maintained balance of water plants and perhaps some fish should not be difficult to look after. There are, however, a number of small jobs that you will need to do from time to time. To keep the levels of oxygen in the water correct and to ensure free growth of the pond plants and healthy fish, you will need to remove algae and other weeds that may clog the surface of the water during the summer and divide any overgrown or overvigorous plants. Most of the routine maintenance, however, is done just once a year, including clearing of foliage that dies back naturally in the autumn, netting the pond to prevent leaves from falling into it from nearby trees, and taking action to prevent the pond from freezing up completely during the winter months. Occasionally you may need to carry out repairs if the pond leaks.

KEEPING PLANTS HEALTHY
Many pond plants are fairly vigorous and grow rapidly once established. Although this means that you quickly achieve a lush covering of vegetation, individual plants may soon outgrow their surroundings.

DIVIDING WATER PLANTS
Overgrown water plants in containers should be divided and repotted or replanted toward the end of spring or in early autumn. Lift and inspect the root ball of each plant. If it has become potbound, remove it from its container and divide by hand or using two hand forks back to back. If the plant has developed a very tight or congested root ball, you will need to use a spade or knife. Repot each clump into a separate container and replant. For more details, *see "Dividing Perennials," p.50.*

REMOVING LEAVES
Occasionally, leaves of pond plants become yellowed or may be damaged by weather conditions or pests. Toward the end of the summer and into autumn many start to die back naturally, too. Dead or deteriorating leaves should be removed promptly before they fall off since they will lower the oxygen content of the water and may also harbor diseases.

OXYGENATORS AND ALGAE
If submerged oxygenators become too vigorous, these may clog up the pond, restricting the movement of fish and the growth of other plants. Duckweed and algae should also be removed regularly.

Maintaining your pond
Keep your pond clear of weeds and dead leaves. Water plants that are large and overcrowded may need dividing. If the water level has dropped, check the pond for leaks.

Excessive weeds

Tear in butyl liner

Weeds between crevices

Yellowing water plants

THINNING WATER PLANTS
However large or small your pool, always thin plants gradually over a period of several weeks – a sudden, drastic change in the quantity of oxygenators or other plants may lead to algae spreading rapidly. Pull pieces of the plant out a few handfuls at a time, or, alternatively, lift each plant completely and trim back the stems by 30–50 percent.

Cutting off yellow leaves
Grasp the plant firmly and use a sharp knife to remove any yellowed or dead leaves, cutting back to healthy, green stems. If yellowing is excessive for the time of year, lift the entire plant to see if there is anything obviously causing the problem.

Removing blanketweed
Algae that form dense mats of growth are usually referred to as blanketweed and should be regularly removed. The easiest way to do this is with a stick. A gentle turning motion should pull out the blanketweed in large quantities.

Removing duckweed
Hold a board vertically and draw it across the surface of the water to skim off excess duckweed. Dispose of the weed with care since it spreads easily – either dig it into a trench, add it to the compost pile, or put it in the garbage.

MENDING POND LINERS

Ponds built using a butyl or other flexible liner may develop a leak – the edge of the liner may have slipped below the original water level or the liner may have been punctured. Drain the pond by bailing it out or using a siphon or electric pump. Lift and store pond plants and any fish temporarily in buckets of pond water. The pond can be refilled after about one hour once it has been securely mended.

Preformed pools may crack, especially if they were badly installed. They are best mended using fiberglass repair compound, but, before setting to work, try to find out

YOU WILL NEED

- Soft cloth • Denatured alcohol • Water-resistant, double-sided tape
- Butyl liner patch

why the pond cracked in the first place – poorly compacted soil around the sides and an inadequately firmed and leveled base are usually the culprits. Mend the crack carefully and ensure the compound is completely hard and dry before refilling.

1 Drain the pond. Clean the damaged area with a soft cloth and denatured alcohol, and allow it to dry completely.

2 Place a length of double-sided, water-resistant tape over the puncture and remove its upper covering.

3 Cut a piece of liner to fit accurately over the tape. Press it down firmly, carefully smoothing out any air bubbles.

MENDING A CONCRETE POND

Repairing a concrete pool is a time-consuming job, but it needs to be done properly since even the tiniest hairline crack may allow a lot of water to escape. It is often difficult to take any effective preventative measures, since ice and subsidence are the most common causes of cracks in concrete ponds.

Drain the pond as above. Examine it carefully for cracks and chipping. You must ensure that all possible sources of leaks are properly repaired and allowed to dry completely before you refill the pond with

YOU WILL NEED

- Chisel • Club hammer
- Wire brush • Trowel
- Mortar • Pool sealant
- Paintbrush

water. Remember that mortar contains toxins that must not be allowed to leach out into pond water, so always cover mortar with a good coat of pool sealant to keep it waterproof.

1 Use a chisel and club hammer to enlarge fine cracks, working along their entire length to create an even crack that will be easier to fill. Clean out loose concrete and dust with a wire brush.

2 Use a builder's trowel to fill in the crack either with mortar or with a commercial pond sealing mixture. Press it firmly into the crack and smooth the surface.

3 When the mortar or sealing mixture is completely dry, brush over the entire filled area with a coat of pool sealant to prevent toxins from leaching out and contaminating the water.

AUTUMN AND WINTER CARE

Throughout autumn and winter, your most important job is to prevent leaves from building up in the pond since they give off noxious gases such as methane that reduce the oxygen levels and harm fish.

AUTUMN MAINTENANCE

Many pond plants die back naturally at this time of year – trim them back so that the dying leaves do not fall into the water and rot. Once this is done, cover the pond with netting to stop leaves from falling in. Black netting is almost invisible, so it will not spoil your pond's appearance.

Netting to catch leaves
From the start of autumn, lay fine mesh plastic netting over the surface of the pond, holding the edges down with bricks, large stones, or pegs and string. From time to time, lift off the netting to clear away the leaves, and remove it completely when all the leaves have fallen.

WINTER MAINTENANCE

Ice over the pond traps gases given off by decaying organic debris, killing fish and other pond animals. Ice can also exert pressure on the sides, which may cause cracking. Try to prevent the water from freezing over (see below), but if it does, melt a hole by standing a pan of hot water on the ice. Never smash the ice if the pond contains fish since this may kill them.

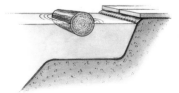

Preventing ice damage
A log or plastic ball left to float on the surface of the pool will slow down the rate at which the whole pond freezes over and, as the ice forms and expands, can absorb some of the pressure, preventing the pool sides from being damaged.

·10·
THE EDIBLE GARDEN

*The flavor of home-grown fruit and vegetables, picked fresh
from the garden, is hard to beat. Whether you have the space
for a separate kitchen garden, or room for just a few choice
crops in containers on the terrace, this chapter will introduce
you to the delights of growing your own.*

A FEAST FOR THE EYE

Even the tiniest garden or backyard is large enough to contain some edible plants. Having your own supply of home-grown fruit, vegetables, or herbs is tremendously satisfying and usually works out cheaper than store-bought alternatives. In addition, you can choose to grow only your favorite varieties and, since minimal time elapses between picking and eating, you will enjoy the fruits of your labor at their tastiest and most nutritious. For advice on how to organize a separate area for edible plants, *see* "Setting Aside a Plot," pp.134–5.

INCORPORATING EDIBLE PLANTS IN THE BORDER

If space is at a premium, a few well-chosen edible plants can always be mixed in among the flower borders or in containers, where their decorative features will complement those of other plants.

It's not just what you grow, but how you grow it that makes the difference. Thyme can make a fragrant, attractive, and useful border edging. Fan-trained fruit takes up little space, can be used as a screen, and is more interesting to look at than when grown in bush- or tree-form. Climbing vegetables can be trained over arches or pergolas to create an unusual feature.

A PLACE FOR HERBS

Herbs often have pretty flowers as well as fragrant foliage – rosemary, thyme, and chives, in particular, would deserve a place in the border even if they were not so useful in the kitchen. It is worth seeking out the many golden, gray, and variegated forms of common herbs, such as sage, to increase the range of color and texture.

VEGETABLES AS DECORATION

As a glance through the seed catalogs will confirm, many vegetable cultivars are in fact highly ornamental. Indeed, the choice is so wide that it is possible to choose cultivars to suit not just your taste buds but also your border designs.

Most lettuces look at home in a border, but for an even more pleasing effect choose salad crops with finely divided or frilled foliage such as endive, or the deep purple-red radicchio. Salad vegetables are fast-growing and can be slipped in among larger plants in the border, or used as compact edging beside a path or lawn.

The common cultivars of runner bean have bright red flowers and produce a mass of foliage, either grown up nets to form screens or freestanding on wigwams. Combine these with white-flowered bean cultivars and perhaps a few sweet peas for extra color with the bonus of scent.

Use ripening tomatoes to add a splash of intense color – particularly cherry tomatoes with large clusters of fruits. If

Restrained color
Here, in a planting suitable for warm climates, a clump of vivid yellow kniphofia stands out against the mound of a citrus bush. This combination relies on a striking contrast in form, coupled with a limited color range, for its impact.

space is limited, choose cultivars bred for use in containers so you can be confident that they won't sprawl too much.

Zucchini, with their large, interestingly shaped leaves, make a striking border feature and look even better when their golden-yellow flowers and rounded, striped fruits appear. Vivid crimson chard stems and the purple foliage of some cultivars of Brussels sprouts also bring a touch of the exotic to borders and make impressive, architectural plants.

MAKING A FEATURE OF FRUIT

There is no disputing that some fruit trees are as good to look at as their fruits are to eat – apples, pears, cherries, and plums look stunning in bloom, and their ripening fruits are equally attractive. Use fruit trees at the back of a wide border, to mark a boundary, or as specimen trees in lawns. Well-trained bush and cane fruits look equally good in borders or as boundaries.

Strawberry plants are pretty either in open ground or tumbling out of containers, and compact varieties make a delicate border edging. Grapevines can be trained over a sunny wall where they quickly impart an air of grandeur, with the bonus of rich, colorful autumn foliage as you harvest luscious bunches of fruit.

An abundance of forms
This typical cottage-garden planting crams together vivid calendulas and nasturtiums, fluffy dill heads, and the purple drumsticks of allium.

SETTING ASIDE A PLOT

If you want to grow a wide range of fruit, vegetables, and herbs, the sensible option is to set aside a separate area for their cultivation. The amount of space you decide to devote to crops will depend partly on how self-sufficient you hope to be, and partly on how much land you have to spare. Of course, there is nothing to stop you from turning the whole of your garden into one large, highly productive plot, packed to bursting with fruit, herbs, and vegetables (see also "A Productive Garden," p.15), but most of us prefer to leave a reasonable amount of space for ornamentals and in which to relax, too.

If you select cultivars carefully, choosing those that crop well but take up relatively little space, and ensuring that you grow only a few plants of each, it is surprising how productive a small area can be. Even if your gardening endeavors are restricted to a balcony or backyard, you will still be able to produce a good selection of edible plants in containers.

SITE AND ACCESS

When choosing a site, you need to find an area where the plants will grow well and be convenient to tend and harvest. Herbs, in particular, should be grown very close to the house so that you don't need to traipse to the end of the garden in the dark if you suddenly decide to use fresh herbs in a supper dish.

A sheltered and fairly sunny, warm spot is best since most fruit, vegetables, and herbs need a great deal of sunlight to grow well and develop a good flavor. If you have a partially shaded wall and border, sweet or sour cherries can be trained to grow up the wall, and lettuces or cabbages planted in well-prepared soil in the border below.

Ornamental divider
Espalier-grown fruit trees are ideal for smaller gardens, producing masses of fruit in a very limited space. In addition to making an attractive, ornamental feature, the splayed espalier form allows air to circulate freely around the developing fruits, helping to keep them healthy.

Square-bed system
Not only does this neat patchwork of crops look extremely attractive, it also makes the plants very easy to tend. The crops in this small space include onions, lettuces, carrots, and parsley. A network of paths between the beds facilitates access from every side and prevents the soil from being compacted by trampling feet.

PLANNING THE PLOT

If you have space, it helps to group plants with similar needs close together – soft fruit bushes, for example, can be protected with netting much more easily if they are all in one place. Many vegetables also benefit from being grown in "family" groups, with beans and peas in one bed, brassicas (including cabbages, cauliflowers, and broccoli) in another, and root crops in a third. This makes it easier to provide them with the growing conditions they need, and establishes the basis for a simple crop rotation – in which the plot is divided into four, and each

family is grown on a different quarter every year in rotation, leaving one quarter at a time free to rest for a season. The main benefit of crop rotation is that it helps prevent the buildup of pests or diseases in a particular area.

Always take into account the effect individual plants will have on each other when deciding how to plant up your plot – if a part of the plot is slightly shady, make sure you give the sunniest position to plants such as tomatoes that really need it. When planting tall crops, such as pole lima beans, sweet corn, or soft fruit bushes, think carefully about where and how much shade they will cast when mature, and avoid growing sun-loving varieties in this area.

CHOOSING FRUIT

Clearly, the most important criterion is the taste of the fruits. There are a large number of delicious varieties which are never seen in stores. Also consider the cropping times of your preferred varieties, and choose several with staggered harvest times to extend the season and avoid short-term gluts.

Lack of space need not be too much of a problem, since many fruit trees are now available on dwarfing rootstocks, which grow very slowly and prevent the tree as a whole from becoming too large. These are ideal for small gardens, but they also allow a good selection of trees to be grown in larger gardens. In addition, many other tree fruits, as well as grapevines, can be kept in check by regular pruning, or trained

o suit the space available, and therefore are suitable for most gardens, regardless of size. The majority of soft fruits, apart from particularly vigorous cultivars of blackberries and hybrid berries, are naturally fairly compact and so make a good choice in a smaller garden.

CHOOSING VEGETABLES AND HERBS

The secret of choosing vegetables is to have a regular look through the seed catalogs, experimenting to find the cultivars that are best suited to your site and tastebuds. New ones are constantly being developed, and older ones reintroduced, so do scan the catalogs carefully every season. If you haven't grown vegetables before, it is a good idea to start with crops that are easy to grow, and then experiment with some of the trickier ones later on.

If you have nowhere to raise young seedlings, select cultivars that can be sown directly into the ground where the crop is to mature – for example lettuce or bush beans. Wherever possible, choose ones with staggered harvest times to ensure you have plants cropping over the longest possible period of time. Where space is at a premium, experiment with techniques that enable you to maximize

Herb garden

Perhaps the most practical – and certainly one of the prettiest – ways to grow herbs is in a parterre. The formal layout shows off a selection of herbs to advantage and keeps the more invasive ones under control. Grown in one place, a range of herbs can be harvested easily.

the number of vegetables that can be grown in a small area (*see* "Making the Most of Your Space," p.137).

You are unlikely to avoid problems with pests and diseases completely but, to minimize their effects, select resistant cultivars. These vary in availability from year to year, so check seed catalogs and racks thoroughly to see which are currently available. Look out for compact cultivars too, since these will be especially suitable for growing in a smaller garden. To add interest, select types with attractive

features – hyacinth and some bush beans produce purple beans instead of the more usual green ones, and salad vegetables are available with a huge variety of leaf color and shape, including red- and frilly-leaved forms.

There are a few basic herbs that most kitchen gardeners would not be without. Chives, rosemary, sage, marjoram, parsley, and mint are all herb garden staples – although mint has such an invasive habit that it is often grown in a container where it can be kept under control. Beyond this, the selection will be determined by your tastes and cooking habits. Many more exotic herbs, such as coriander and fennel, will grow well in a sunny, sheltered spot, giving you a fresh, tasty, summer-long supply for a fraction of store prices.

GROWING EDIBLE PLANTS IN CONTAINERS

Windowboxes, pots, grow bags, and even hanging baskets can all be used to raise vegetables and herbs as well as some fruits. Growing edible plants in this way allows you to keep them conveniently close to the house, and you could even have a mini-kitchen garden on a balcony or windowsill. All container-grown crops should be kept under an extremely close watch, and they need regular feeding and watering if they are to thrive.

Herbs can be quite productive in pots or even a hanging basket, especially if you concentrate on the smaller ones such as chives, thyme, parsley, and savory. With their fragrant foliage, pots of herbs also make an attractive cluster by the back door.

Some small cultivars of tomato, both upright and trailing, have been developed for containers and small spaces. Beans, lettuces, peppers, and potatoes all respond surprisingly well to the confines of a container, and zucchini and carrots will also crop well provided they are grown in a deep container which gives them plenty of soil mix around their roots.

Container-grown fruits, with the exception of strawberries, need plenty of root space, so large containers are essential if these plants are to thrive.

Picture of health

Well-tended, healthy vegetables are a lovely sight. To produce crops of this quality, the soil must be rich and fertile, and the plants given regular attention. Close spacing gives maximum produce from minimum space, but the site must be kept weed free and well fed and watered, or the competition could prove too much.

GROWING VEGETABLES

Even if your garden is tiny, you can still find room for some vegetables. The larger the space you set aside, the greater the selection you can raise, but even if you cannot devote a whole bed to vegetables, you can grow a few of your favorites among the flowers in an ornamental border. There are several ways of producing the maximum crop of vegetables from a small space – such as planting two sorts together that ripen at different times, or sowing leafy vegetables close together and harvesting them when they are young and still small. You can even grow some in containers – ideal if you have only a balcony, roof garden, or patio. Vegetables grow well on most soils, but will produce higher yields if the soil is improved by digging, manuring, and fertilizing. A sunny, sheltered site will increase the size and quality of the crop. So long as your vegetables have enough space and are well watered and fed, you can expect delicious, fresh produce from your garden. For how to grow specific vegetables, *see* "Vegetables Crop by Crop," pp.138–41.

SOWING AND EARLY CARE

Check the seed packet for the best time to sow, the recommended method and depth of sowing, and suggested site. The packet should also mention how long it will take for the seeds to germinate and for the vegetables to be ready to harvest, so retain seed packets for future reference.

SOWING METHODS

Seeds can be sown in three ways – directly where they are to mature, into a seedbed, or into pots or trays. Sowing directly into the ground where the crop will mature is generally the simplest option. Add manure and fertilizer to the soil, then rake to remove all lumps before sowing. If sowing in dry soil, water the drill, sow, and cover the seeds with the soil, which acts as a mulch, keeping the moisture where the seeds need it. If the soil is very wet, wait for a few days or cover the area with a cloche or clear plastic until it dries out slightly. To assist drainage, sprinkle sand

in the base of the drill before sowing. If the ground where the vegetables are to mature is not clear, sow in a seedbed – a spare area of prepared ground – and transplant the seedlings to the newly cleared area. Sowing into pots or trays is useful for half-hardy vegetables since the seedlings can be raised in a protected environment until it is warm enough to plant them out (*see* "Sowing in a Tray," p.53).

After sowing, some vegetables can be left to mature, but most need to be thinned or transplanted elsewhere.

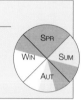

YOU WILL NEED

- Manure •Fertilizer •Rake
- Watering can •Stakes
- String •Board •Hoe
- Seeds •Hand fork
- Plastic bag

(SPR / SUM / AUT / WIN)

Sowing in a drill
Use two stakes and a piece of string to mark the position of the drill. Stand on a board to avoid compacting the soil, and draw the point of the hoe along the string. Sow the seeds as thinly as possible, cover with soil, firm down, and water.

Thinning
When the seedlings are large enough to handle, thin them out, leaving twice as many as you need. Two or three weeks later, thin them again to the optimum spacing. Remove the weakest seedlings without disturbing the roots of the remaining ones: either use a hand fork carefully or pinch off the young seedlings at ground level. Water well.

Transplanting
Crops grown away from the vegetable plot need to be transplanted into their final positions when they are still young. Use a hand fork to ease out the young plants, then place them in a plastic bag so they do not lose moisture. Transplant immediately into moist, weed-free soil. After transplanting, water gently to settle the soil around the roots.

Staking
A few vegetables, including some tomatoes, peppers, and eggplant, need staking as they develop to keep them stable and to allow enough light and air to reach the crop. Push in a stake beside each plant when it is young, taking care not to damage the roots. Tie in the stem at regular intervals as the plant grows.

MAKING THE MOST OF YOUR SPACE

By a careful choice of cultivars, good timing, and imaginative sowing combinations you can get the maximum return from the smallest plot. Closer-than-recommended spacing often works well, provided watering and feeding are regular.

To save space, sow two different crops in a single drill – this is known as intersowing (*see* right). Sow a slow-growing crop, such as carrots or parsnips, at well-spaced intervals, and a fast-growing crop, such as lettuces or radishes, in between. The rapid-maturing crop will be ready for harvesting before the slower one needs the space. On a larger scale, fast-growing vegetables can be sown under or around tall, slow-growing vegetables – this is known as intercropping. Make spacings between the rows larger than normal, so neither crop is cramped. Green beans, zucchini, and pumpkins crop well under sweet corn.

Many salad crops can be sown densely and harvested as seedlings (*see* below). The plants will usually sprout again for a second or third crop. This method, known as cut-and-come-again, suits some lettuces, spinach, and endive.

1 *Prepare a drill, then sow 3 or 4 parsnip seeds every 4in (10cm). Sow radish seeds between the parsnips about 1in (2.5cm) apart. Cover the seeds, firm down gently, and water in well.*

2 *Harvest the radishes after about a month. Pull them up carefully so that the roots of the parsnips are undisturbed, then water the drill well. The parsnips should now have room to mature fully.*

Harvesting cut-and-come-again crops

Use a sharp knife or pair of scissors to cut the foliage just above the lowest leaves, leaving about 1in (2.5cm) of stem to resprout. Cut-and-come-again crops are usually harvested when they reach a height of about 2–6in (5–15cm), depending on the crop grown.

LOOKING AFTER YOUR VEGETABLES

All vegetables grow better and crop more heavily if they are well looked after. Keep the weeds down from seed sowing through to harvesting because they will compete with the plants for water, nutrients, and light. Hand weed around seedlings; once the vegetables are larger, remove weeds with a hoe. Early evening is the best time to water to minimize evaporation – though if a plant is wilting, water it at once. Irregular watering is a common cause of crop failures. Most vegetable crops need feeding during the growing season. For specific requirements, *see* "Vegetables Crop by Crop," pp.138–41. Certain vegetables, such as beans, zucchini, and peppers, will produce a bigger crop if they are harvested regularly.

PROTECTING AGAINST COLD
Extend the growing season by protecting against cool temperatures and chilling or drying winds. A cover raises the soil temperature, enables young plants to be planted early on in the season, and allows crops to ripen at the end of the season. It also protects against pests. Adjust or remove covers from time to time for extra ventilation.

GROWING VEGETABLES IN CONTAINERS

Many vegetables can be grown in containers, making an attractive and productive display for balconies, roof gardens, and patios. Shallow-rooting vegetables, such as lettuces, can even be grown in a windowbox, but others need a deeper pot or a grow bag to give them more space for their larger roots. Tomatoes, cucumbers, and peppers are all easily raised in grow bags and need slightly less watering than they would in a pot.

Container-grown vegetables often need more careful attention to ensure temperatures and light levels are suitable, especially in sunny, sheltered sites. They will also need to be fed and watered more frequently to meet their needs.

Tomatoes in a grow bag
Grow bags can be used either in or outside the greenhouse. Because little of the soil is exposed, water is better retained around the roots.

Bottle-base cloche
For seedlings and small plants, a clear plastic bottle, with the top removed, makes a good mini-cloche.

Low polytunnel
Insert wire hoops at 1ft (30cm) intervals with a stake at each end. Lay clear plastic over the hoops and tie to the stakes. Stretch string over the top of each hoop and tie at the base.

Perforated films and fleeces
Lay these loosely over the crop to protect it from cold and pests. Weigh down or tuck in the edges.

VEGETABLES CROP BY CROP

Once you have decided which vegetables to grow in the coming season, you will need to check that you are able to supply each with the conditions it requires. The chart on the next four pages gives you general guidelines about what each vegetable needs, concentrating on crops that do not take up too much space and should produce a good yield without too much work on your part. To ensure a healthy crop, provide the right conditions for germination and maintain the plants carefully — especially by watering, feeding, and protecting them as they need it. Use the chart to choose vegetables that crop in succession, providing a supply of fresh produce over a longer period and avoiding a glut.

CROP	EASE OF GROWING	SITE AND SOIL	FROST PROTECTION NEEDED	SOWING NEEDS: WHERE, WHEN, TEMPERATURE NEEDED	HOW TO SOW	SPEED OF GERMINATION	TRANSPLANTING & THINNING
SUMMER LETTUCES	☆ ☆☆	☀ ▢ ◐	early to midspring until last frost	Spring; late summer 50–68°F (10–20°C)	thinly in rows 12in (30cm) apart; thinly	▲	♛♛ ♛♛
WINTER LETTUCES	☆☆	☀ ▢ ◐	late autumn to winter	Late summer to midautumn 50–60°F (10–15°C)	thinly in rows 12in (30cm) apart	▲	♛♛ ♛♛
CHARD	☆ ☆☆	☀ ☀ pH ▢	–	Spring; mid- to late summer 61–4°F (16–18°C)	thinly in rows 12in (30cm) apart	▲▲	♛♛ ♛♛
BROCCOLI	☆	☀ pH ▢ ◐	–	Spring to early summer 50–60°F (10–15°C)	thinly in rows 2ft (60cm) apart	▲	♛♛ ♛♛
ZUCCHINI	☆ ☆☆	☀ pH ▢ ◐	for early sowings	Late spring to early summer 65–70°F (18–21°C)	thinly 2–3 seeds per pot	▲	♛♛ ♛♛
PUMPKINS/WINTER SQUASH	☆☆	☀ ◐	until no risk of frost	Late spring 65–70°F (18–21°C)	thinly 2–3 seeds per pot	▲	♛♛ ♛♛
CUCUMBERS	☆☆	☀ ▢ ◐	until no risk of frost	Late spring 65–70°F (18–21°C)	18–30in (45–75cm) apart in twos	▲	♛♛
SWEET CORN	☆☆	☀ ▢ ◐	until no risk of frost	Spring 65–70°F (18–21°C)	2in (5cm) apart	▲▲	♛♛

KEY TO SYMBOLS

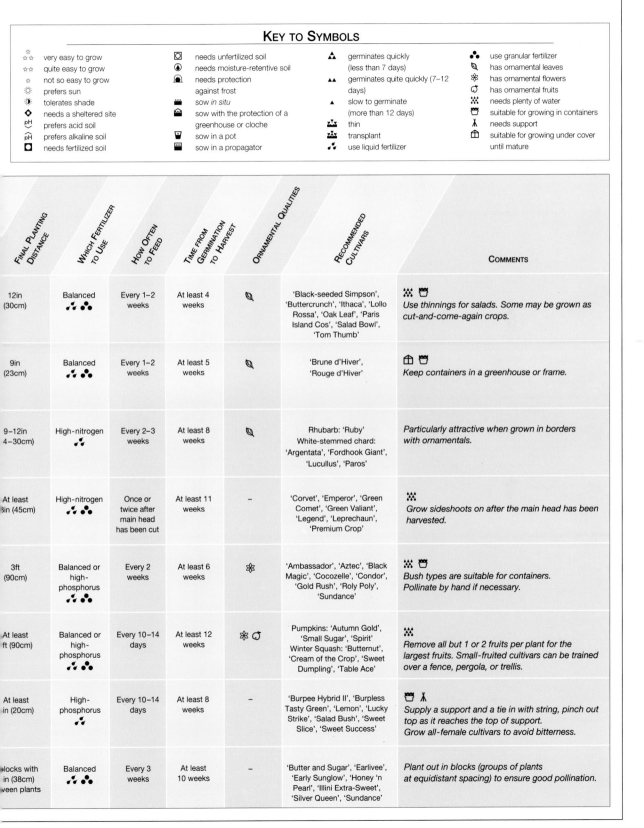

☆☆☆	very easy to grow	
☆☆	quite easy to grow	
☆	not so easy to grow	
☼	prefers sun	
☼	tolerates shade	
◇	needs a sheltered site	
pH	prefers acid soil	
pH	prefers alkaline soil	
▢	needs fertilized soil	

▢	needs unfertilized soil
◉	needs moisture-retentive soil
⌂	needs protection against frost
▤	sow *in situ*
▥	sow with the protection of a greenhouse or cloche
▯	sow in a pot
▦	sow in a propagator

▲	germinates quickly (less than 7 days)
▲▲	germinates quite quickly (7–12 days)
▲	slow to germinate (more than 12 days)
⣿	thin
⣿	transplant
⦂	use liquid fertilizer

•	use granular fertilizer
✎	has ornamental leaves
✳	has ornamental flowers
⭕	has ornamental fruits
⣿	needs plenty of water
▭	suitable for growing in containers
人	needs support
⊞	suitable for growing under cover until mature

Final Planting Distance	Which Fertilizer to Use	How Often to Feed	Time from Germination to Harvest	Ornamental Qualities	Recommended Cultivars	Comments
12in (30cm)	Balanced ⦂ •	Every 1–2 weeks	At least 4 weeks	✎	'Black-seeded Simpson', 'Buttercrunch', 'Ithaca', 'Lollo Rossa', 'Oak Leaf', 'Paris Island Cos', 'Salad Bowl', 'Tom Thumb'	⣿ ▭ *Use thinnings for salads. Some may be grown as cut-and-come-again crops.*
9in (23cm)	Balanced ⦂ •	Every 1–2 weeks	At least 5 weeks	✎	'Brune d'Hiver', 'Rouge d'Hiver'	⊞ ▭ *Keep containers in a greenhouse or frame.*
9–12in (4–30cm)	High-nitrogen ⦂	Every 2–3 weeks	At least 8 weeks	✎	Rhubarb: 'Ruby' White-stemmed chard: 'Argentata', 'Fordhook Giant', 'Lucullus', 'Paros'	*Particularly attractive when grown in borders with ornamentals.*
At least 18in (45cm)	High-nitrogen ⦂ •	Once or twice after main head has been cut	At least 11 weeks	–	'Corvet', 'Emperor', 'Green Comet', 'Green Valiant', 'Legend', 'Leprechaun', 'Premium Crop'	⣿ *Grow sideshoots on after the main head has been harvested.*
3ft (90cm)	Balanced or high-phosphorus ⦂ •	Every 2 weeks	At least 6 weeks	✳	'Ambassador', 'Aztec', 'Black Magic', 'Cocozelle', 'Condor', 'Gold Rush', 'Roly Poly', 'Sundance'	⣿ ▭ *Bush types are suitable for containers. Pollinate by hand if necessary.*
At least 3ft (90cm)	Balanced or high-phosphorus ⦂ •	Every 10–14 days	At least 12 weeks	✳ ⭕	Pumpkins: 'Autumn Gold', 'Small Sugar', 'Spirit' Winter Squash: 'Butternut', 'Cream of the Crop', 'Sweet Dumpling', 'Table Ace'	⣿ *Remove all but 1 or 2 fruits per plant for the largest fruits. Small-fruited cultivars can be trained over a fence, pergola, or trellis.*
At least 8in (20cm)	High-phosphorus ⦂	Every 10–14 days	At least 8 weeks	–	'Burpee Hybrid II', 'Burpless Tasty Green', 'Lemon', 'Lucky Strike', 'Salad Bush', 'Sweet Slice', 'Sweet Success'	▭ 人 *Supply a support and a tie in with string, pinch out top as it reaches the top of support. Grow all-female cultivars to avoid bitterness.*
blocks with 15in (38cm) between plants	Balanced ⦂ •	Every 3 weeks	At least 10 weeks	–	'Butter and Sugar', 'Earlivee', 'Early Sunglow', 'Honey 'n Pearl', 'Illini Extra-Sweet', 'Silver Queen', 'Sundance'	*Plant out in blocks (groups of plants at equidistant spacing) to ensure good pollination.*

CROP	EASE OF GROWING	SITE AND SOIL	FROST PROTECTION NEEDED	SOWING NEEDS: WHERE, WHEN, TEMPERATURE NEEDED	HOW TO SOW	SPEED OF GERMINATION	TRANSPLANTING/THINNING
TOMATOES	☆☆	☼ ▢◉	until last and before first frosts	Early to mid-spring at least 65°F (18°C)	singly at least 2.5cm (1in) apart; in twos	▲▲	⁙
CHERRY TOMATOES	☆☆	☼ ▢◉	until last and before first frosts	Early to mid-spring at least 65°F (18°C)	singly at least 2.5cm (1in) apart; in twos	▲▲	⁙
SWEET PEPPERS	☆☆	☼ ▢	until last and before first frosts	Spring 65–70°F (18–21°C)	½–¾in (1–2cm) apart; in twos	▲▲▲	⁙
GREEN BEANS (BUSH)	☆ ☆☆	☼ ◉	until no risk of frost	Late spring to early summer 70°F (21°C)	9in (22cm) in rows 24in (60cm) apart	▲▲	⁙
RUNNER BEANS	☆ ☆☆	☼ ◉	until no risk of frost	Spring to early summer at least 70°F (21°F)	6–9in (15–22cm); 9in (22cm) apart	▲▲	–
PEAS	☆☆	☼ ▢ ◉	until no risk of severe frost	Midspring at least 50°F (10°C)	6in (15cm); rows 2–4½in (5–11cm) apart	▲▲	–
CARROTS	☆☆	☼ ▢	–	Spring at least 45°F (7°C)	thinly in rows	▲▲▲	⁙
POTATOES	☆☆	☼ ◉ ▢ pH	Hill up, and protect foliage	Early to mid-spring at least 60°F (15°C)	in rows 12in (30cm) apart	▲▲▲	–
ONIONS	☆☆	☼ ▢ ◉	–	Mid- to late spring 50–59°F (10–15°C)	plant sets 6in (15cm) apart; rows 12in (30cm) apart	▲▲▲	–
LEEKS	☆	☼ ▢ pH	–	Early to mid-spring at least 44°F (7°C)	thinly in rows	▲▲▲	⁙

Final Planting Distance	Which Fertilizer to Use	How Often to Feed	Time from Germination to Harvest	Ornamental Qualities	Recommended Cultivars	Comments
At least in (45cm)	High-phosphorus	Every 2 weeks	At least 9 weeks	–	'Beefsteak', 'Better Boy', 'Celebrity', 'Early Girl', 'First Lady', 'Golden Boy', 'Roma', 'Rutgers'	Cultivars available for greenhouse or outdoor use, some suitable for both.
least 18in in) in growing s or singly in (25cm) pots	High-phosphorus	Every 2 weeks	At least 8 weeks	♂	'Patio', 'Pixie', 'Gold Nugget', 'Sun Gold', 'Sweet 100', 'Sweet Million', 'Yellow Pear'	Trailing or dwarf upright cultivars are available.
18in (45cm)	High-phosphorus	Every 2 weeks	At least 8 weeks	♂	'Bell Boy', 'California Wonder', 'Cherry Sweet', 'Gypsy', 'Hungarian Wax', 'Purple Beauty', 'Sweet Banana'	Red, yellow, green, orange, and other-colored cultivars are available. Pick young fruits often, allowing only a few to ripen on each plant.
s for first sowing	Balanced	Once at planting out or seedling stage	At least 7 weeks	–	'Bush Blue Lake', 'Derby', 'Gold Crop', 'Roma II', 'Royal Burgundy', 'Tendergreen Improved'	Tall-growing (pole) cultivars may be more productive but require support.
s for first sowing	Balanced	Once at planting out or seedling stage	At least 10 weeks	❋	'Prize Winner', 'Red Knight', 'White Knight'	Has an attractive climbing habit.
s for first sowing	Balanced	Once at seedling stage	At least 9 weeks	–	'Green Arrow', 'Laxton's Progress', 'Lincoln', 'Little Marvel', 'Oregon Sugar Pod', 'Sugar Anne', 'Sugar Snap'	Push in twiggy branches around plants for support or grow on netting. Pick frequently for the largest crop.
2–3in –7.5cm)	Balanced	Once at seedling stage	At least 10 weeks	–	'Danver's Half-long', 'Gold Pak', 'Imperator', 'Lady Finger', 'Red Cored Chantenay', 'Royal Chantenay', 'Thumbelina'	Must have loose soil to produce straight roots.
or planting	Balanced	Before planting	At least 8 weeks	–	'Cayuga', 'Cherokee', 'Kennebec', 'Lady Fingers', 'Norgold Russet', 'Red Pontiac', 'Yukon Gold'	Hill up to prevent tubers from greening and to avoid frost damage. Main-crop potatoes are very space-consuming.
or planting	–	–	At least 12 weeks	–	'Benny's Red', 'Carmen', 'Lucifer', 'Norstar', 'Sweet Sandwich', 'Walla Walla Sweet', 'White Sweet Spanish'	Can also be grown from seed.
9in (24cm)	High-nitrogen	Before planting and 2–3 times in growing season	At least 16 weeks	–	'King Richard', 'Large American Flag', 'Otina', 'Pancho'	Very hardy: may be harvested for much of the winter if mulched heavily.

GROWING HERBS

By growing your own herbs, you will not only add new dimensions to your cooking but also fragrant and beautiful foliage and flowers to your garden. Many herbs are attractive all year: some, such as borage and chives, have pretty flowers, while others are worth growing purely for their foliage, which often gives off delightful wafts of scent when brushed against or crushed. Herbs usually love sunny, well-drained sites, but in a shady spot they soon grow leggy and may lose their flavor. Whatever the size of your garden, it is easy to find enough space for a selection of your favorite herbs. They are ideal for growing, individually or combined, in a range of containers, such as windowboxes, pots, or planters. Try growing them in a traditional herb garden (*see* p.135), among vegetables, as ornamental path or border edgings, or in gaps between paving slabs (*see* "Planting in Crevices," p.93, and "Planting in the Middle of Paving," p.101). If possible, position herbs close to the house so that they are easily accessible for harvesting.

PLANTING A STRAWBERRY JAR

Strawberry jars provide the well-drained conditions that herbs need and give you the opportunity to grow a selection in a small area. Try some of the many herbs with variegated or unusually colored foliage. Choose a frostproof pot large enough to hold several plants, but not so large that it will be too heavy to move when full of soil mix. Most herbs flourish in containers, but always check the labels to ensure that the plants will not grow too large. Mint, for example, soon outgrows a container, while rosemary may grow into a sizable shrub unless it is regularly trimmed. Remember to water and feed the herbs regularly during the growing season.

YOU WILL NEED

- Strawberry jar
- Soil mix • Trowel
- A selection of herbs
- Watering can

SPR • SUM • AUT • WIN

1 Fill the jar with soil-based or soilless mix up to the first planting hole. Firm the mix gently, adding more if necessary.

Keep the root ball intact.

2 Plant each herb through a planting hole. Start at the base and work upward, adding more soil mix after each layer of planting.

3 Plant the top of the jar last, after firming down the soil mix. Check that none of the plants has been dislodged, and then add soil mix to within about ¾in (2cm) of the rim. Water thoroughly but slowly so that the water penetrates right to the base without washing away the soil mix. If the soil mix level sinks, top it up. Add a little mulch.

Leave space at the top for watering.

Chives

Rosemary

Sweet basil

Upright plants for the top

Golden-variegated sage

Lemon verbena

Curled-leaved parsley

Golden-variegated thyme

4 When the rosemary is larger, remove the chives to give it more space.

Trailing plants for the sides

PLANTING HERBS AS EDGING

Most herbs create a neat as well as useful edging next to a path or lawn. Here their aromatic qualities come into their own when brushed against or crushed. Select those that keep a compact form or are easily cut back if they outgrow their position. The best edible ones to choose are chives, sage, thyme, and parsley.

Herb edgings can be planted with just one type of herb but are more useful, and often more attractive, with two different ones. More than two with uneven heights and shapes may look scruffy. Choose herbs that you use regularly, and avoid invasive plants, such as mint, and large or woody ones, such as bay and rosemary.

1 *Chives and variegated sage look wonderful together, and neither will outgrow its position too quickly. Plant the herbs at the suggested spacings and not too near the edge of the border.*

2 *Trim off dead or dying foliage and water in the herbs well. Keep them watered and fed throughout the growing season.*

HARVESTING AND STORING

Herbs can be harvested throughout the growing season but are usually at their best just before flowering. For storing, pick fresh sprigs at their prime, preferably on a dry morning, when the foliage is no longer wet with dew but before it has been subjected to the hot, drying sun. Choose the healthiest-looking leaves since any that are damaged may deteriorate in storage and lose their taste. When harvesting, consider the health, shape, and appearance of the parent plant, removing lopsided stems first.

Drying
Tie the stems in bunches and hang them in a warm, well-ventilated room. When dry, strip the foliage from the stems.

STORING
The easiest methods are drying, freezing, or bottling. Deal with the herbs as soon as possible after harvesting; otherwise, they become limp and can lose some of their more subtle scents and flavors.

Bottling in oil
Wash and dry the herbs and crush them to release their flavor. Put them into a bottle or jar, add oil, then seal.

PROLONGING THE SEASON

Many herbs die back over the winter, but with a little extra effort you can persuade them to keep producing fresh leaves. Parsley, mint, coriander, and chives respond well to being removed from open ground, potted up, and put on a sunny window-sill. In early autumn, dig up strongly growing plants, divide them, and replant in pots of soil-based mix. Keep them in good light, and they will produce new growth.

Broadleaved parsley

Potting up
Transplant into fresh soil mix, trim off any damaged or sickly parts, water thoroughly, and place on a frost-free, sunny windowsill. Apply liquid fertilizer occasionally.

Whole mint leaf

Borage flower

Chopped chives

Freezing
Half-fill each compartment of an ice cube tray with fresh herbs. Top up with water and freeze.

PLANTING MINT

Mint becomes invasive very quickly but can be contained by planting it in a large flower pot sunk in the ground. This way there should be no problems with drying out and the mint can grow well without swamping nearby plants. Every spring, lift, divide, and repot the plant.

1 *Dig a hole and nestle the pot into it so that the rim of the pot is just beneath the soil surface.*

2 *Place the mint in the pot, firming down the soil around the plant. Water well.*

PLANTING AND PRUNING FRUIT TREES

Once you have chosen and planted a fruit tree, you need to prune it regularly so that it produces a good crop of ripe, healthy fruits. In the first couple of years, the aim is to form a basic, permanent framework of branches. After that, prune to keep this framework balanced and open so that it produces a constant supply of fruiting wood. Fruit trees can be pruned and trained into a variety of forms, but the simplest of these is the bush, since it is most similar to the way a fruit tree grows naturally. It forms a graceful, compact tree ideal for most gardens. All fruit trees – from apples and pears to plums, peaches, and citrus fruits – can be grown in this way, and all are pruned using the same basic method. If your garden already has an established but neglected fruit tree, you will need to renovate the tree – once this is done, follow the routine pruning method given below.

CHOOSING AND PRUNING A FRUIT TREE

Buy and plant your tree in late autumn or early spring, and start formative pruning in winter or early spring. Some fruit trees, including apples, need to be planted with a compatible cultivar nearby so that they can pollinate each other; without this they will not fruit. For details of compatible trees, check with your supplier. It is best to buy a one-year-old tree with several vigorous, undamaged branches – although thin and flexible at first, pruning in the first couple of years will thicken them up. For how to plant, see "Planting and Staking a Tree," p.43.

BASIC PRUNING GUIDELINES

All fruit trees need careful and regular pruning to keep them in good condition and to help keep disease at bay. This is usually done annually. For a bush tree, the aim is to encourage a straight trunk, supporting a bowl-shaped system of branches growing upward and outward allowing light and air to reach the center (see "Year of

planting" and "Following year," below). Always prune back to a healthy-looking bud; this stimulates sideshoots to form along the branch. Choose a bud that points in an outward direction so that the resulting shoot will grow to keep the center of the tree open and its shape balanced. Remove shoots growing downward or toward the center of the tree, cutting out any damaged or diseased stems at the same time.

If the tree fruits on small spurs along the branches, prune the ends by one-third of the new growth, and new sideshoots to five or six buds to encourage more spurs to form. If it fruits toward the tips of the branches, remove some sideshoots that have already borne fruit to ensure a supply of new ones (see "Routine pruning," below).

THE BEST TIME TO PRUNE

• Apples: late winter for bush trees, summer for trained trees (e.g. espaliers).
• Pears: late winter for bush trees, just after midsummer for trained trees.
• Plums: midsummer for bush and trained trees.
• Peaches and nectarines: midsummer after fruiting for bush and trained trees.
• Apricots: late summer after fruiting for bush and trained trees.
• Sweet cherries: early summer, then midsummer after fruiting for bush and trained trees.
• Sour cherries: midsummer after fruiting for bush and trained trees.
• Citrus: after fruiting for bush trees.

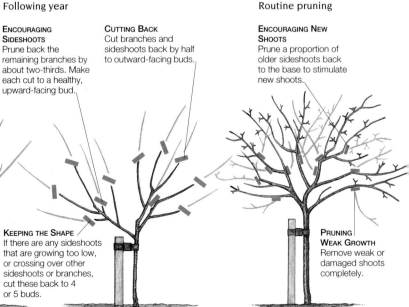

Year of planting

Following year

ENCOURAGING SIDESHOOTS
Prune back the remaining branches by about two-thirds. Make each cut to a healthy, upward-facing bud.

CUTTING BACK
Cut branches and sideshoots back by half to outward-facing buds.

Routine pruning

ENCOURAGING NEW SHOOTS
Prune a proportion of older sideshoots back to the base to stimulate new shoots.

FORMING THE BASIC SHAPE
Cut the central shoot back to a good, strong branch about 30in (75cm) from the base, leaving three or more well-spaced, healthy branches just below the cut.

KEEPING THE SHAPE
If there are any sideshoots that are growing too low, or crossing over other sideshoots or branches, cut these back to 4 or 5 buds.

PRUNING WEAK GROWTH
Remove weak or damaged shoots completely.

RENOVATING A NEGLECTED FRUIT TREE

An old, gnarled fruit tree is, potentially, a lovely focal point in a garden and gives even a fairly new garden a feeling of maturity. It makes sense to save this sort of tree, unless it is unsafe or severely diseased. Usually all that is needed is a program of renovation which can be carried out over a couple of years.

For apples and pears the best time to prune is in late winter, but for plums, cherries, and other tree fruits most of the renovative pruning should be done in summer. Renovation consists of pruning away all overcrowded, diseased, dead, or crossing shoots and branches, and removing any unwanted sideshoots that are growing from the trunk (see also "Cutting off a Branch," p.49).

Crossing branches
Prune out crossing branches since they crowd the center of the tree and may rub. Prune back to the point of origin or to a strong sideshoot.

Overcrowded branches
Overcrowding makes the crown congested, providing ideal conditions for many diseases to develop. Prune to open up the center of the tree.

Weak, unproductive wood
Any branches that are weak or spindly, with bare, unproductive areas, should be removed to concentrate vigor into the remaining growth. Either cut them out altogether or trim them back to a vigorous shoot.

Dead wood
Dead branches can be dangerous as well as unfruitful. They are more likely to snap than healthy ones and, if left on the tree, they may allow dieback to spread to other parts. Cut right back to areas of vigorous growth.

Diseased wood
Remove any diseased, canker-infected wood. Prune out any small or weak branches or take them back to completely healthy wood. If in doubt, trim away too much rather than risk leaving any diseased wood behind.

RECOMMENDED FRUIT TREES

APPLES
Plant two kinds for cross-pollination.
• 'McIntosh' bears its large, slightly tart fruits in September. The tree is very cold- and drought-resistant.
• 'Jonathan' has big, tasty fruits good for cooking. It ripens in late September, and the plant resists disease.
• 'Lodi' is famous for its yellow-green fruits, excellent for cooking, which ripen in August.

PEARS
Plant two kinds for cross-pollination.
• 'Kieffer' begins bearing when young and resists fire blight. The golden fruits ripen in September.

• 'Clapp's Favorite' is good for eating fresh and for canning. The red-blushed fruits ripen in early August.

PLUMS
Japanese plums need a pollinator; Europeans do not.
• 'Green Gage', a European cultivar, ripens in September.
• 'Stanley Prune' is a dark purple-black European prune plum with a bluish cast. It ripens in early September.
• 'Santa Rosa' bears purple-red fruits in mid-August. Japanese.

SWEET CHERRIES
Sweet cherries need a pollinator, except 'Stella'.
• 'Black Tartarian' is popular for its flavor and for its usefulnes as a pollinator. Its big, dark fruits ripen in in mid-June.

• 'Stella' bears juicy, red-black fruits good for both fresh eating and canning in June. It is self-fertile and a good pollinator.

SOUR CHERRIES
These do not need a pollinator.
• 'Montmorency' crops heavily in July. The scarlet fruits hold up well when cooked.
• 'Early Richmond' bears a week or more ahead of most sour cherries. Its juicy fruits are borne when the tree is young.

PEACHES AND NECTARINES
Most peaches do not need a pollinator; nectarines are self-pollinating but bear more heavily if cross-pollinated.
• 'Reliance', hardier than most, bears its freestone fruits in late August.
• 'Belle of Georgia' produces very sweet,

white-fleshed peaches in August.
• 'Mericrest' nectarine bears its freestone fruits heavily and when young, in July.

APRICOTS
Apricots bear more heavily when cross-pollinated.
• 'Sungold' and 'Moongold' are among the hardiest apricots and are good pollinators for each other; ripe in August.

CITRUS FRUITS
Most citrus are self-fertile.
• 'Ponderosa' lemon bears huge fruits at an early age, and grows well in containers.
• 'Valencia' orange, the world's most popular juice orange, produces its fruit in summer.

GROWING SOFT FRUIT

Many soft fruits are easy to grow, and their brightly colored fruits hang temptingly on the plant as they ripen. You need only a few plants to provide a delicious crop throughout the summer. Soft fruits can be divided into three types – bush fruits (borne on bushes that can be single- or multi-stemmed), cane fruits (produced on tall canes) and strawberries (the odd ones out since they are not woody and die down in winter). Good formative pruning is needed to establish healthy and productive soft fruit bushes, whereas careful training and support is required for fruiting canes. Strawberries need protection from bird damage and diseases. The season of cropping for soft fruit can, with a little careful planning, span several months since there are early, late, and midseason varieties of most fruits. For details about aftercare, *see* "Maintaining and Harvesting Fruit," pp.150–51.

PLANTING AND PRUNING SOFT FRUIT BUSHES

Red- and whitecurrants and gooseberries are usually grown as single-stemmed bushes – with their shoots forming an open-centered bush, growing from a short, single stem about 4in (10cm) long. Blackcurrants and blueberries naturally form multistemmed bushes, producing their new growth from below ground level.

Choose a one-year-old bush that has several vigorous, healthy shoots, and plant in the same way as for shrubs (*see* "Planting a Container-grown Shrub," p.42). Once established, soft fruit bushes need regular and careful pruning if they are to fruit well.

PRUNING BLACKCURRANTS AND BLUEBERRIES

The first year's pruning is drastic and stimulates plenty of new shoots to establish the multistemmed shape. After that, routine pruning consists of removing all crowded, crossing, or weak shoots and any that are growing too close to the ground. Remove a proportion of old, fruited wood each year; older wood can be recognized easily since it darkens with age, being pale brown when new, grayish when two years old, and black when older.

Blueberries need less detailed pruning than blackcurrants: you only need to remove weak, crossing, or damaged growth. For more about how to prune, *see* below.

PRUNING GOOSEBERRIES, REDCURRANTS, AND WHITECURRANTS

For a single-stemmed bush, create a clear stem by removing shoots growing within 4in (10cm) of soil level, then prune the tips of the rest of the shoots. Routine pruning consists of removing enough old wood each year to maintain an open shape.

WHEN TO PRUNE
• Blackcurrants: late winter.
• Blueberries: early spring.
• Gooseberries: winter while dormant.
• Red- and whitecurrants: winter while dormant.
• Blackberries: autumn after fruiting.
• Summer-fruiting raspberries: summer after fruiting.
• Autumn-fruiting raspberries: late winter.

AVOIDING PROBLEMS
On gooseberry and blackcurrant bushes, prune out any shoots that show signs of powdery mildew (*see* "Plant Doctor," p.162). Removing these as soon as you see them should prevent the infection from spreading.

Routine pruning

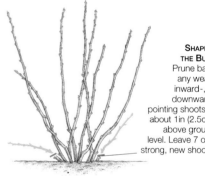

CUTTING TO THE BASE
Remove a proportion of old, fruited stems to the base to encourage new shoots.

Year of planting

CUTTING BACK
Cut all the shoots back to leave just one bud above ground level.

Following year

SHAPING THE BUSH
Prune back any weak, inward-, or downward-pointing shoots to about 1in (2.5cm) above ground level. Leave 7 or 8 strong, new shoots.

PRUNING FOR SHAPE
Leave young, healthy shoots spaced evenly.

OPENING OUT THE CENTER
Prune out old and crossing branches.

ENCOURAGING UPWARD GROWTH
Prune out low-growing branches.

PRUNING AND TRAINING RASPBERRIES

Raspberries fruit on the previous year's wood; the fruiting canes need to be trained so that they are well spaced and accessible, and the newly developing canes, which will fruit the following year, trained in as they grow. To achieve this they should be grown and trained on a permanent, sturdy support; this will also provide an attractive, ornamental feature or divider for your garden. Prune summer-fruiting raspberries right after harvesting. Cut each cane that has fruited back to ground level, and remove any straggly, damaged, or diseased canes. Remove

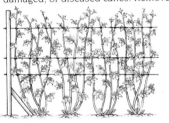

Post-and-wire system

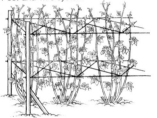

Parallel-wire system

suckers that develop too far from the main row as you notice them to prevent the row from becoming messy.

DIFFERENT TRAINING METHODS

A single row of canes on posts and wires is useful for small areas. Place the posts 10ft (3m) apart, and stretch galvanized wire tautly and horizontally at 2½ft (0.75m), 3½ft (1.1m), and 5ft (1.5m) from ground level. Weave strong twine between the wires and canes to keep them in place. The alternative parallel-wire system is easier to maintain since the canes are supported by

Pruning raspberries
After harvesting, cut all the canes that have borne fruit back to the base. Remove weak new canes, leaving several strong, healthy ones on each plant. Tie these in to the support.

a system of crossing string or wire; however, it is unsuitable if the garden is windy or the cultivar vigorous. Position the posts 10ft (3m) apart, in two rows about 2½ft (0.75m) apart. Run two galvanized wires horizontally along each row of posts, one at 2½ft (0.75m) and another at 5ft (1.5m) from ground level. Criss-cross string or wire horizontally between the wires.

AUTUMN-FRUITING RASPBERRIES

These fruit later than other raspberries, continuing until the first hard frosts. The canes grow and bear fruit in the same year. Pruning is therefore different from the method used for summer-fruiting raspberries, and a little easier; simply cut back all canes to ground level toward the end of winter.

Pruning autumn-fruiting raspberries
In late winter, before any new shoots appear, cut back all canes to ground level. This will stimulate the growth of new canes, which will bear fruit the following autumn.

PRUNING AND TRAINING BLACKBERRIES AND HYBRID BERRIES

Prune blackberries and hybrid berries as for raspberries, by cutting out all the old fruited wood and keeping new growth that will fruit the following year. In early spring, prune back the tips of any cold-damaged canes to healthy wood.

Blackberries and hybrid berries usually need more secure training in than raspberries since they tend to be more vigorous and produce longer canes. Attach the support wires to posts or along a fence – this is particularly useful in a small garden.

TRAINING METHODS

The main aim when training is to separate the one-year-old canes from the new, current season's canes. Two good ways of training are the weaving method (*see* right) and the fan method. The former is

most suitable for vigorous plants but requires a large area. The latter is ideal for a small garden since it takes up very little space: after pruning, train the current season's canes into a fan shape and tie them in, leaving a gap in the center where the new canes will develop next year. The following year, these can be trained into a fan shape to replace the fruited shoots.

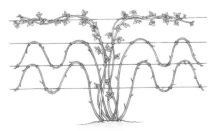

Weaving method
After cutting out the old fruited canes, tie in the current season's best growth, weaving the canes in groups in and out of the wires. The following year, tie the new canes in the center along the top wire.

Canes evenly spaced

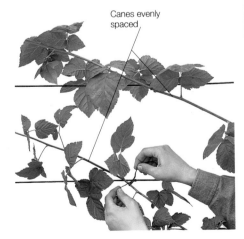

Tying in blackberries
After pruning out the old, fruited canes, tie in the new canes to the wire according to your chosen training method. Tie them firmly, but not too tightly, so that they have room to develop.

PLANTING AND GROWING STRAWBERRIES

Strawberries can be grown in the open, in a large cold frame, under cloches, or even in the greenhouse. Choose a selection of early-, mid-, and late-season plants to extend the cropping season for as long as possible. A humus-rich, well-drained soil suits strawberries best – add plenty of well-rotted manure or compost before planting, plus a balanced fertilizer. Space the plants 15–18in (38–45cm) apart, with rows 30–36in (75–90cm) apart.

Water regularly throughout the growing season. The period during and immediately after flowering is particularly important so that the fruits set well. Each plant will produce runners – new plants borne on long stalks from the crown. Remove these for the best crop (*see* right). To use the runners for propagation, pin them down to root *in situ*, or root them into pots of soil mix. Plant out as soon as they have a good root system.

Slugs (*see* p.162) can devastate a crop. For how to protect strawberries against birds, *see* p.150. For protecting flowers and young berries against frost, *see* p.160.

Planting depth
When planting, make sure the crown of the plant is at soil level. If planted too high it may dry out, and if too low the plant may not crop well.

Mulching with straw
As the strawberries mature and hang down toward the soil, put a straw mulch around each plant to prevent the fruits from touching the soil – don't use too much straw since it may restrict air movement. Protecting the fruits in this way may also reduce weed growth around the plants.

Removing runners
Pinch out runners as they appear or cut them out using a sharp knife or pruners to minimize damage to the parent plant.

CUTTING BACK FOLIAGE

After fruiting, cut off the old foliage – leave about 4in (10cm) of leaf stem since cutting too close to the crown could damage young, developing leaves. The sheared stems will help provide winter protection. At the same time, clear away all debris, old straw, and weed growth.

Before

After

RECOMMENDED SOFT FRUITS

STRAWBERRIES
Most strawberries are self-fertile, although cross-pollination is often beneficial.
• 'Surecrop' (Junebearing) bears a big crop of large, juicy fruit and resists disease.
• 'Honeoye' (Junebearing) is famous for its sweetness, juiciness, and vigor.
• 'Fort Laramie' (everbearing) is hardier than most and holds up to summer heat. Long, numerous runners make it a good choice for hanging baskets and short trellises.

CURRANTS
Currants are self-fertile.
• Red Lake' (red) bears large crops of dark red fruits in long clusters and ripens in July.

• 'White Dutch' (white) is a July-fruiting cultivar with a medium-sized, well-flavored crop.
• 'Ben Sarek' (black) bears large, acidic berries on a compact bush. It crops in July and resists powdery mildew.

GOOSEBERRIES
Gooseberries are self-fertile.
• 'Welcome' produces slightly tart green berries with a touch of pink in July. The densely foliaged plants grow best in partial shade.
• 'Pixwell' bears sweet, dark pink-red fruits in July, is very hardy, and and resists disease and drought. The stems are nearly thornless.

BLACKBERRIES
Most blackberries are self-pollinating but bear more heavily when cross-pollinated.

• 'Darrow' produces a large crop of big berries on 4–5ft (1.2–1.5m) canes in July.
• 'Black Satin' is a thornless cultivar which ripens its fruits in mid-July. Pick after the fruits lose their shine.

RASPBERRIES
Raspberries are self-fertile.
• 'Latham' (red; summer-fruiting) produces plentiful crops in July. This cultivar is vigorous, disease-resistant, and adaptable.
• 'Fall Gold' (gold; July and Sept) is prized for its unusual golden fruit which may be harvested until frost.
• 'Black Hawk' (black; summer-fruiting) is good for areas with hot, dry summers, and it resists disease. Firm, abundant fruits ripen in July.

HYBRID BERRIES
Hybrid berries are self-fertile.
• 'Royalty' produces purple fruits in late July on tall 5–6ft (1.5–2m) canes.
• 'Tayberry' bears big fruits, similar to loganberries, and are purple when ripe.

BLUEBERRIES
Plant two kinds for cross-pollination.
• 'Dwarf Northblue' is hardier than most and bears its crop in June on 2ft (60cm) bushes.
• 'Jersey' bears its medium-sized fruits on 4–6ft (1.2–2m) bushes in large crops in June.
• 'Tifblue' is a good selection for the South. It is vigorous and bears late in the season.
• 'Hybrid Patriot' produces large, slightly flattened fruit in July.

GROWING GRAPES

Having a fruit-laden grapevine is the stuff of many gardeners' dreams. Trained vertically, a grapevine will form a beautiful wall of foliage; it can be grown over a sturdy support such as a pergola, or in the roof space of a greenhouse. If the grapes are to ripen outside, unless your garden is in an area with reliably warm, long summers, choose an early- or mid-season cultivar; late-season cultivars are unlikely to ripen in cooler climates. In a greenhouse you should be able to provide the warmth needed to ripen the fruits, but allow the temperature to drop in winter since the dormant grapevine needs to be chilled to fruit well the following year. Provide adequate ventilation, especially in winter and after the fruit has set, to avoid diseases such as mildew. If the grapevine is well maintained and is suited to its conditions, you should be rewarded with a crop of juicy fruit for eating or winemaking.

PRUNING AND TRAINING A GRAPEVINE

For the first couple of years, winter pruning is aimed at thickening the central stem – prune to a bud near ground level at planting, and the following winter prune the new growth on the leader by two-thirds.

ANNUAL PRUNING

When the leader reaches the height you want, cut it back to two buds of new growth each winter and cut back all the sideshoots from the previous summer to one strong bud. As the vine grows older, growth around these sideshoots may become congested, and you may need to saw off these woody stubs. By early summer flower trusses should be visible – these will develop into bunches of grapes. Pinch out any weak flower trusses, leaving one well-developed truss per lateral. Prune back all the laterals with flower trusses leaving about two leaves beyond the flower truss. Cut back any laterals without any flower trusses to five or six leaves.

TRAINING

Train the main vertical stem up the support and secure it firmly, but not too tightly. Every summer tie in the horizontal shoots that develop on both sides of the main stem to cover the support.

Summer pruning

Leader

Lateral

FRUITING LATERALS
Cut these back to 2 leaves beyond the developing bunch of grapes.

FLOWER TRUSSES
Pinch out weak flower trusses to concentrate the plant's energies on fewer, larger bunches.

LATERALS WITHOUT FLOWER TRUSSES
Pinch these back to about 5 or 6 leaves.

Winter pruning

PRUNING LATERALS
Cut the laterals back to the first strong bud using a sharp pair of pruners to make a clean cut.

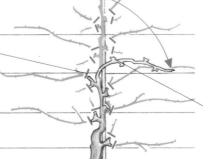

PRUNING THE MAIN STEM
Once this has reached the height you want, cut it back to 2 buds of new growth each winter.

BENDING DOWN THE MAIN STEM
Bend over the upper half and tie it in horizontally. Return it to the vertical once shoots have started to form.

INCREASING THE SIZE OF THE FRUITS

Feed, water, and mulch the grapevine as described on p.150. Select the bunches of grapes to leave one bunch every 12in (30cm) of stem, and thin the berries within each bunch if they are too densely packed (see "Thinning Fruits," p.151). Try to avoid handling the ripe or ripening fruits since they are easily damaged. If leaf growth is very dense, lightly thin the foliage slightly toward the end of summer so that the bunches receive enough sunlight to ripen properly.

Removing leaves
Remove or tie back any leaves that are casting shade on ripening grapes, but do not remove too many because some shade is necessary to prevent the fruits from being scorched by direct, strong sunlight.

MAINTAINING AND HARVESTING FRUIT

Most types of fruit will crop reasonably well and remain healthy with minimal care. But for the best crop, and to keep the plants well-balanced and in top condition, a little more care is called for. Precise needs vary from plant to plant according to its age and how it has been trained, but feeding, watering, mulching, and pest and disease control are usually all required on a regular basis. Additional jobs, such as fruit thinning and protecting the plant against adverse weather conditions, including extremes of drought, cold, and waterlogging, may also be necessary.

The small amount of effort needed to keep your plants in the best possible condition really pays dividends when it comes to harvest time. Having taken the time to cultivate healthy and productive plants, make the most of the fruits of your labors by harvesting and storing them with equal care.

WATERING, MULCHING, AND FEEDING

A regular supply of water is essential for flowers to bloom and healthy fruits to develop. When watering, pay particular attention to young plants and those sited on light, free-draining soils.

One of the best ways to reduce the amount of water you need to apply is to use a bulky layer of mulch. Apply it in spring after heavy rainfall or after thorough watering. Well-rotted manure, compost, coarse peat, spoiled hay or straw, and bark chips all make effective mulches (*see also* p.46).

Routine feeding is always essential if the plants are to continue to crop well. Apply a balanced fertilizer in early spring – the rate is usually 3–4oz/sq yd (105–140g/sq m), but varies according to the formulation. Too much fertilizer can cause poor growth, and too much nitrogen in particular encourages soft foliage, which may be damaged by diseases and pests and is prone to scorching.

On certain soils, nutrient deficiencies may develop. The most common deficiencies affecting fruit are magnesium, potassium, phosphorus, nitrogen, and calcium. Nutrient deficiencies usually cause dis-colored and blotchy foliage or fruits. Always seek specialist advice to identify and treat a suspected deficiency.

> ### REDUCING FEEDING NEEDS
> When growing a fruit tree in a lawn, keep the area immediately surrounding the base of the trunk free of grass to reduce the tree's need for fertilizer. Keeping this part clear will also make it much easier to mow.

Mulching an apple tree
A 3in (8cm) layer of mulch prevents too much moisture being lost from the soil around the roots by evaporation. It also suppresses weeds and, as long as the area is weeded before the mulch is applied, it may even prevent their regrowth. Apply the mulch to moist soil, preferably over the whole root area, which usually extends a little farther than the outermost spread of the branches. Leave a small area clear around the trunk.

PROTECTION FROM BIRDS AND RABBITS

Birds can be one of the worst pests in a fruit garden. As they search for insects and spider eggs to eat, they may damage the fruit buds, causing poor growth and sometimes dieback. Ripe fruits are also frequent targets. If your fruit is planted in one area, a fruit cage should provide good protection from birds; small bushes, cane fruit, or trees can be netted individually using special fruit netting. Rabbits may remove bark and even girdle woody stems. To prevent damage, any susceptible tree or bush should be fitted with a commercial spiral plastic tree guard.

Netting
Protect small fruits, such as strawberries, by using a fruit cage. To make one, use four stakes each capped with an upturned flower pot. Lay netting over the top and anchor it firmly.

Pot on top of stake holds netting in place and allows you to adjust it without damaging the mesh.

Lift sides of cage for harvesting.

PROTECTION AGAINST PEACH LEAF CURL

Peaches and nectarines are often infected by peach leaf curl fungus. The fungal spores responsible may be carried by winter rain. Plastic sheeting is the best protection and needs to be in place by midwinter.

Sheltering a peach fan
Erect an open-sided, heavy-duty, clear plastic shelter to cover the branches.

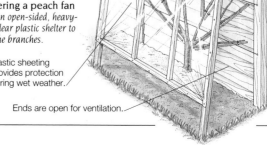

Plastic sheeting provides protection during wet weather.

Ends are open for ventilation.

THINNING FRUITS

Tree fruits and grapes may need thinning if they have set a very large, heavy crop. It is tempting to leave all the young fruitlets in place, but, if you do, you will not get the best quality and flavor or the largest possible fruit size.

Thinning is also vital for the health of the whole plant – under the weight of a heavy crop, branches can split or break. Fruits on young trees, especially apples and pears, should always be thinned, since a heavy crop too early can seriously restrict the tree's growth in future years.

Grapes should be thinned down to one bunch per shoot, or there will not be room enough for each bunch to develop fully. If you want to cultivate particularly large grapes, the individual fruits can be thinned within each bunch as they develop, using a sharp pair of pruners.

Before thinning
Apples shed any imperfect and infertile fruits naturally in early summer. After this you can thin them further – the cluster of fruitlets shown here is too tightly packed, and not all of the apples would be able to develop to their optimum size if left growing on the tree.

After thinning
Use pruners to remove the central fruit in each cluster and remove all that are very small, damaged, or malformed. On dessert ("eating") cultivars aim to space the clusters about 4–6in (10–15cm) apart. On culinary ("cooking") cultivars space them 6–9in (15–22cm) apart.

HARVESTING

Most fruits crop over a period of several weeks or even longer. For eating fresh, harvest them only when they are ripened to perfection. It is usually easy to tell when soft fruits are ripe by looking at their color – to keep pace with ripening, you will need to harvest every them day or two. Tree fruits, such as apples and pears, should come away easily in your hand when ripe – hold the fruits firmly and then twist. If they do not come away easily, leave them on the branch. Ripe peaches, nectarines, apricots, and plums should also come away easily – handle them gently. Cut cherries and grapes from the tree or vine using sharp pruners or scissors, so that you do not tear the bark or damage the fruits when you handle them. If you intend to store some of the fruits, harvest them just before they are fully ripe.

Harvesting strawberries
For eating fresh, pick strawberries by pinching through the stalk to avoid bruising the fruits. For jam, pull them away, leaving the stalk on the plant.

Harvesting dessert grapes
When the bunch is fully ripe, use a sharp pair of pruners to cut it away from the vine. Cut to leave about 2in (5cm) of woody stem on either side of the bunch, giving it a "handle." In this way you can avoid touching the individual grapes on the bunch any more than is necessary since this will spoil the bloom (the powdery fruit coating).

STORING

Only fruits in perfect condition should be stored, regardless of which method you are using. Apples and pears can be stored fresh, preferably when very slightly underripe. Soft fruits must be harvested when completely dry if they are to store well; they are best frozen or used in preserves.

Wrapping apples
Wrap each fruit in a piece of tissue paper, taking care not to bruise it. Put the fruits in a slatted wooden tray or shallow cardboard box (below). This method can also be used for pears.

Storing in a plastic bag
Put slightly underripe apples or pears in a clear plastic bag with ventilation holes and fold over the end. Store in a cool, dark place.

Harvesting apples
Grasp the fruit and twist – if the stalk breaks easily and the fruit comes free, it is ripe; if not, leave it. Harvest pears the same way.

Harvesting blackberries
Pull the berry away, leaving the stalk and core. If it does not come away, it is not ripe. Harvest raspberries the same way.

Harvesting cherries
Use a sharp pair of scissors to cut the stalk close to the branch, but not so close as to damage the bark.

·11·
GREENHOUSES AND FRAMES

The protection provided by a greenhouse or even simple sheets of plastic, plus the boost of a heater, is all you need to extend the growing season and the range of plants in your repertoire dramatically. This chapter offers advice on selecting, installing, and maintaining suitable structures.

CHOOSING COVER

Greenhouses are an expensive purchase initially, but by extending the growing and cropping season, they increase the scope for gardening. They can also save you money in the long term since they allow you to raise your plants from seed and to overwinter whole plants or cuttings of summer favorites.

Greenhouses vary tremendously in size, shape, construction, quality, and price – although it is probably worth spending a little more than the minimum. Site your greenhouse in a sheltered yet open position, away from trees and shade.

A greenhouse is a long-term investment, but if you want to have some of its benefits without all of the cost, frames (also known as cold frames) and cloches can go part of the way to extending the growing season and allowing you to raise plants from seed.

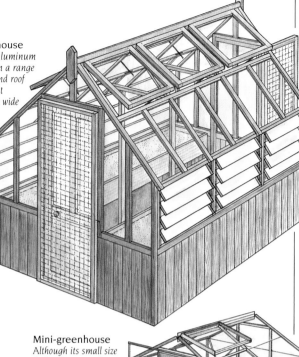

Traditional span greenhouse
This has either a wooden or aluminum framework and is available in a range of sizes; it should have side and roof ventilators. Its shape makes it easily accessible and allows a wide range of plants to be grown. Shelves or staging can easily be added, and one or two in-ground borders may be included. If you intend to overwinter tender plants and raise plants in spring, orient your greenhouse east to west. To make the best use of summer light, orient it north to south.

Lean-to greenhouse
A wooden or aluminum lean-to greenhouse is useful where space is limited – if built over a door it can also be used as a small garden room. It will benefit from the warmth retained by the house wall, and its limited glazed surface means that heating and water systems are cheaper to install and run.

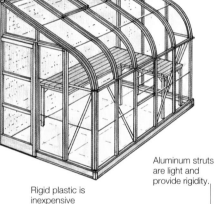

Mini-greenhouse
Although its small size limits the range of uses and the number of plants you can grow, a mini-greenhouse is highly recommended for those with a limited budget or a tiny garden. Lean-to versions are also available and best situated against a sunny fence or wall.

The sides of a wooden frame retain heat well.

Rigid plastic is inexpensive and lasts well.

Aluminum struts are light and provide rigidity.

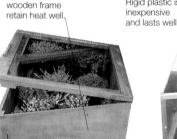

Frames
Use plastic or wooden frames for prolonging the growing season, and for growing on and hardening off seedlings. Raise or slide the plastic or glass top for access and ventilation.

Cloche
A cloche normally consists of sheets of glass clipped together. It is used to warm soil before sowing or planting, to protect from weather and pests, and to prolong the cropping season.

Use a cloche to protect seedlings.

Fleece-covered tunnel
Use strong wire hoops to support a tunnel of woven polypropylene fleece, which allows light and air to reach the plants while insulating and protecting plants and seedlings.

Corrugated tunnel
A sheet of corrugated clear plastic is held in shape by a rigid plastic stabilizer. This type of tunnel is relatively expensive but lasts well.

INSIDE THE GREENHOUSE

Whatever the size or shape of your greenhouse, it makes sense to make the very best use of the available space. Often a greenhouse stands unused for part of the year. For the rest of the year some parts may be crammed with plants while others are left empty and neglected. If adequately equipped with shelves and benches, a huge range of plants – including tropical specimens, cacti, vegetables, and others – can live together in the greenhouse, each being suited to the conditions in a specific part. In a heated greenhouse you can add to the natural temperature variations, and so to the range of growing conditions, by partitioning off a section and heating this to a higher temperature. Light levels can also be controlled to some degree by using shading or blinds, while vents enable you to control temperature and humidity to suit the plants you are growing.

EQUIPPING YOUR GREENHOUSE

Even the simplest greenhouse needs some basic equipment. A convenient water supply is a great help, especially in warm weather, and insulation is essential to reduce heating costs. Automatic vent openers, shading, and perhaps a thermostatically controlled heater all help you to maintain the conditions you need (*see* "Controlling Temperature and Humidity," p.157). A maximum-minimum thermometer enables you to check temperature fluctuations.

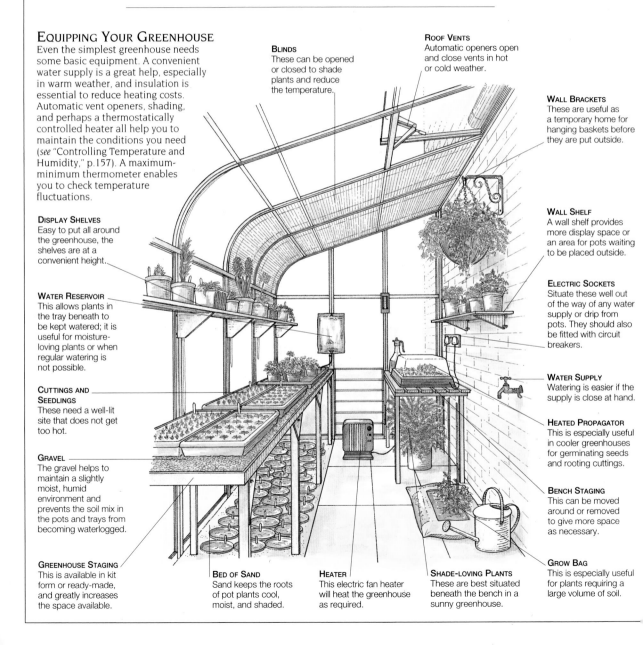

BLINDS
These can be opened or closed to shade plants and reduce the temperature.

ROOF VENTS
Automatic openers open and close vents in hot or cold weather.

WALL BRACKETS
These are useful as a temporary home for hanging baskets before they are put outside.

WALL SHELF
A wall shelf provides more display space or an area for pots waiting to be placed outside.

DISPLAY SHELVES
Easy to put all around the greenhouse, the shelves are at a convenient height.

WATER RESERVOIR
This allows plants in the tray beneath to be kept watered; it is useful for moisture-loving plants or when regular watering is not possible.

ELECTRIC SOCKETS
Situate these well out of the way of any water supply or drip from pots. They should also be fitted with circuit breakers.

CUTTINGS AND SEEDLINGS
These need a well-lit site that does not get too hot.

WATER SUPPLY
Watering is easier if the supply is close at hand.

HEATED PROPAGATOR
This is especially useful in cooler greenhouses for germinating seeds and rooting cuttings.

GRAVEL
The gravel helps to maintain a slightly moist, humid environment and prevents the soil mix in the pots and trays from becoming waterlogged.

BENCH STAGING
This can be moved around or removed to give more space as necessary.

GREENHOUSE STAGING
This is available in kit form or ready-made, and greatly increases the space available.

BED OF SAND
Sand keeps the roots of pot plants cool, moist, and shaded.

HEATER
This electric fan heater will heat the greenhouse as required.

SHADE-LOVING PLANTS
These are best situated beneath the bench in a sunny greenhouse.

GROW BAG
This is especially useful for plants requiring a large volume of soil.

DIFFERENT GREENHOUSE ENVIRONMENTS

The greenhouse temperature will determine which plants you can grow. In general, the higher the temperature, the higher the humidity and watering needs – you might consider installing an automatic watering system. All greenhouses benefit from good winter insulation and effective summer shading.

TROPICAL OR WARM GREENHOUSE

This should be maintained with a daytime winter temperature of at least 60°F (15°C) and a night-time temperature of not below 55°F (13°C). Use an electric or fuel-fired heater (natural gas or propane is safest) with a thermostat in winter, with shading and automatic vents in summer to prevent overheating. These conditions are suitable for growing tropical and sub-tropical plants, both ornamental and edible.

TEMPERATE GREENHOUSE

This should be maintained with a minimum daytime winter temperature of 50°F (10°C) and a night-time temperature of not below 45°F (7°C). Use a heater with a thermostat in winter, and vents and shading in summer to keep temperatures down. These conditions suit half-hardy and tender pot plants and vegetables.

COOL OR FROST-FREE GREENHOUSE

This should be maintained with a minimum daytime winter temperature of 41°F (5°C) and a night-time temperature of not below 36°F (2°C). Use a heater fitted with a thermostat in winter, and provide good ventilation all year. Hose down the floor as necessary to decrease temperatures and increase humidity. These conditions

Collection of cacti
This specialist collection of cacti and succulents needs the protection of a greenhouse to develop and flower to its full potential, but tolerates fairly cool greenhouse conditions. Regular ventilation keeps the air circulating, and shading is essential in summer to prevent leaves from being scorched. Under the greenhouse bench is the best place for plants that dislike direct sunlight and tolerate shade.

are suitable for overwintering frost-tender plants and starting seedlings early in the year. Extra heat will be needed for propagation; a small, heated propagator is ideal for this.

UNHEATED GREENHOUSE

With no heating costs, this is the cheapest type of greenhouse to run; however, the range of plants you can grow is much narrower than in other types, especially in cold climates. Good ventilation is essential to prevent diseases from building up. When necessary, ventilate in the day and close the vents when temperatures drop at night. These conditions are suitable for starting seedlings early so that they are ready to plant out after the last frosts, and for growing many leafy vegetables out of season. It may be worth installing an alarm as a safeguard in cold weather.

ORNAMENTAL PLANTS FOR DIFFERENT TYPES OF GREENHOUSE

TROPICAL OR WARM
Maidenhair fern (*Adiantum raddianum*) ❦ ❁
Golden trumpet (*Allemanda cathartica*) ❦ ❁
Zebra plant (*Aphelandra squarrosa*) ▲❁
Begonias [many] ❦ ❧ ♂ ❁
Caladium x hortulanum ❦ ❁
Bleeding-heart vine (*Clerodendrum thomsoniae*) ❧ ❁
Lipstick plants (*Columnea*) ❧ ❁
Flame violets (*Episcia*) ❦ ❁
Euphorbias [many] ❦▲❁
Gardenia (*G. jasminoides*) ❦ ❁
Hoyas (*H. bella, H. carnosa*) ❧ ❁
Impatiens, incl. New Guinea hybrids ❦ ❁❁
Musa acuminata 'Dwarf Cavendish' ❦ ❁
Peperomias ❦ ❁

Staghorn fern (*Platycerium bifurcatum*) ❦ ❁
Madagascar jasmine (*Stephanotis floribunda*) ❧ ❁
Tillandsias ❦ ❁

TEMPERATE
Hot-water plants (*Achimenes*) ❦♂ ❁
Bird's-nest fern (*Asplenium nidus*) ❦ ❁
Begonias [many] ❦ ❧ ♂ ❁
Queen's tears (*Billbergia nutans*) ❦ ❁
Cacti [many] ❦
Clivia miniata ♂ ❁
Cyclamens ♂ ❁
Angels' trumpets (*Datura*) ▲❁❁❁
Persian violet (*Exacum affine*) ❁❁
Hibiscus rosa-sinensis ❁ ❁
Amaryllis (*Hippeastrum*) ♂❁

Red morning glory (*Ipomoea coccinea*) ❁❁
Kalanchoes ❦ ❁
Myrtus (*Myrtus communis*) ▲❁
Passion flowers (*Passiflora*) ❧ [most ❁]
Christmas cactus (*Schlumbergera bridgesii*) ❦ ❁
Bird of paradise (*Strelitzia reginae*) ❦ ❁
Streptocarpus ❦ ❁
Tibouchinas ❦ ❁

COOL OR FROST-FREE
Abutilons ❦❁❁
Mimosas (*Acacia*) ▲❁❁
Agapanthus ♂
Asparagus fern (*A. densiflorus*) ❦ ❁
Bougainvilleas ❧❧❁
Calceolarias ❁ ❁
Camellias ▲ [some ❁] ⁿ

Chinese trumpet creeper (*Campsis grandiflora*) ❧ ❁
Cestrums ▲❁❧❧❁
Lemon (*Citrus limon*) ▲ ❁
Fuchsias ❁ [some ❁]
Genista canariensis ❁❁
Transvaal daisies (*Gerbera*) ❦ ❁
Jasmines (*Jasminum*) ❧ ❧ [some ❁]
Chilean bellflower (*Lapageria rosea*) ❧ ❁
Bay (*Laurus nobilis*) ▲❁
Daffodils (*Narcissus*) ♂
Geraniums (*Pelargonium*) ❦ ❁
Pittosporum tenuifolium ❁▲❁
Cape leadwort (*Plumbago auriculata*) ❁ ❁
Primroses (*Primula*) ❦ ❁ [some ❁]
Butterfly flowers (*Schizanthus*) ❁ ❁
Cineraria (*Senecio x hybridus*) ❁ ❁

MAINTAINING YOUR GREENHOUSE

Greenhouses may provide a controlled, protected environment for plants to grow in, but these same conditions are also ideal for diseases and pests to thrive. Many of these, for example spider mites, are tiny and easily go unnoticed until they reach serious levels. Good hygiene should therefore be high on your list of priorities – by keeping the greenhouse clean and neat, many pests and diseases need never become a problem, and at the same time you will be providing better growing conditions for your plants. Keep a regular check on the state of the greenhouse framework, along with any ventilation, watering, or heating systems. Any damaged areas or functional problems should be dealt with before they have a chance to become serious. Regular checking need not take long, but, combined with prompt action, it can save a lot of damage in the long run.

WATERING SYSTEMS

If you are unable to water the plants in the greenhouse regularly, it may be worth investing in an automatic watering system, such as a trickle irrigation system. For occasional use, there are numerous small gadgets you can buy, most of which work by tapping water from a reservoir and gradually releasing it into the pot or tray. For short periods of time, you can also place plants on capillary matting, with one edge laid in a dish or reservoir of water to draw up moisture as the plants need it. For plants in larger pots, cut a small wick from capillary matting and insert it through the drainage holes when planting. It will protrude onto the matting below and allow the plant to obtain water.

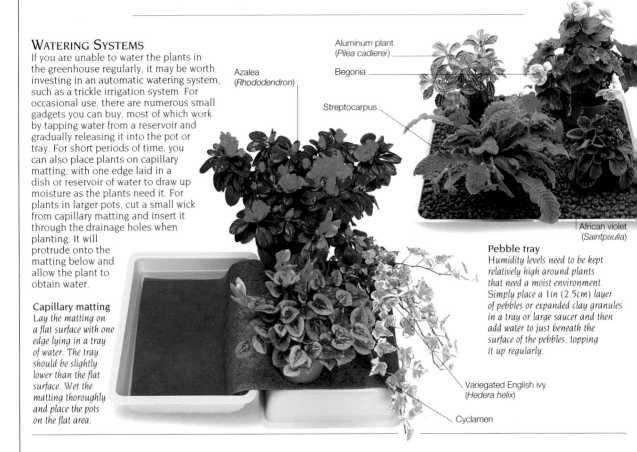

Azalea
(*Rhododendron*)

Aluminum plant
(*Pilea cadierei*)

Begonia

Streptocarpus

African violet
(*Saintpaulia*)

Capillary matting
Lay the matting on a flat surface with one edge lying in a tray of water. The tray should be slightly lower than the flat surface. Wet the matting thoroughly and place the pots on the flat area.

Pebble tray
Humidity levels need to be kept relatively high around plants that need a moist environment. Simply place a 1in (2.5cm) layer of pebbles or expanded clay granules in a tray or large saucer and then add water to just beneath the surface of the pebbles, topping it up regularly.

Variegated English ivy
(*Hedera helix*)

Cyclamen

HYGIENE IN THE GREENHOUSE

Keep conditions in your greenhouse as hygienic as possible. Have a thorough cleanup every autumn: clear out the plants while you scrub down the glass and frame both inside and out.

Throughout the year, sweep the floor and staging as needed to remove fallen leaves and plant debris since these often carry fungal spores and provide a perfect site for fungi or pests to overwinter. Pinch out dead and dying foliage, flowers, and stems promptly since they may cause dieback. Remove weeds from pots and gravel to keep air circulating well and prevent competition for moisture and nutrients. As you finish with pots and trays, scrub them out so that they are clean and ready to use again. Keep your water source clean so that it does not harbor diseases.

Removing algae from glass
First wet the algae thoroughly to loosen the deposits, and then scrub them off with warm soapy water and a scrubbing brush. A plastic plant label is useful for cleaning between panes of glass where algae have accumulated.

CONTROLLING TEMPERATURE AND HUMIDITY

The temperature and humidity of the greenhouse will need to be adjusted according to the needs of the plants you grow. Electric heaters with a built-in fan and thermostat ensure good air circulation. Kerosene heaters are cheaper but may lack thermostats and emit plant-toxic fumes if not well maintained. Gas-fired heaters can often be run off an existing central heating system. Good insulation moderates cold temperatures and reduces heating costs. Automatic vents that adjust in response to temperature changes are useful all year. A white shading wash and internal or external blinds reduce summer temperatures, as can hosing down the floor, which also raises humidity.

Blinds
Blinds provide valuable shade and help to keep temperatures from rising within the greenhouse. If the greenhouse is full, exterior blinds are easiest to operate since they cannot damage tall plants.

Shading washes
These are specially formulated paints. Dilute in water, then apply to the roof and sides of your greenhouse to provide shade and prevent overheating. Wash off toward the end of summer.

Bubble plastic insulation
This can be bought in lengths and cut to the width you need. It lets plenty of light through and has good insulation properties. To mount the plastic, pin it to the roof apex using drawing pins or special fixtures. Roll down the sheet of plastic with the raised bubbles next to the glass to trap the most air, and pin it again at the base.

RENOVATING WOODEN GREENHOUSES

With a wooden greenhouse, you need to maintain the frame in good condition. Clean the wood each year and treat it with preservative every one to three years; avoid using one that is harmful to plants, such as creosote. Repair small rotting areas with wood filler.

1 Cut or chisel out rotting areas of the framework, taking it back to sound wood. If the damaged area is very large, remove it and replace it with a completely new length of wood.

2 Fill the excavated area with plastic wood filler. Allow it to dry, and then treat the entire framework with a wood preservative.

BIOLOGICAL CONTROLS

These are a range of predators and parasites that naturally feed on certain pests, keeping them at bay without the need for chemicals. Most are suitable for using in greenhouses. Biological controls are available for pests such as spider mites, whiteflies, mealybugs, vine weevils, scale insects, aphids, slugs, and leaf miners. For more details on identifying pests, see "Plant Doctor," pp.161–8.

A daytime temperature of at least 70°F (21°C) is usually necessary if the predators and parasites are to breed and feed faster than the pests. Introduce predators or parasites before the infestation becomes severe, or there may be too many for the controls to cope with. There is, however, no point introducing them before the pest appears since without the pest, the predator and parasite populations will die out. Suppliers send out the biological controls in different forms and will advise as to how many of which type of control you need. Most controls are small and some are barely visible to the naked eye, so it may be hard to determine how well they are working – look for signs of improvement on the plants, for a decrease in the number of pests visible, and, with parasites, for signs of the parasitized pest.

Whitefly control
Sold as eggs in a plastic tube, the parasitic wasp Encarsia formosa parasitizes the juvenile, or scale stage of the whitefly. The whitefly is killed and another wasp develops inside the scale.

Vine weevil control
This sponge is about 1 x 2in (2.5 x 5cm) and contains at least 30,000,000 nematodes. When mixed with water, this can be used as a drench around plants infested with vine weevil grubs.

Spider mite control
The microscopic predatory mite Phytoseiulus persimilis feeds on all stages of the spider mite, including its eggs.

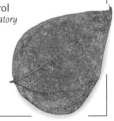

APPENDICES

This section of the book provides you with essential backup information. It is divided into three sections. The first, "Winter Protection," describes how to protect tender and other vulnerable plants against damage from snow, cold, and wind. This is followed by "Plant Doctor," which covers how to treat plants that have problems with pests, diseases, and disorders, and gives advice on how to avoid these problems in the first place. Finally, there is a glossary of key gardening terms.

WINTER PROTECTION

There is a lot to be said for choosing plants that will thrive in your garden whatever the weather, but this restricts your choice of plants enormously. If you want to include some favorite tender plants, winter protection will often be needed. The measures you can take to safeguard against wind, frost and cold, and snow range from temporary overnight covers to more elaborate insulation that stays in place over the winter.

PROTECTION AGAINST FROST AND COLD

You can save yourself a lot of effort by planning your planting carefully: always avoid planting potentially tender plants in known frost pockets – site them in sheltered areas. For more information about identifying frost pockets, *see* "Microclimates," p.22. Young plants are more prone to winter damage than fully established ones, so protection may be needed only for the first few years. Never feed too late in the season since this stimulates soft, new growth that can be damaged by the cold. Plants that flower early in the year often need protection more than those that flower later.

Move tender plants in containers into a sheltered spot when winter arrives, since the roots can easily freeze and die. Alternatively, wrap the pots in insulating material. This has the added benefit of protecting the pot itself, which may crack or crumble in a severe winter. Protect

Protecting a large pot
If a container is too heavy to move into shelter over winter, wrap it up well using an insulating material tied securely in place with string. It should provide good protection until spring when the pot can be unwrapped.

Use burlap, bubble plastic, newspaper, or even old curtains as insulating material.

roses from extreme cold by mounding soil around their bases before the temperatures drop very low, covering the stems as much as possible. Remove the mounded soil (and any additional covering) in spring.

Many plants can protect themselves if not neatened up too much – a herbaceous

perennial that is left alone and allowed to die back naturally with its crown protected by dead foliage is far less likely to be damaged in the winter than one that is cut back and left exposed. If the dead foliage is inadequate or it looks too messy, apply a light mulch of dry leaves or bark chips heaped directly over the crown.

Mounding up soil around roses
Mound up the soil to 5–6in (12–15cm) around the crown. In severe winters, increase the insulation by adding a layer of straw, holding it in place within a cylinder of chicken wire or newspaper.

Graft union

Protecting plants with burlap
Protect the blossoms of early-flowering wall plants and climbers from frost using woven nylon netting or burlap. Attach the burlap or netting to the plant's support wires, and roll it up or down over the plant as required.

Protecting crowns of herbaceous perennials
Wedge dry leaves or bark chips between the remains of the stems, so that they are held firmly in place. Alternatively, use chicken wire or old woody prunings to make a loose "cage" to hold the mulch in place.

Protecting plants with straw
Cover the plant with a layer of strong netting or chicken wire. Pack with straw to create an insulating "jacket" and wedge more straw between the plant and the wall. This protects against cold and wind while providing ventilation.

PROTECTION AGAINST SNOW

Snow can cause a lot of damage, particularly if followed soon afterward by wind. Its sheer weight can snap foliage and stems or branches of small plants, hedges, and trees. In areas with heavy snowfalls, watch out for and protect any young plants that may be crushed, or branches that may be broken by a thick layer of snow.

SHRUBS AND TREES

Hedges and evergreen shrubs or trees are often forced apart and bent over by a heavy fall of snow and, even when this does not actually break the branches, the shape of the plant or hedge may be spoiled permanently. Clipping a hedge so that the sides taper slightly toward the top will help avoid this problem (see "Hedges," pp.84–5). Providing protection for plants prone to snow damage is always worthwhile, although most damage can be limited

in the first place by simply brushing the snow off the branches at regular intervals, and always before it has frozen. Snow removal like this is, however, advisable only for larger and sturdier woody plants since more delicate ones could be easily damaged.

SMALL PLANTS

A covering of snow forms an effective insulating layer when it falls on top of many small, compact plants, providing

them with some protection against very low temperatures and chilling winds. If further protection is needed, there are various ways to achieve this.

A very light snowfall can be kept off plants by laying several layers of newspaper over them. Polytunnels and cloches can also be used to protect small plants, and these should be strong enough to withstand a slightly heavier weight of snow. Use snow frames (below) if you need greater protection.

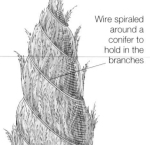

Wire spiraled around a conifer to hold in the branches

Using a snow frame
In areas of high snowfall it may be worth constructing a snow frame, made using cross-braced panels of plywood, to place over vulnerable plants.

Using wire around a conifer
Evergreens including small trees and conifers can often be carefully wired, using galvanized wire, so that their branches are held together and cannot be forced apart by snow. This treatment should also help prevent damage from unusually strong winds.

PROTECTION AGAINST WIND

Wind can cause foliage to go brown, wither, and even die. Plants with variegated or golden foliage are particularly vulnerable. Symptoms are usually most obvious on the exposed side of the plant. Plants with small, thickened, waxy leaves, such as barberries and hollies, are usually able to withstand wind, as are certain deciduous trees, notably mountain ash, willows, and hawthorn. To protect small or young shrubs, use burlap supported by sturdy stakes, or a commercial windbreak. For the long term, plant strategically sited trees and hedges to shelter an exposed garden.

TEMPORARY PROTECTION

Early-flowering shrubs or those that bloom during cold spells are easily spoiled by inclement conditions and may never flower if their buds are damaged by a sudden frost. Woven horticultural fleece draped over the plant on frosty nights provides an excellent lightweight protection. Use old net curtains for a similar, though slightly less insulating, effect, taking care not to squash young stems, buds, or blooms, and tying them to branches to keep them in place.

Polytunnels are usually used to protect low-growing plants, such as lettuces and strawberries, from extreme weather

conditions such as frost, snow, and chilling winds. They cause little reduction in light and, provided they are adequately ventilated, they work very well. Polytunnels are available in a range of sizes, are fairly inexpensive to buy, and are easy to store. Provided they are cleaned up regularly, they should function well for several seasons. After a few years the plastic may degrade or tear but is easily replaced. Newspaper makes a good temporary insulation against early or late frosts. It deteriorates fairly quickly in wet weather, but in most conditions it can be used for several consecutive frosty nights.

Permeable windbreaks
Commercial windbreaks are suitable for large, exposed areas and may be helpful for reducing problems of wind in the entire garden. They should be erected rather like a fence around the affected area and held in position by wooden stakes.

Polytunnels
Polytunnels are easily made by pushing sturdy wire hoops firmly into the ground and stretching a length of clear plastic over the hoops. Ventilate the polytunnel by raising one or both sides of the plastic on warm days.

Newspaper
Drape newspaper over dwarf shrubs, herbaceous perennials, and crops such as potatoes, which have young growth that is easily frosted. Anchor the edges securely by weighing them down with bricks or large stones, or by mounding up with soil.

PLANT DOCTOR

This page provides general guidelines about how to control and avoid plant problems. The following six pages deal with a selection of pests, diseases, and disorders. To make it easier for you to diagnose any problem your plants may have, these pages are arranged according to the part of the plant that is most commonly affected, such as the flowers or leaves. Many problems affect several plant parts; symbols next to the name of each plant problem provide a quick-reference guide to all the parts of the plant that may be affected. Fruits and vegetables have their own section, which covers problems that affect both edible and nonedible parts of the plants. Identification and control of weeds is dealt with at the end of this section.

> **KEY TO SYMBOLS USED IN THIS SECTION**
> ❧ Leaves ✿ Flowers ❦ Stems or whole plants ✸ Roots ♂ Fruits

PLANT PROBLEMS AND HOW TO CONTROL THEM

A pest is an insect or animal that damages plants, usually by chewing, sucking the sap, or biting leaves or stems, sometimes producing swellings. A disease is caused by a fungus, bacterium, virus, or closely related organism; it may result in a wide range of symptoms, such as discoloration, distortion, leaf drop, or even plant death. A disorder is not caused by a living organism but by a nutritional deficiency or poor growing conditions.

ORGANIC CONTROLS

Many plant problems can be controlled organically by providing healthy growing conditions and encouraging natural predators. If you are following these principles in your garden, you will want to avoid using any chemicals since they may harm beneficial insects as well as pests. Organic controls are often available as an alternative, in the form of traps, or

treatments such as soap and pyrethrum dust; these need to be applied carefully and selectively to be effective and avoid harming beneficial insects. For details of biological controls, *see* p.157.

CHEMICAL CONTROLS

Chemical controls are available as pesticides to control snails, insects, mites, and their young, and fungicides and bactericides that control diseases caused by fungi and bacteria. Choose the one most appropriate for the problem, and follow the instructions – not all products are suitable for use on every type of plant.

Spray or apply chemicals sensibly and at the advised rates: young plants, seedlings, and plants stressed by drought or heat may all be adversely affected by chemicals applied at the wrong strength or at an unsuitable time of day – when in direct sunlight, for example.

TIPS FOR AVOIDING PROBLEMS

- Always buy good-quality plants that appear to be in perfect health: check stems, leaves, and roots.

- Grow plants in suitable conditions: consider soil type, exposure, amount of sun, and temperature. Plant or sow carefully and maintain the plants well.

- Observe good hygiene: use sterilized soil mix and clean water, remove rotting leaves and debris, and sort out any pest or disease infestation quickly.

- Where possible, rotate vegetables to avoid buildup of problems in the soil. Choose resistant cultivars.

- Keep a watch for problems and treat them before they get out of hand.

BENEFICIAL GARDEN CREATURES

Knowing which insects and other creatures are on your side makes sense; these creatures will help to keep pest levels down without any effort on your part. Some creatures are essential to the plant's productivity or ability to reproduce – pollinating insects such as honeybees, for example. Others are important in controlling pests; some larger creatures, such as skunks, birds, frogs, toads, and shrews, eat pests that live close to or on the ground.

The numerous beneficial insects include ladybugs and their larvae, hoverfly larvae, lacewings and their larvae, and ground beetles. There are also minute wasps that parasitize certain pests such as aphids. Even common wasps and ants

are of use since they prey on many insect pests. Spiders and centipedes, too, will help to keep pest levels down since they catch and consume insects that could damage plants. For how to introduce beneficial insects to your greenhouse, *see* "Biological Controls," p.157.

Growing a wide range of plants, especially those with open or daisylike flowers, will attract beneficial insects into your garden, particularly hoverflies and bees. Decrease damage to these insects by using chemicals only when essential. Treat an insect or pest only if you are sure it is causing damage. If in any doubt, check its identity and work on the principle of "innocent until proven guilty"!

Common garden spider
Spiders' webs trap many garden insects.

Ladybug
Ladybugs and their larvae feed on aphids.

Centipede
Centipedes (not to be confused with millipedes which have two pairs of legs per segment) feed on pests that dwell in the soil.

Hoverfly
Hoverflies and their larvae feed on aphids. The flies also pollinate flowers.

Lacewing
Lacewing larvae eat aphids.

LEAF PROBLEMS

CATERPILLARS 🔍 ❋

Symptoms and cause Holes appear in leaves and occasionally flowers, caused by caterpillars of many butterflies and moths. These may be found, often hidden under the leaves, with pellets of excreta present on or beneath the plant. Some caterpillars produce webbing; some feed in groups, others are solitary. Most have a fairly restricted host range.

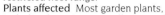

Cabbage caterpillars

Plants affected Most garden plants, including brassicas, as well as greenhouse and indoor plants.
Control Pick by hand, or spray with *Bacillus thuringiensis* (Bt, a biological control), or insecticidal soap, or carbaryl.

SLUGS AND SNAILS 🔍 ✿

Symptoms and cause The leaves become full of holes and may even be stripped. Bulbs and tubers may have visible tunnels. Silvery slime trails may be visible on the leaves, stems, or on the ground. These are left by slugs and snails which feed mostly at night and in wet weather.

Leaf eaten away

Plants affected Seedlings, herbaceous perennials, annuals, shrubs, climbers, bulbs, vegetables, including potatoes, and many fruits.
Control Cultivate the soil to expose eggs, and clear organic debris under which slugs hide. Use liquid or pelleted slug killers, or the nematode parasite of slugs as a biological control agent.

BEETLES 🔍 ❋ ✹

Symptoms and cause Holes or pits in foliage, flowers, or buds, caused by various beetles which may be visible. The damage may kill the plant.
Plants affected Roses, lilies, asparagus, eggplants, hibiscus, potatoes, beans, and leafy vegetables.
Control Remove beetles and clear the garden of debris. Spray with Bt, insecticidal soap (for larvae), rotenone, or carbaryl.

LEAF MINERS 🔍

Symptoms and cause Linear, irregular, or blotchy areas (mines), usually white or brown, in foliage. Leaves do not fall. Caused by larvae of flies, moths, beetles, and sawflies.
Plants affected Perennials (especially chrysanthemums), trees, and celery.
Control Pick off affected leaves or squash the larvae within. Spray with dimethoate or malathion when you see signs of damage.

APHIDS 🔍 ❋ ✹ ✿

Symptoms and cause Leaves may be distorted by various species of aphids, which may range in color from green to brown or black, sucking the plant sap. Stems, buds, flowers, and roots may be affected, too. A sticky excreta (honeydew) may be found on the leaves, or beneath the plant, even if the pests are no longer in evidence. This may become colonized by a black, sootlike mold.

Leaves distorted

Plants affected Nonwoody, green growth on almost all plants.
Control Aphids can be controlled by several predators, or spray with insecticidal soap, malathion, pyrethrum or rotenone, or a systemic such as dimethoate.

POWDERY MILDEWS 🔍 ❋ ✹ ♂

Symptoms and cause Powdery white fungal growth usually on upper surfaces of leaves. Leaves may be distorted and then die or drop. Mildew may also be visible on stems, flowers, and fruits. It is caused by fungi which thrive on plants that have a dry root environment but are in humid air.

Powdery mildew

Plants affected Trees, shrubs, climbers, annuals, perennials, vegetables, fruits (grapes and gooseberries), and greenhouse plants.
Control Remove affected plant parts. Keep plant roots moist and avoid overhead irrigation. Spray with a fungicide, such as dinocap, sulfur, or captan.

SPIDER MITES 🔍 ✹

Symptoms and cause Leaves are covered with pale mottling and may fall. Fine webbing may appear over infested plants, which may die. Most commonly caused by the greenhouse (or two-spotted) spider mite, which is less than 1/16in (1mm) long.
Plants affected Almost all plants under glass. Outdoors, melons, cucumbers, apples, beans, and roses are most at risk.

Mottling on leaf

Control Infestation is difficult to detect and may not be noticed until it is advanced, and many strains of mite are resistant to pesticides. Spray with malathion, dimethoate, or insecticidal soap. In the greenhouse, try using predatory mites, maintain high humidity, or dislodge with a strong stream of water.

SCALE INSECTS 🔍 ✹

Symptoms and cause Small raised bumps appear on the leaf undersides and stems. The foliage is coated with a sticky excreta (honeydew) which may also be blackened with sooty molds. The insects, including soft scale and San Jose scale, may be brown, yellow, or gray, and oval, pear-shaped, or circular (*see also* p.164).

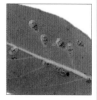

Soft scale

Plants affected Trees, shrubs, climbers, cacti and other succulents, fruits, and greenhouse plants.
Control Spray with dormant oil in late winter, or malathion or acephate in early to midsummer, but year-round in greenhouses.

LEAF SPOTS 🔍

Symptoms and cause Spots appear on foliage. If caused by bacteria, the spots may be angular, with a yellow edge. Fungal spots have concentric zones and an area of pinprick-sized, fungal fruiting bodies; black, brown, or gray spots may cover most of the leaves, which may drop.
Plants affected Trees, shrubs, roses, perennials, annuals, bulbs, vegetables, and fruits.
Control Remove affected parts. Spray fungal spots and blackspot with triforine, bacterial spots with Bordeaux mixture.

Blackspot on rose

RUSTS 🍃

Symptoms and cause Small brown or orange (occasionally buff) pustules or spores appear, usually on the undersides of the leaves, each one corresponding to a discolored (usually yellowed) patch on the upper leaf surface. The leaf may then distort and start to die. The rust fungi responsible are spread by rain splash or air currents and are especially damaging in wet weather.

Brown spores

Plants affected Most plants.
Control Remove and destroy affected leaves, or entire plants if severe. Remove alternate hosts, for example red cedars for cedar-apple rust. Spray with a fungicide, such as a ferbam and sulfur mixture.

VIRUSES 🍃 ❀

Symptoms and cause Poor growth, distortion, and discoloration are common. Flecks, mottles, streaks, spots, or ring-spots, usually yellow in color, appear on the leaves or flowers. Sometimes leaves pucker and distort, and flowers fail to appear. General stunting is occasionally followed by death. Viruses are minute particles that can be found anywhere in the plant. They are usually spread from infected sap by handling, by sap-feeding pests (including aphids), or by propagation tools. Some viruses are seed-borne.

Ring spots

Plants affected Most flowering plants, including bulbs.
Control There is no cure, so minimize spread: destroy affected plants, control virus-carrying pests, and maintain hygiene.

FLOWER PROBLEMS

THRIPS ❀ 🍃

Symptoms and cause Pale or white flecks on petals and leaves give the affected areas an overall silvery white appearance. Buds may fail to open. Cream-colored nymphs and black or brown adult thrips ¹⁄₁₆in (2mm) long may be visible.

Silvery petals

Plants affected Many plants including roses, cyclamens, chrysanthemums, gladioli, onions, and geraniums.
Control Thrips like hot, dry conditions so regular watering and ventilation will help. Predatory mites are useful. Spray with an insecticide, such as dimethoate.

BOTRYTIS (GRAY MOLD) ❀ ✽

Symptoms and cause Discolored spots or patches appear on the petals, followed shortly afterwards by gray, fuzzy fungal growth. This fungus often attacks via wounded or damaged tissue. Soon the whole flower rots and the mold may spread to the rest of the plant (*see also* p.166).

Discolored patches

Plants affected Trees, shrubs, perennials, annuals, bulbs, vegetables, and fruits.
Control Clear up all debris, then cut out and remove all affected areas, including flowerheads if necessary. Improve ventilation and spray with a fungicide containing captan or ferbam.

BLOSSOM WILT ❀ ✽

Symptoms and cause Flowers turn brown and wither, but remain on the plant. Adjacent leaves may discolor, too. Tiny, raised, buff-colored pustules appear on affected areas and may later appear on the damaged bark. The wilting is caused by a fungus; its spores are easily spread in wet weather and carried on air currents, entering the plant through the flowers.

Wilted blossom

Plants affected Azaleas and many fruit trees, including cherries, apples, pears, and quinces.
Control Prune out and destroy all infected areas before the dieback spreads to other parts of the plant, then spray with a suitable copper-based fungicide.

BLINDNESS ❀

Symptoms and cause The flower buds develop only partially or not at all and are empty or contain malformed flowers. Prolonged or repeated drought is usually responsible. On camellias and rhododendrons, the problem may be caused by drought in the previous year at the time when the buds were being formed. Another likely cause, particularly with naturalized bulbs, is inadequate feeding or overcrowding.

Undeveloped buds

Plants affected All plants, but those subjected to erratic watering, especially in containers, are most at risk.
Control Normally the problem can be avoided (and affected plants restored) by regular watering, mulching, and feeding.

PROLIFERATION ❀

Symptoms and cause Flower buds, or flower stems, often topped with an additional flower bud, develop and grow through the center of the affected flower. Early damage to the growing point of the bud by frost or insect attack is the most common cause of proliferation. If the problem appears for several seasons, the plant may be suffering from a virus.

Affected rose

Plants affected Mainly roses, especially the older varieties, but also other ornamentals and fruit trees.
Control Virus-infected plants should be destroyed. On other affected plants, areas with proliferation can be pruned out.

POLLEN BEETLES ❀

Symptoms and cause In spring and summer small black beetles appear, usually in large numbers, on and within flowers. Pollen beetles eat the pollen of the flower but do not damage the plant.
Plants affected The flowers of many garden plants including sweet peas, roses, daffodils, runner beans, and squash.
Control Insecticides are not recommended since they may cause damage to flowers and

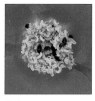
Pollen beetles

pollinating insects. To remove the beetles from cut flowers, place the flowers in a dark garage or shed near a light source – the pollen beetles will fly out of the flowers toward the light.

STEMS OR WHOLE PLANTS

CANKER ❧
Symptoms and cause Symptoms vary with the host plant and the organism responsible. Raised, loosened, often concentric rings of bark may be seen close to a wound or a bud, with fungal pustules nearby. The bark may appear to sink inward but remains virtually intact. Gumming or oozing may also occur. The canker, which can be caused by a variety of fungi and bacteria, may result in dieback.
Plants affected Many woody plants including apples, pears, beeches, poplars, cherries, and plums.
Control Cut off affected branches or parts of branches, then spray the remainder of the plant with a suitable fungicide or bactericide.

Fungal pustules

WOOLLY APHIDS ❧
Symptoms and cause In spring a white growth, like a small cotton ball, may be seen on the bark. It first appears in bark cracks and old pruning wounds on larger branches, but then spreads to newer, softer growth. Rounded swellings may develop and, on close inspection, gray-black aphids may be visible among the white waxy fibers. Woolly aphids suck the sap from the bark and secrete the white, fluffy threads.
Plants affected Apples, pyracanthas, and cotoneasters.
Control As soon as the aphids become visible, spray the plant with pirimicarb, diazinon, or dimethoate.

Fluffy white growth

CROWN GALL ❧
Symptoms and cause Irregular, wartlike, often rounded swellings develop on or burst out from the stems. The galls are usually woody and although the rupture of the stem may cause some dieback, the plant is rarely killed. Crown gall is caused by a type of bacterium, which is particularly prevalent in poorly drained soils. The bacteria usually enter the plant through stem wounds.
Plants affected Trees, shrubs (especially roses), cane fruits, and various woody perennials.
Control Cut out and destroy any affected stems. Improve soil drainage and avoid or minimize injuries to the plant.

Distorted crown

FUNGAL FRUITING BODIES ❧
Symptoms and cause Fungal growths, often bracket- or shelflike, appear on trunks, branches, buttress roots, or the ground beneath the tree. Different fungi on the same plant vary in appearance. Some are perennial, while others die with the first frosts. The crown may become thin, and dead wood may develop. Some fungi cause internal damage while others live purely on dead woody material and cause little harm.
Plants affected Most mature trees and shrubs, as well as woody perennials and woody climbers.
Control Seek professional advice, especially if a weakened tree poses a potential hazard. Remove fruiting bodies to limit spread.

Fungal brackets

ARMILLARIA ROOT ROT ❧
Symptoms and cause The plant loses vigor. Gum or resin, as well as cracks, may appear on conifers. A creamy white mycelium develops beneath the bark at the base of the stem or trunk and on large roots. Black fungal strands may grow through the soil and cling to or penetrate the bark. The cause is one or more species of fungus.
Plants affected Trees, shrubs, woody climbers, and some woody perennials; it is most common on the West Coast.
Control Remove plants with their roots. Sterilize the soil and do not plant trees and shrubs for a couple of years. Then choose resistant plants, such as yews and beeches.

Fruiting bodies

SCALE INSECTS ❧
Symptoms and cause Stems are encrusted with various species of scale insect, such as mussel scale and soft scale. Often raised and brown or gray in color, the insects may be oval, circular, or pear-shaped. White, slightly fluffy egg deposits may also be present. Stems may be sticky with excreta (honeydew) that may then become covered with a black, sooty mold (see also p.162).
Plants affected Trees, shrubs, fruits, and succulents including cacti.
Control Spray in late winter (except succulents) with dormant oil. Spray with acephate or malathion, preferably when the newly hatched scale nymphs are present.

White egg deposits

FOOT AND ROOT ROTS ❧
Symptoms and cause Various soil- and water-borne fungi cause stem bases to discolor and shrink inward. Stems and foliage wilt, discolor, and die off, lower leaves first. Roots blacken and rot.
Plants affected Many plants, including seedlings, bedding plants, tomatoes, cucumbers, peas, sweet peas, and beans.
Control Fungi build up because of poor hygiene and wet soil. Unsterilized soil mix, dirty pots, and using unclean water worsen the situation. Maintain strict hygiene. Remove affected plants or rotate susceptible plants.

Rotting roots

CROWN ROT ❧
Symptoms and cause Various fungal and bacterial organisms cause plants to wilt, and the crowns of the plants may rot.
Plants affected Perennials mainly, but also trees, shrubs, annuals, bulbs, vegetables, and fruits.
Control Avoid planting too deeply or injuring the crown; keep it free of debris. If the affected area is removed, it may be possible to save the plant.

STEM BORERS ❧
Symptoms and cause A hole appears in the stem. This leads into a tunnel which may contain larvae. Often droppings and sawdust accumulate around the hole. Infested branches may seem unharmed but snap easily, or die.
Plants affected Many woody plants including fruit trees, lilacs, and ashes.
Control Prune out infested stems, and kill the larvae.

REPLANT PROBLEMS/SOIL SICKNESS ❧

Symptoms and cause Viruses, soil-borne fungi, nutrient depletion, and soil-dwelling nematodes all cause affected plants to grow poorly. They may show signs of dieback, and have small, discolored roots.
Plants affected Roses (especially on certain rootstocks), and fruit trees.
Control Change the soil to a depth of at least 18in (45cm) and to a width of at least the spread of the plant's roots.

DROUGHT ❧

Symptoms and cause Foliage and soft stems wilt and turn brown due to drought, followed by leaf drop and dieback. Growth is poor, flowering and fruit set is reduced, fruits are small and cracked. Injured roots and compacted soil worsen the problem.
Plants affected All plants, particularly those that are young, in containers, or in a light, sandy soil.
Control Water regularly and adequately, and apply a mulch.

RABBITS ❧

Symptoms and cause Plants are eaten away, sometimes down to ground level, especially during cold weather. Tree bark toward the base of the trunk is gnawed.
Plants affected A wide range of low-growing plants, young trees, and shrubs.
Control Trees and shrubs may be protected by spiral plastic tree guards. Chicken-wire fences, which must be at least 3ft (1m) high and sunk 1ft (30cm) below the ground, may also be used, either around the entire garden, or to protect individual trees and shrubs. Repeated applications of commercial repellants may provide a limited degree of protection, but their effectiveness will be reduced during wet weather or when plants are growing rapidly.

Plants eaten away

ROOT PROBLEMS

CUTWORMS ✳ ❀

Symptoms and cause Taproots may be severed and cavities develop in root crops, causing plants to wilt and die. Stem bases and the foliage of low-growing plants may also be gnawed. This is caused by caterpillars of several species of moth. Known as cutworms, the caterpillars are up to 1¾in (4.5cm) long, and brownish cream in color.
Plants affected Perennials, annuals, root vegetables, and lettuces are most at risk.
Control Destroy cutworms and protect young plants with aluminum foil collars pushed into the soil.

Cutworm

VINE WEEVILS ✳ ❧

Symptoms and cause Plants wilt and discolor, then collapse and die. Roots of woody plants, cuttings, and seedlings may be gnawed, and bulbs, corms, and tubers eaten into by vine weevil larvae. Larvae are up to ½in (1cm) and white. Adult weevils are beetle-shaped with a gray-black body.
Plants affected Shrubs, perennials, annuals, and bulbs, especially fuchsias, begonias, cyclamens, impatiens, sedums, primroses, strawberries, and container plants.
Control Remove or squash any larvae or adults. Use a biological control (see p.157), or treat with permethrin.

Vine weevil larvae

WIREWORMS ✳ ❧

Symptoms and cause Tunnels up to ⅛in (3mm) in diameter appear in the flesh of roots or tubers and at the stem base of seedlings. Some plants may wilt and die. Wireworms, the small, orange-yellow larvae of click beetles, may be visible; they are most troublesome on newly cultivated land, particularly if it was previously grassland.
Plants affected Potatoes and other root crops, perennials, annuals, and bulbs.
Control Destroy any wireworms found. Leave crops in the ground for as short a time as possible. Treat soil with chloropyrifos + diazinon, or water susceptible plants with diazinon. Cultivate the ground regularly so that the problem declines.

Wireworms

CLUBROOT ✳ ✎

Symptoms and cause Roots become swollen and distorted, growth is poor, and foliage wilts and may discolor, particularly in hot weather. The slime mold that causes this is usually found in poorly drained, acidic soils and is spread via boots and tools. It can remain in the soil for over 20 years.
Plants affected Wallflowers, stocks, and brassicas, such as Brussels sprouts, rutabagas, radishes, and cabbages.
Control Discard affected plants. Keep the area clear of weeds and improve drainage, adding lime to deter infection. Dip plants in a commercial chemical dip at planting.

Distorted roots

VERTICILLIUM WILT ✳ ❧

Symptoms and cause Vascular tissue within both stems and roots shows brown stripes beneath the bark. Woody plants wilt but take several years to die. The cause is a species of fungus, usually found in soil, on plant remains, or on new plants.
Plants affected A wide range of greenhouse and garden plants.
Control Remove affected plants and the surrounding soil. Always clean tools thoroughly after use on suspect or diseased plants. Avoid buildup of weeds or growing susceptible plants in the area, since these may harbor infection or show signs of dieback.

Striped stains

PHYTOPHTHORA ROOT ROTS ✳

Symptoms and cause Foliage becomes sparse and discolored. Dead areas on the stem are stained a bluish black color by the fungus responsible, which is common in water-logged soils.
Plants affected Trees, shrubs, and woody perennials, but especially maples, apples, yew, and heathers.
Control Improve drainage. Dig up and destroy affected plants.

DAMPING OFF ✳ ❧

Symptoms and cause Fungi cause stem bases and roots to darken and rot, and seedlings to collapse. A fluffy white growth may appear on plant remains.
Plants affected Seedlings of all plants.
Control Avoid by using clean containers, sterilized soil mix, and clean water. Water seedlings with captan, thiram, or zineb as a preventative measure.

FRUIT AND VEGETABLE PROBLEMS

SCAB ♂ 🗨

Symptoms and cause Dark brownish green, scabby patches on the surface of the fruits, which may crack and become distorted. Foliage may blister and drop early. The fungi that cause scab spread rapidly in wet weather and may overwinter on infected leaves and shoots.
Plants affected Apples, pyracanthas, pears, citrus, and loquats are all susceptible.
Control Plant resistant varieties. Clear up and destroy fallen leaves and fruits, keep the plant open-centered by pruning, and prune out infected shoots. Spray with a suitable fungicide, such as thiram.

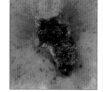
Scab on apples

CALCIUM DEFICIENCY ♂

Symptoms and cause On apples, where the problem is known as bitter pit, the flesh is scattered with brown flecks and may taste bitter; the skin may be pitted. On tomatoes, and sometimes peppers, it is called blossom-end rot: a dark brown, sunken, often leathery patch appears at the blossom end of the fruit. The rest of the fruit ripens normally. Calcium deficiency in the fruits, caused by dry soil, makes cells collapse and discolor.
Plants affected Apples, tomatoes, eggplants, and peppers.
Control Regular, thorough watering is essential but, if the trouble persists, spray with calcium chloride.

Bitter pit

CODLING MOTHS ♂

Symptoms and cause Holes, usually surrounded by brown, powderlike droppings, appear toward the blossom end of the ripe fruits. These are caused by the pale caterpillars of the codling moth, which may be found feeding in the core of the fruit. When mature, they bore through the fruit, leaving the tunnel filled with droppings.
Plants affected Apples and pears.
Control Catch the male moths (to reduce mating) in pheromone traps hung from the trees between the end of spring and midsummer. Spray with permethrin or carbaryl in early summer (when males appear in the traps) and then repeat the application after about three weeks.

Droppings on apple

BROWN ROT ♂

Symptoms and cause Soft, brown patches, usually circular, develop on the fruit surface and penetrate the flesh. Creamy white, raised pustules, often arranged in concentric circles, develop over the rotting area. Affected fruits either disintegrate or become mummified; some fruits drop while others remain on the tree. Fungi are the cause; their spores are carried from the pustules either by insects or on air currents. Only damaged fruits become infected.
Plants affected Cultivated fruits, especially apples, plums, peaches, nectarines, and pears.
Control Pick off and discard any affected fruits immediately.

Rotting pear

GRAY MOLD (BOTRYTIS) ♂ ❦

Symptoms and cause Discolored patches develop on the plant. Stems, fruits, and other parts may be affected and sink inward, later becoming covered in a fuzzy, gray, fungal growth. Fruits rot rapidly and affected stems die back. The mold is caused by a fungus whose spores are spread by rain or water splash and on air currents (*see also* p.163).
Plants affected All plants, but those with soft- or thin-skinned fruits or stems are most susceptible. Plants that have been damaged also run a greater risk of infection.
Control Avoid injuring plants, clear up debris, and improve air circulation, since cool, damp conditions encourage disease spread. Spray with a suitable fungicide containing captan or ferbam.

Fungal growth

APPLE MAGGOTS ♂

Symptoms and cause Brown tunnels wind through the fruit. The surface of the fruit is distorted and pitted. The fruit may fall early. Larvae of the apple maggot, a black fly ¼in (6mm) long are the cause; they emerge from the fallen fruit and pupate in the soil over winter.
Plants affected Apples, plums, cherries, and blueberries.
Control Dispose of fallen fruits immediately. Spray young fruits with diazinon or methoxychlor.

SCAB ON POTATOES ✱

Symptoms and cause Raised, scabby patches appear. The potato may develop normally, or the flesh may become cracked and distorted. Scab is found in most soils, especially those that are sandy, light, and contain a lot of lime.
Plants affected Potatoes.
Control Avoid adding additional lime. Dig in bulky organic matter to improve soil texture. Grow scab-resistant cultivars, such as 'Cayuga'.

POTATO LATE BLIGHT ✱ 🗨 ❦

Symptoms and cause Sunken patches of rot develop on the skin with the flesh beneath stained reddish brown. The rot is dry at first, but secondary, soft-rotting bacteria often invade, reducing the tuber to a slimy mass. The haulms and foliage may be affected, too. It is caused by fungal spores in the air and soil.
Plants affected Potatoes.
Control Hill up potatoes deeply, avoid overhead watering, and clear up debris. Plant resistant cultivars, such as 'Kennebec' or 'Cherokee'. When warm, moist weather is forecast, apply a preventative spray of a copper-based fungicide.

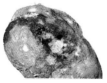
Reddish brown staining

CABBAGE ROOT MAGGOTS ✱ ❦

Symptoms and cause Plants wilt and discolor. Seedlings die and root crops are tunnelled into by white larvae up to ¼in (3mm) long.
Plants affected Brassicas, such as cabbages, cauliflowers, turnips, rutabagas, and radishes.
Control Lay carpet padding, cardboard, or roofing felt around the plants, or use chlorpyrifos + diazinon.

CARROT RUST FLIES ✱ ❦

Symptoms and cause Orange-brown tunnels in mature roots, caused by carrot rust fly larvae. Foliage starts to discolor and plants may die.
Plants affected Carrots, parsnips, parsley, and celery.
Control Keep out female flies with a clear plastic fence at least 24in (60cm) high. On seed rows use chlorpyrifos + diazinon or diazinon crystals; use a diazinon drench on plants.

RASPBERRY FRUITWORMS ♂

Symptoms and cause Female raspberry beetles lay eggs on the flowers in early to midsummer; these hatch into larvae that tunnel into the fruits. The stalk ends of infested fruits become dry and brown and the brownish white larvae, up to ¼in (6mm) long, may be visible. Droppings and damage from feeding may be found in the inner plug.
Plants affected Raspberries, and occasionally blackberries and hybrid cane fruits.
Control Spray raspberries with malathion, permethrin, or rotenone when the first pink fruits appear. Spray blackberries when the first flowers open and loganberries when 80 percent of the petals have fallen. Raspberries may need a second application. To reduce the risk to bees, spray at dusk.

Eggs and larvae

BIRDS ON FRUIT ♂

Symptoms and cause Peck marks appear in the flesh of ripe fruits, such as apples, cherries, and peaches. Smaller fruits may disappear without trace. Brown rot infection often follows injury (*see* p.166). Blackbirds and starlings are often responsible, but other birds may cause damage, too.
Plants affected Tree and soft fruits, and the fruits on ornamental trees and shrubs.
Control Use fruit cages or install permanent netting.

HORMONE WEEDKILLER DAMAGE ♂

Symptoms and cause Peculiarly shaped fruits, such as elongated tomatoes, form. The fruits are usually hollow and, although safe to eat, may taste unpleasant. This is caused by hormone or growth-regulator weedkiller contaminating watering cans, or drifting onto nearby plants when it is being applied.
Plants affected Many plants.
Control Reserve one watering can or sprayer for weedkillers.

LAWN PROBLEMS

MOLES

Symptoms and cause Burrowing moles cause molehills – heaps of finely turned soil – which appear on the lawn and occasionally in flower beds or other cultivated areas. The roots of small plants or seedlings growing in the area may be disturbed, with the whole plant sometimes being upturned or buried completely.
Plants affected Young plants, seedlings, and lawns.
Control Moles are effectively controlled by trapping, although they may be deterred by barriers cutting off their tunnels. Push metal sheets about 1ft (30cm) vertically into active tunnels.

Molehill

SNOW MOLD

Symptoms and cause Yellowish patches develop on the lawn. In moist weather, a white or pink fungal growth appears; this is encouraged by excessive use of nitrogen fertilizers and poor aeration. Commonly seen in late autumn and into winter, especially where lawns have been walked on when covered with snow.
Plants affected Lawns, particularly those with a high proportion of annual bluegrass.
Control Improve maintenance, aerate and scarify regularly, and avoid using high-nitrogen feeds in late summer or autumn. Treat with thiophanate-methyl.

Fungal growth

CATS AND DOGS

Symptoms and cause Lawns and other grassed areas may be disturbed or damaged by the feces and urine of cats and dogs. Foliage can be scorched and large brown patches appear on the lawn.
Plants affected Lawns, garden plants, and seedlings.
Control Fence off areas of the garden. Protect individual plants or small areas using netting. Regular watering will help deter cats but not dogs.

WHITE GRUBS

Symptoms and cause Brown patches appear and expand rapidly. Dead grass is loose and can be rolled up like a carpet. Larvae of June beetles, Japanese beetles, Asiatic garden beetles, and rose chafers up to 1in (2.5cm) long, white with orange-brown heads, feed on grass roots.
Plants affected Lawns and other grassed areas.
Control Drench affected areas with diazinon.

DROUGHT

Symptoms and cause Straw-colored patches appear on the lawn and the whole lawn may become discolored due to inadequate watering or prolonged hot, dry weather.
Plants affected Lawns, particularly those on free-draining, sandy soils.
Control Regularly water the lawn in the early evening; allow the grass to grow longer than normal to increase drought resistance. Feed regularly.

RED THREAD

Symptoms and cause Tiny, pale pink to red, gelatinous threads of fungus appear between blades of grass, which later become bleached. Known as red thread, it is worst after heavy rain, when the lawn lacks nitrogen, or is compacted and in need of aeration.
Plants affected Lawns, particularly those with a high proportion of fine grasses.
Control Feed, scarify, and treat with thiophanate-methyl.

SLIME MOLDS

Symptoms and cause Clusters of beige, orange, or white fruiting bodies smother the grass, and spores are then released, giving a gray appearance; the grass looks unsightly but is not harmed. Slime molds, soil-inhabiting microorganisms that feed on decayed matter are the cause. They thrive during periods of heavy rain and are most common in late spring and early autumn.
Plants affected Lawn grasses, and occasionally other plants.
Control Hose down the area with a forceful spray. Rake thoroughly to reduce thatch, which holds water and encourages molds.

Affected grass

TOADSTOOLS

Symptoms and cause Fungal fruiting bodies appear on the lawn, usually with a toadstoollike shape, sometimes forming a circle or fairy ring. If growing on buried tree roots, they will cause little damage. Fairy rings, however, disfigure a lawn: two lush circles form one inside the other, then the grass in between the circles dies off, with a white fungal growth among the grass and in the soil beneath the ring.
Plants affected Lawns and other grassed areas.
Control Brush off the fungi as they appear. Remove buried wood where fungi appear. There is no chemical control for fairy rings.

Fairy ring

WEEDS

A weed is usually defined as any plant that grows where it is not wanted. To most of us, however, a weed is an uncultivated plant, small or large, that is invasive, competes with cultivated plants, and self-seeds freely. Remove weeds – especially annual ones – before they set seed. Many perennial weeds have fleshy roots that enable them to persist even if top-growth is killed off. Most weeds can be treated by digging out the whole root system or using a weedkiller.

Hairy bittercress
This common, annual weed develops very quickly. The explosive mechanism of seed dispersal can spread seeds as far as 1yd (1m) or even farther if the seeds are carried on the wind. Hoe or pull before they set seed, or use glyphosate.

Goutweed
This common perennial weed is difficult to control since its underground stems spread just beneath the soil surface, stifling other plants as they grow. A layer of organic matter, black plastic, or carpeting may smother the weed after several seasons. Weedkillers, including dichlobenil and glyphosate, may be effective.

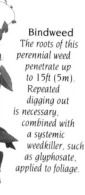

Bindweed
The roots of this perennial weed penetrate up to 15ft (5m). Repeated digging out is necessary, combined with a systemic weedkiller, such as glyphosate, applied to foliage.

Dock

Root sections of this perennial weed will regenerate if left in the soil. Use a suitable weedkiller – according to whether the weed is in a lawn or border.

Japanese knotweed
Rapidly growing to a height of about 6ft (2m), this perennial weed is extremely invasive and difficult to control. Use a weedkiller then dig deeply, removing all the underground parts to prevent them from regenerating.

Oxalis
Some species of this perennial develop bulbils around the base (right) – these separate to form new plants. Remove in spring or early summer. The other species eject seeds from seed pods: remove before the seeds ripen.

Thistles
Canada thistle is the most common form of this perennial weed. The plant spreads by lateral roots and can regenerate from any root sections left in the ground after weeding. Digging, removal of top-growth, and the use of weedkillers, such as glyphosate, can control thistles.

Nettles
Both annual (right) and perennial species are common. Remove both types before the seeds develop. Dig out the creeping roots of the perennial nettle; it may need several applications of weedkiller before it is killed.

Horsetail

The roots of this perennial weed are difficult to destroy since they can penetrate to a depth of 6ft (2m) or more. Digging and removal of top-growth, combined with the use of weedkillers, may be effective.

Quackgrass
This invasive perennial weed spreads by creeping roots. If broken while being lifted out, each segment will regrow. Control with a suitable weedkiller.

OTHER WEEDS

• Dandelion is a perennial weed that spreads by seeding, or can regenerate from pieces of root left in the soil after hand-weeding. Remove the entire root or treat with a suitable weedkiller – the type of weedkiller will vary according to whether the dandelion is in a border or lawn (see also p.65).

• Kudzu is an extremely fast-growing perennial vine, particularly in the Southeast. Remove as much top-growth as possible and spray regrowth with glyphosate.

• Stinking cucumber is a long-running vine that is common from Nebraska to California and Mexico. Its vigorous growth quickly engulfs smaller plants. Pull out as much as you can.

• Lamb's-quarters and quickweed are annual weeds that grow and set seed rapidly. Remove them before they have a chance to set seed.

• Deadly nightshade is a perennial weed that may be controlled by regular hoeing; rapid removal is essential since it is highly poisonous, especially the fruits.

• Poison ivy and poison oak contain a strong skin irritant. Pull the plants out only if you are sure you are not sensitive to them, or spray with glyphosate.

GLOSSARY

*Words in italics within a definition
have a separate entry.*

Aerate Alter soil texture and
structure by creating more air
spaces, often by spiking.

Annual A plant that completes
its life cycle (flowering, setting
seed, and dying) within one
year.

Backfill Replace soil or *soil mix*
around roots after planting.

Bedding plants Plants (usually
annuals, but sometimes *biennials*
and *perennials*) that are used for
temporary, often showy, display.

Biennial A plant that produces
leafy growth in the first year
and then flowers, sets seed,
and dies the next.

Broadcast Scatter seeds or
fertilizer, usually directly onto
the soil surface.

Bud A swelling on a plant
stem containing embryonic
leaves or flowers or both. A
growth bud produces leaves or
a shoot. A **fruit bud** produces
flowers then fruits.

Bulb A group of swollen,
modified, underground leaves
that act as a storage organ.

Cloche A structure used to
protect plants from unsuitable
weather conditions – usually
made from clear glass or
plastic supported on a metal
or plastic framework.

Compost An organic material
resulting from the rotting down
of organic material from the
kitchen and garden.

Contact action The action
of a pesticide, fungicide, or
herbicide that kills or damages
its target on contact.

Corm An underground, bulb-
like, swollen stem or stem base.

Crown The part of a *herbaceous
plant* where the stems meet the
roots and from where new
shoots develop. Also the upper
branch structure of a tree.

Cultivar A cultivated variety of
a plant as distinct from a wild,
naturally occurring plant.

Cutting A piece of stem, root,
or leaf that, if taken at the

correct time of year and
prepared in the correct way,
should grow to form a new
plant.

Damp down Wet the floor of a
greenhouse or conservatory to
help increase the humidity and
lower the temperature.

Deciduous Losing leaves every
year in autumn and winter.

Dieback The death of tips
of shoots, usually caused by
damage or disease.

Dormancy The temporary
stopping or slowing of growth,
usually in winter.

Drill A narrow (usually
straight) furrow in the soil
in which seeds are sown.

Ericaceous Lime-hating,
needing conditions of pH 6.5
or less.

Evergreen Retaining leaves
throughout the year.

F1 hybrid A first-generation,
vigorous plant bred by crossing
two specially selected plants.
Seed of F1 hybrids does not
come *true to type*.

Fertilizer A plant food (usually
in concentrated form), naturally
or synthetically produced, that
is applied to the soil or to plant
foliage. A **balanced** fertilizer
contains a mix of nitrogen,
phosphorus, and potassium.
A **complete** fertilizer contains
both these and other nutrients.

Formative pruning A method
of pruning used to ensure that
a tree or shrub develops the
desired shape and branch
formation from an early age.

Graft union The point on
a tree, shrub, rose, or woody
climber where the top-growth
has been grafted onto the
rootstock.

Half hardy Not able to
withstand frost (often applied
to *annuals*).

Harden off Acclimatize
a young plant raised in a
protected environment to
cooler conditions.

Hardy Able to withstand frost
and cold and therefore grow
outside throughout the year.

Heel in Plant trees, shrubs,
or *herbaceous plants* temporarily
before placing them in a
permanent position.

Herbaceous plant One with
top-growth that is soft, not
woody, and (usually) dies
back over winter.

Inorganic Not of plant or
animal origin, i.e., a mineral
or a synthetically produced
material.

Leader The main, central stem
of a plant. Also a branch tip
that extends the branch system
as it grows.

Leaf node The point where
a stem bears a leaf or leaf *bud*.

Organic Of plant or animal
origin, containing carbon. Also
a gardening method that
avoids nonorganic materials.

Perennial A plant, usually
herbaceous, that lives for at least
three years.

pH A measure of acidity.

Pinch out Remove the growing
tip of a shoot to encourage
sideshoots to form and to
restrict extension growth.

Pollination The transfer of the
male pollen onto the female
stigma, often carried out by
insects, especially bees, or
by air movement.

Rhizome A swollen stem that
grows horizontally, producing
roots and shoots.

Rock plant Any plant that,
because it is compact and non-
invasive, is suitable for growing
in a rock garden.

Rootstock A plant used to
provide a root system for the
top-growth of another plant
that is grafted onto it.

Routine pruning Pruning
carried out regularly to
maintain the shape and health
of a plant and ensure good
growth.

Seedbed An area of level,
well-prepared soil set aside
for seed sowing.

Semi-evergreen Retaining
most or almost all foliage for
most of the winter.

Soil mix A growing medium
available in different forms:
cuttings soil mix has a light,
free-draining texture to
encourage rapid rooting of
cuttings; **ericaceous** (or acidic)
soil mix has a low pH and is
suitable for growing acid-loving
plants; **multi-purpose** soil mix
has a texture and level of
nutrients that make it suitable
for most uses and for a wide
range of plants; **potting** soil
mix is suitable for plants or
seedlings that are being grown
on in pots; **planting** soil mix
encourages good root growth
of newly planted trees and
shrubs; **seed** soil mix has a
structure and nutrient
composition ideal for raising
seedlings from seed.

Spot-treat Apply a pesticide
or weedkiller to specific areas
of a plant or to individual
plants or weeds.

Spur A short branch of fruit
buds that develops on a mature
branch of a fruit tree.

Succulent Fleshy. Also a
plant with fleshy, water-storing
leaves and/or stems.

Systemic action The action
of a pesticide or fungicide
whereby it is absorbed by the
roots or leaves and *translocated*.

Taproot A thick root, usually
growing straight down.

Tender Injured or killed
by cold weather and frost.

Top-dress Apply fresh *fertilizer*,
soil, or *compost* to the soil
around a plant or to a lawn.

Translocated The internal
process whereby nutrients or
weedkillers are carried from
one part of a plant to another.

True to type As applied to
seed, producing plants the
same as the parent plant from
which the seed was collected.

Tuber A swollen root, usually
underground, that stores food
material and water.

Variegated Marked with one
or more colors. Often used to
describe leaves with white,
yellow, or cream markings.

Viable Capable of germinating
or growing.

INDEX

ACKNOWLEDGMENTS

AUTHOR'S ACKNOWLEDGMENTS
Diana Mitchell and the rest of the DK team for
unending help and patience. Justina Buswell
for her wordprocessing help.

DORLING KINDERSLEY WOULD LIKE
TO ACKNOWLEDGE:
Diana Mitchell for location assistance.
The staff at the RHS Garden, Wisley, and
at the RHS Plant Centre, Wisley.
Daniel Pearson for the garden designs
on pp.14–15. Hilary Bird for the index.

For props and locations: Challenge Fencing,
Cobham; Defenders Ltd, Ashford; English
Woodlands Biocontrol, Petworth; Fargro Green
Team, Littlehampton; Edwina Head, RHS Plant
Centre, Wisley; Roger Hill Carpentry and Joinery,
Richmond; Lynkon Aquatic, Lincoln;
Rolawn (Turf Growers) Ltd, York; Silverlands,

Chertsey; Two Wests and Elliott Ltd, Chesterfield;
World of Water, Chertsey.

For additional assistance: Mark Bracey;
Steve Gorton; Link Hall; Stephen Josland;
Madeleine Ladell; Sarah Lillicrapp; Fergus Muir;
Tim Ridley; Ina Stradins; Glenda Tyrrell;
William C. Uber; Joe Williamson.

PHOTOGRAPHY CREDITS
Camera Press 106tr, 107tl.
Camera Press/Linda Burgess 109tc.
Neil Campbell Sharp 118, 120tr.
Eric Crichton 11tr & bl, 17cr & bl, 37bc,
   38tr, 39bl, 40tr, 41tc, 63br, 67bc, 87br,
   120bl, 122br, 135tr.
Garden Picture Library/Densey Clyné 69br.
Will Giles 16cr, 105bc.
John Glover 9tr, 36, 38tl, 41bl, 54, 55bc, 86,
   119br, 133br.

Derek Gould 40b, 87bl.
Jerry Harpur 55tr, 108tr.
Neil Holmes 122tr.
Andrew Lawson 10tr, 10bl, 68bl, 69tr,
   107tr, 119tr, 121tr, 121br.
Clive Nicholls 95tr (Turn End, Bucks),
   105tr (Old School House, Essex), 108bl.
Tim Sandall 69bc.
Elizabeth Whiting & Associates 109br.
Steve Wooster 2, 8, 9bl, 18, 20br,
   37tr, 41tr & br, 67tr, 68tr, 94, 95bc, 104,
   132,133tr, 134bc, 158.

ILLUSTRATION CREDITS
Karen Cochrane
Martine Collings
Simone End
Will Giles
Sandra Pond
John Woodcock